Warriors of Untouchable: Ambedkar and Gandhi

Warriors of Untouchable: Ambedkar and Gandhi

A.S. Pabla

2008

CYBER TECH PUBLICATIONS
4264/3, Ansari Road, Daryaganj, New Delhi-110002 (India)
Ph.: 011-23244078. Fax: 011-23280028
E-Mail: cyberpublicationsdelhi@yahoo.com

WARRIORS OF UNTOUCHABLE: AMBEDKAR AND GANDHI

A.S. Pabla

First Edition 2008

Published by :

G.S. Rawat for Cyber Tech Publications
4264/3, Ansari Road, Daryaganj, New Delhi-110002 (India)
Ph.: 011-23244078. Fax: 011-23280028
E-Mail: cyberpublicationsdelhi@yahoo.com

Printed at : **Amit Enterprises**, Maujpur, Delhi, (9810878184)

Preface

For those who appreciate any comparison of Ambedkar's importance to Dalits with that of anti-racist leaders to Black America, we may say that he was a combination of the scholar W. E. B. duBois, the slave rebel Frederick Douglas and the radical teacher/leader Malcolm X.. His born on 14 April 1891 to a Mahar family in Mhow, Maharashtra, Ambedkar rose to become an exemplary scholar, statesman and revolutionary leader in modern India. Fondly remembered today by Dalits as Babasaheb, Ambedkar is a figure whose greatness the rest of India is still struggling to understand. Ambedkar ranks easily amongst the most highly educated and erudite leaders of India.

He spent many years studying a host of subjects ranging from economics and anthropology to politics, law and religion, in colleges and universities such as Elphinstone College, Bombay where he earned a B.A., Columbia University, USA, from where he earned an M.A. and a Ph.D., London University where he earned a D.Sc. and entrance to the Bar from Grey's Inn, London. Much of Ambedkar's education was made possible by financial support from the Gaikwad of Baroda who was known for his financial contributions to reformers and educators in what was the Bombay Presidency during colonial times. Yet, Ambedkar's education did not grant him the status of a fellow human being when he returned to India. Untouchability, practiced by an overwhelming majority of caste Hindus as well as other religious communities, stigmatized him in the most pernicious ways.

—Author

Contents

1

INTRODUCTION

For those who appreciate any comparison of Ambedkar's importance to Dalits with that of anti-racist leaders to Black America, we may say that he was a combination of the scholar W. E. B. duBois, the slave rebel Frederick Douglas and the radical teacher/leader Malcolm X.. His born on 14 April 1891 to a Mahar family in Mhow, Maharashtra, Ambedkar rose to become an exemplary scholar, statesman and revolutionary leader in modern India. Fondly remembered today by Dalits as Babasaheb, Ambedkar is a figure whose greatness the rest of India is still struggling to understand. Ambedkar ranks easily amongst the most highly educated and erudite leaders of India.

He spent many years studying a host of subjects ranging from economics and anthropology to politics, law and religion, in colleges and universities such as Elphinstone College, Bombay where he earned a B.A., Columbia University, USA, from where he earned an M.A. and a Ph.D., London University where he earned a D.Sc. and entrance to the Bar from Grey's Inn, London. Much of Ambedkar's education was made possible by financial support from the Gaikwad of Baroda who was known for his financial contributions to reformers and educators in what was the Bombay Presidency during colonial times. Yet, Ambedkar's education did not grant him the status of a fellow human being when he returned to India. Untouchability, practiced by an overwhelming majority of caste Hindus as well as other religious communities, stigmatized him in the most pernicious ways. His own analysis refuted an understanding of untouchability as a racial oppression. He argued instead that it arose as a social, political, religious, and economic separation and denigration of practitioners of Buddhism in the historical period of renascent Hinduism (see his book The Untouchables, 1948). For Ambedkar, Buddhism represented the historical revolutionary experience in India, while Hinduism represented the counter-revolutionary experience seeking to bring back an orthodoxy founded upon the caste system. Such an understanding of Hinduism was one of the main causes of Ambedkar's strong differences with Gandhi's approach to the struggle against oppressive practices such as untouchability.

Throughout his active political life spanning more than three decades, Ambedkar spearheaded an alternative movement against the evils of the caste system—an alternative that was much more radical in content and modern in vision than the one that Mahatma Gandhi nurtured and led by example. The difference in their approaches is brought out by Dr. Eleanor Zelliot, a pioneer historian of Untouchables/Dalits in Maharashtra: Ambedkar's programs were intended to integrate the Untouchable into Indian society in modern, not traditional ways, and on as high a level as possible. This goal stood in marked contrast to Gandhi's "Ideal Bhangi" (Harijan, 23 November 1936) who would continue to do sanitation work even though his status would equal that of a Brahmin.

Ambedkar's ideal for the depressed (classes) was to "raise their educational standard so that they may know their own conditions, have asportation to rise to the level of the highest Hindu and be in a position to use political power as a means to that end." Both reformers had a vision of equality, but for Ambedkar equality meant not only equal status of the Varnas, but equal social, political, and economic opportunity for all. Ambedkar planned his programmes to bring the Untouchable from a state of "dehumanization" and "slavery" into one of equality through the use of modern methods based on education and the exercise of legal and political rights.

Ambedkar's adaptation of western concepts to the Indian scene is also reflected in the terms he used to justify Untouchable political rights: democracy, fraternity, and liberty. In his Marathi speeches, Ambedkar conveyed the implication of these concepts in a single word, manuski, that was readily understood by the most illiterate Mahar villager. Although manuski's literal meaning is "humanness", it serves to evoke feelings of self-respect and human attitudes towards one's fellow humans.

Ambedkar himself delineated his differences through minute study of Gandhi's vision of an ideal society and the specific practices which Gandhi upheld throughout his life. It is worth quoting a couple of paragraphs from his essay titled Gandhism: The Doom of the Untouchables, which forms part of his larger book titled What the Congress and Gandhi have done to the Untouchables.

DR. BHIMROA AIMS AND OBJECTIVES

While formulating the objectives, the Sangh took note of the present international outlook towards development which overwhelmingly emphasise on improvement in quality of life than mere development of per capita income. The central aim therefore is not limited to social upliftment of the Harijans, but economic emancipation of the poor by eliminating all forms of exploitation through capacity building among the target population and conscientisation of the masses with the help of basic education and self-employment. The basic parameters of quality of life are education, health and environment and specifically in these three spheres, the poor including the Harijans are grossly deprived. Keeping in view above mentioned development paradigm of the international institutions, the Sangh framed following objectives:-

(i) To secure human development irrespective of caste, creed, sex and religion.

(ii) To bring about growth and development of the children on holistic concept.

(iv) To disseminate popular education in lieu of elitist education of the present day, so as to ensure "Education for All."

(v) To promote vocational education and training leading to income generation.

(vi) To develop an integrated health care system and sanitation on community based sustainable programmes Strategies were formulated on the basis of stated Aims and objectives. The central strategy is to concentrate on child welfare and development with the belief that childhood is that segment of life when mind, bodies and personalities are formed and even the slightest deprivation during this period can lead to life-long impairment resulting in fundamental distortion in human development. Benefiting from the hindsight of Gandhiji who founded the Sangh and laid emphases on basic education, sanitation and gram Swaraj, the HSS, Bengal carefully blended western institutional framework with Indian cultural heritage and developed its own brand of institutions which are common with other NGOs but with the basic difference that all of them are innovative, community based and thus sustainable even without the guidance of the HSS, Bengal.

(vi) The central aim therefore is not limited to social upliftment of the Harijans, but economic emancipation of the poor by eliminating all forms of exploitation through capacity building among the target population and conscientisation of the masses with the help of basic education and self-employment.

OUTREACH

During last 20 years, the HSS, Bengal has achieved a spatial outreach in 17 districts of West Bengal where it has 210 branches/associates, the maximum number of branches/ associates (37) being in the Midnapur district and the minimum (05) in the districts of north and south Dinajpur and Purulia. These 210 branches/associates have covered 1050 villages comprising of 2. 5 lakh people. Only district left out is Calcutta where the need for the programme is comparatively less. HSS however is contemplating child development activities in selected slum areas of Calcutta metropolis provided funds are forthcoming. Attempts are also being made to increase the outreach in Purulia and districts of North Bengal where concentration of poor and backward scheduled caste and tribe population is highest. As funds would permit there would be progressive escalation of activities and outreach in those districts over the next reporting year.

Programmes: Programmes now being implemented by the HSS, Bengal can be sub-divided into three areas viz, Education, Health and sanitation and income generation. Each programme is embellished by the inputs of the other programmes is embellished by the inputs of the other programmes and there are deliberate overlapping among them, they are follows:

(A) Education:
- (i) Creche
- (ii) Balwadi
- (iii) Ashram Vidyalaya
- (iv) Centre for Information Technology.

(B) Health and Sanitation:
- (i) Child Health
- (ii) Smokeless Chullah
- (iii) Low-cost Latrines
- (iv) Prevention of arsenic contamination

(C) Housing

(D) Income Generation:

(E) Consumer Activities

(F) Special Programmes

HARIJAN

In the Indian caste system, a Dalit, often called an untouchable, is a person who does not have any varnas. Varna refers to the Hindu belief that most humans were created from different parts of the body of the divinity Purusha and according to which part they were created from it defines their social standing for issues such as who they can marry and what jobs they can do. Dalits fall outside varnas system and have historically been prevented from doing any but the most menial jobs. They are also known as outcastes. Included are leather-workers (called chamar), poor farmers and landless labourers, scavengers (called bhangi or chura), street handicrafters, folk artists, clothes washers (dhobi) etc.

TERMS ASSOCIATED WITH THE DALIT CASTE

Dalit is the latest and currently most politically correct of many terms used for the caste. Offensive terms used mostly in the past include chura, bhangi, neech, kanjjar, and mirasi. Whereas the terms chura and bhangi are profession-based terms for scavengers, they can serve as general terms for the low-born; others are actual names of the caste. Harijan was a term for untouchable, coined by Mahatma Gandhi, which means Children of God-Hari is another name for the god Vishnu. It is now considered patronizing. The term can also be attributed to Dalit castes of Pakistan called the Haris, who are a group of mud-hut builders. Neo-Buddhist Dalits try to make 'Harijan' appear as a disgrace to all Dalits as it comes from a Hindu name. This term had already been used, in a different form, by the medieval philosopher Ramanuja who uplifted many backward caste peoples: as Thirukulattar, or People of Holy Clan. (He was probably the first to allow the untouchables into temples, albeit for limited periods).

The word 'Dalit' comes from the Marathi root dal, and means 'held under check', 'suppressed', or 'crushed', or, in a looser sense, 'oppressed'. Maharashtrian Dalit Activist and poet Namdeo Dhasal made it a symbol of pride to fight against social injustice. He said:

> "*Yes, I do feel that the fight to eradicate caste has to be fought by Dalits and caste Hindus together carrying forward the tradition of Adi Shankara, which got broken somewhere in between.*"

It is possible that Dr. Ambedkar borrowed this term from Swami Vivekananda from his quote, "Deena-Dalita-Dukhi Devo Bhava!" ("Service to the weak, the downtrodden and the suffering masses itself is the worship of God").

Another term used for the Dalits was Matanga named after Maharshi Matanga, a Matanga Bhil and guru of Bhakta Shabari. In fact, Dalits are often addressed as 'Matanga 'in passages like Varaha Purana 1. 139. 91.

Dr. B. R. Ambedkar, a Dalit, and one of the leaders of the Indian independence movement, is considered the chief architect of the Indian Constitution, in which Article 17 abolishes untouchability. Ever since, under the aegis of the Constitution of India, a 'Reservation System' (privilege in education and other services given only to the Dalits) has been implemented for the benefit of the 'Dalits' which is a step towards affirmative action.

The terms scheduled castes/scheduled tribes (SC/ST) and non-caste tribes are also used in the Indian legal system to refer to this social group in India.

SOCIAL BACKGROUND AND ORIGINS

In the context of traditional Hindu society, Dalit status has often been historically associated with occupations regarded as ritually impure: namely, any occupation involving killing, handling of animal cadavers or night soil (human feces). Engaging in these activities was considered to be polluting to the individual who performed them, and this pollution was considered to be 'contagious'. As a result, Dalits were commonly banned and segregated from full participation in Hindu social life (they could not enter the premises of a temple), while elaborate precautions were sometimes observed to prevent incidental contact between Dalits and other Hindus.

Historically, there may not have been clear demarcation between Dalit castes and the Sudra castes. Dalits are not a single identifiable race or caste. Instead, like the rest of the Hindu society, they are divided into various sub-castes known as 'jatis. One study found some association between caste status and genetic markers seeming to indicate a more European lineage.

Dalit diversity may be due to newly outcaste individuals or communities over the years. It is noteworthy that somet mes, regional tribes that are considered Dalits are sometimes seen by Indians as racially distinct. In both northern and southern India it is different. For example, in North India, in places such as Rajasthan they are usually lighter because Rajasthan was invaded several times by white tribes. In addition they also have different colour of eyes and sometimes hair. As a result in superstition, it is said to never trust a cat-eyed person. Then, in South India, they are often regarded as more closely related to Tibetans, Burmese, Khmers, Thais, and other Southeast and East Asians.

Many Dalits who have converted to other religions in the past few centuries continue to retain their Dalit heritage. In the 1991 census, Dalits numbered just over 130 million and constituted more than 16% of India's population.

Discrimination against Dalits is not limited to the Hindu community. This situation is exacerbated by the fact that non-Hindu Dalit groups have traditionally not been recognized as Scheduled Castes under hiring quota laws. The Dalit Muslims or "Arzal" (also called Mojahir in Pakistan), as well as Dalit Christians form an integral part of the caste system in South Asia among Muslims and Christians. Many Dalit Muslims are discriminated against by the upper-caste "Ashraf" Muslims, and Dalit Christians discriminated against by upper caste Christian priests and Nuns.

Some Dalits have successfully integrated into urban Indian society, where caste origins are less obvious and less important in public life. In rural India, caste origins are more readily apparent and Dalits remain excluded from local religious life, though this exclusion in its severity is in fact fast diminishing due to changing social norms of acceptable behaviour.

Dalits and similar groups are also found in Nepal, Pakistan and Bangladesh.

DALITS AND INDIAN POLITICS

Mahatma Gandhi made it part of the Indian National Congress's mission to eradicate untouchability. For this reason, untouchability has been officially abolished in India, although the social practice still exists today, particularly in rural villages.

In these villages, Dalits are still not allowed to let their shadows fall upon a non-Dalit caste member (particularly a Brahmin, for fear of ritually contaminating them), and they are still required to sweep the ground where they walk to remove the 'contamination' of their footfalls. In some of these villages, rural Dalits are forbidden to worship in temples or draw water from the same wells as caste Hindus, and they usually live in segregated neighbourhoods outside the main village.

In urban areas and most villages the old concepts of a rigid caste system and untouchability usually no longer exist, though most Indians still voluntarily hold on to their caste origins, which is intended to reflect that their ancestors belonged to their castes with a sense of pride in the duties and responsibilities as required by the caste rules. In matrimonial matters, whether the wed couple is Dalit or non-Dalit, caste identity is a practical near-must.

This is, however, ignored by inter-caste couples, who marry ignoring castes but due to an attraction on the basis of education or economic status, of either or both members of the couple.

While the Indian Constitution has duly made special provisions for the social and economic uplift of the Dalits, comprising the so-called scheduled castes and tribes in order to enable them to achieve upward social mobility, these concessions are limited to only those Dalits who remain Hindu. There is a demand among the Dalits who have converted to other religions that the statutory benefits should be extended to them as well as social relief to "overcome" historical injustices.

Another major politically charged issue with the rise of Hindutva's role in Indian politics is that of religious conversion. This political movement alleges that conversions of Dalits are due not to any social or theological motivation but to allurements like education and jobs. Critics argue that the inverse is true with laws banning conversion, and the limiting of social relief for these backward sections of Indian society being revoked for those who convert. Bangaru Laxman, a Dalit politician, was a prominent member of the Hindutva movement. Another political issue is over the affirmative action measures taken by the government towards the uplift of the Dalits by implementation of quotas in government jobs and university admissions aimed at improving Dalit representation. About 8% of the seats in the National and State Parliaments are reserved for Scheduled Caste and Tribe candidates, a measure sought by B. R. Ambedkar and other Dalit activists in order to ensure that Dalits would obtain a proportionate political voice.

ON GANDHI'S VIEW ON THE RELATIONSHIP BETWEEN LANDLORDS AND TENANTS

Mr. Gandhi does not wish to hurt the propertied class. He is even more opposed to a campaign against them. He has no passion for economic equality, referring to the propertied class Mr. Gandhi has quite recently said that he does not wish to destroy the hen that lays the golden egg. His solution for the economic conflict between the owners and the workers, between the rich and the poor, between the landlords and the tenants, and between the employers and the employees is very simple. The owners need not deprive themselves of their property. All that they need to do is to declare themselves Trustees for the poor. Of course, the Trust is to be a voluntary one carrying only a spiritual obligation.

ON GANDHI'S SUPPORT FOR THE HINDU CASTE SYSTEM, ALBEIT DEVOID OF UNTOUCHABILITY

The social ideal of Gandhism is either caste or varna. Though it may be difficult to say which, there can be no doubt that the social ideal of Gandhism is not democracy. For whether one takes for comparison caste or varna both are fundamentaly opposed to democracy (p. 297).... Gandhism is a paradox. It stands for freedom from foreign domination, which means the destruction of the existing political structure of the country. At the same time, it seeks to maintain intact a social structure which permits the domination of one class by another on a hereditary basis which means a perpetual domination of one class by another.

The importance of Ambedkar has been recently attacked by certain intellectuals who seem to resent the celebration of Ambedkar on the national level. Dalit assertion is inevitably dealt with violence, both physical as well as ideological. Such times as these demand a nuanced understanding of the different roles which both Gandhi and Ambedkar played in reconstituting an independent India which would be truly free. For, it may be argued that regardless of the real differences between these two inspiring figures of India's struggle for freedom, both of them would represent a severe blow to the foundations of religious fundamentalism as we have come to experience in our midst.

DALITS AND RELIGION

Hindu Dalits (Harijans): Many Dalits continue to debate whether they are 'Hindu' or 'non-Hindu'. Missionaries have initiated several Dalit organizations. In some regions of India and Nepal, missionaries have been successful among the Dalits, both in Eastern India and Nepal, many Dalits have come under the combined influence of Maoists and the missionaries, even attacking and murdering Hindus.

Traditionally, Hindu Dalits or Harijans have been barred from many activities that were seen as central to Vedic religion and Hindu practices of orthodox sects. Among Hindus each community has followed its own variation of Hinduism. The wide variety of practices and beliefs observed in Hinduism makes any clear assessment difficult.

Some of the movements in Hinduism have welcomed Dalits into their fold. The Satnami movement was founded by Guru Ghasidas a Dalit himself. In addition, other Hindu groups have reached out to the Dalit community in an effort to reconcile with them, with productive results. On August 2006, Dalit activist Namdeo Dhasal engaged in dialogue with the Rashtriya Swayamsevak Sangh in an attempt to "bury the hatchet".

In addition, the "Pandaram" are an order of Dalit Hindu priests (a task traditionally reserved for the Brahmins) based largely in Nepal and parts of South India. These Pandaram priests maintain the same tradition as the Brahmin priests, including using Sanskrit for the rituals (a language traditionally reserved for the Brahmins). They perform religious ceremonies from weddings to death rituals. They are not generally as well trained as the Brahmin priests, but are highly respected within their community and are addressed reverentially. Also, Hindu temples are increasingly more receptive to Dalit priests, such as Suryavanshi Das, the Dalit priest of a notable temple in Bihar.

Another popular Harijan includes Babaji Palwankar Baloo, who joined the Hindu Mahasabha and was both a politician and a cricketer. He was an independence fighter.

However, extremist far-right militia groups such as the Ranvir Sena, largely run by upper-caste landlords in backward areas of the Indian state of Bihar, oppose equal treatment of Dalits and have resorted to violent means to suppress them. The Ranvir Sena is considered a terrorist organization. On the other side, extremist groups run by small minority of Dalits such as the "Dalit Panthers Movement" have committed violent acts against Brahmins and middle-caste people.

In Pakistan, a predominantly Muslim nation, more than 60% of the 1. 4 million Hindu minority are Dalits.

Muslim Dalits (Arzal): Muslim society in India can also be separated into several caste-like groups. Descendants of indigenous lower-caste converts are discriminated against by "noble", or "ashraf", Muslims who can trace their descent to

Arab, Iranian, or Central-Asian ancestors. There are several groups in India working to emancipate them from upper-caste Muslim discrimination. The Dalit Muslims are referred to by the Ashraf and Ajlaf Muslims as Arzal or "ritually degraded". They were first recorded in the 1901 census as those "with whom no other Muhammadan would associate, and who are forbidden to enter the mosque or to use the public burial ground". They are relegated to "menial" professions such as scavenging and carrying night soil. Babasaheb Ambedkar, a renowned Dalit activist and the framer of the Constitution of India, wrote about the Dalit Muslims and was extremely critical of their mistreatment by upper-caste Muslims quoting that "Within these groups there are castes with social precedence of exactly the same nature as one finds among the Hindus".

In Pakistan, there are estimated to be 6.8 million Mayazurs (bonded labourers) in Punjab and another 7.5 million in Sindh. Although the Pakistani Supreme Court has ruled bonded labour unconstitutional and the National Assembly has passed laws prohibiting it, these laws remain largely unenforced due to the influence of large landlords. Furthermore, the AIBMM is striving to achieve the SC status for India's Muhajirs.

Sikh Dalits: Master Tara Singh himself helped uplift the Sikh Dalits. K.P. Singh a Dalit activist in UP was himself a Sikh. Kanshi Ram himself was of Sikh background although converted because he found that Sikh society did not respect Dalits and so became a neo-Buddhist. The Mazhabi are one Dalit of the Punjabi Dalits that are treated as outcastes from mainstream Sikh society and not allowed to enter Sikh temples. Jivan Singh, a friend of Guru Gobind Singh was a Dalit.

Christian Dalits: Converts to Christianity (facilitated by the influence of missionaries) have historically retained the caste system in their communities though many Christian leaders publicly reject caste. Joseph D'Souza, President of the All India Christian Council, has publicly pushed for a complete rejection of caste through partnership with Dalits across the country. A 1992 study of Catholics in Tamil Nadu showed that

Dalit Christians face segregated churches, cemeteries, services and processions. They also face economic and social hardships due to the discrimination by upper-caste priests and nuns. One famous Dalit activist with the nom-de-plume of Bama Faustina has written books that provide a first-hand account of the discrimination against them by nuns and priests in South India.

DALITS AND NEO-BUDDHISM

In Maharashtra, Uttar Pradesh and a few other regions, Dalits have come under the influence of the neo-Buddhist movement initiated by Ambedkar. Some of them have come under the influence of the Neo-Buddhist and Christian Missionaries and have converted away from Hinduism into religions such as Christianity and Buddhism in what they have been told is an "attempt to eliminate the prejudice they face". Activists such as Udit Raj have claimed that such conversion will solve all discrimination problems faced by Dalits. Such claims have been criticized as "fragile at best". The conversion attempts have also been criticized by Hindu advocacy groups as "unhelpful" as Casteism is a complex dynamic that extends across all religions in India. However, the Constitution of India guarantees religious freedom and their right to choose their religion, although controversies related to mass-conversions have led to laws being passed against them in some states in India. Since then, several Christian converts have reconverted back into Hinduism as the conversions did not award them the financial rewards that the missionaries lured them with.

RESISTANCE TO THE SOUL: GANDHI AND HIS CRITICS

Looking back at the twentieth century, as it is almost at its end, it has been marked by the bloodiest conflicts ever known to Humankind. From the death and destruction, the annals of history will forever manifest those who contributed to the barbarous events and those who attempted to resist the inhumane acts of aggressors. Belonging to the latter, one personality seems to stand out amongst the lot of humanitarians and peace loving people-Mohandas Karamchand Gandhi. Although Gandhi was a remarkable nationalist leader, he was less concerned with the ends of his actions and more with the means of achieving independence for India.

Gandhi believed in the idea of nonviolent resistance and civil disobedience. These two elements of Gandhi's plan for Indian Independence, stemmed from his philosophy of Satyagraha or soul force. When most nationalist movements of the twentieth century were being executed through the use of violence, Gandhi sought to employ a method that opposed the practice or the advocacy of violence to achieve political goals. His method was based on "Truth, Love and Self-suffering". It was through this method that any adversity could be conquered. By sacrificing one's self to your opponent's wrath without violent retaliation, your opponent would give in because of the commitment to self-sacrifice on the part of the Satyagrahis (Person practising Satyagraha).

Gandhi utilized this method of Soul Force to achieve political reform in South Africa, independence in India and to transform himself into the person that he wanted to be. Gandhi's methods gained him tremendous praise from people worldwide, including his adversaries and served as a catalyst for the mass movement towards ending the British Raj. Long after Gandhi's assassination, Gandhi and his ideas are still admired for their humanitarian and almost saintly attributes. Some revere Gandhi "...as perhaps the greatest figure of the last nineteen hundred years", while others have made serious criticisms of his ideas and methods. Rajani Palme Dutt, saw Gandhi's actions as a method of protecting the interests of the Bourgeoisie in India during a time of uncertainty. K. Sarwar Hasan contests that Gandhi's political ideas and actions based on Hindu doctrine alienated the Muslims of India.

Hindu Nationalist V. D. Savarkar, thought that Gandhi's methods contradicted the religious outlook of Hinduism and jeopardized Hindu political interests as well. The leader of "The

All Indian Depressed Class Federation" and "Untouchable", B. R. Ambedkar contends that Gandhi was a proponent of the Caste System and an antagonist towards progress that would have benefited all of India, especially the depressed classes. These men set forth a plethora of strong criticism against a man who was simply searching for the truth. It will be the goal of this work to answer these criticisms, when possible, through the use of Gandhi's ideas and historical fact.

Dutt construes a Marxist view of Gandhism and contends that Gandhi's methods were not as altruistic as they appeared to be. These methods were a means of protecting the privileges of Indian landlords and Bourgeoisie that were being jeopardized by the unbridled force of the common masses. "Non-violence" is seen as a design, constructed and utilized to restrain this force that struck fear into the hearts of the landed class and to harness the force of the masses to compel the British to make concessions. When the Rowlette act was passed in 1919 it added to the atmosphere of dissatisfaction among the Indian people. At the end of World War I many Indian people expected civil liberties to be restored.

The Rowlatt act was in favour of continuing the "war time vigours". This act caused widespread unrest and strikes in India. Dutt claims that it was Gandhi's primary intention to utilize civil disobedience and nonviolence to stop the civil unrest and strikes. The Rowlatt act and its reforms had at first been accepted by Gandhi and the Congress. Once the violence erupted, Gandhi and congress shifted their positions and assumed the leadership role of the mass movement. This was done because the members of Congress, the Bourgeoisie, were worried about the violent masses turning against them. So, Gandhi planned a program of "Non-violent non-cooperation" to cope with this matter. It would be the middle-class that would spearhead the movement while the masses were supposed to resort hand spinning, weaving and non-payment of taxes. This plan is perceived by Dutt as a scheme to eliminate the possibility of the masses posing a threat to the landed class.

The change in the position of Congress in reference to the Rowlatt, was accompanied by another phenomenon. Congress ceased to be just an organization of self-government with in the British empire but it transformed itself into a modern political party that was leading the masses into a struggle against the British. Like any other political party, Congress was bent on protecting their interests. Non-violent rhetoric "was an attempt to conciliate the interests of the masses with the big bourgeoisie and landlord interests which were opposed to any decisive mass struggle. "Dutt believes this became more obvious after the Chauri Chaura incident in which peasant rioters killed a group of policemen and Gandhi subsequently withdrew his support for the movement.

The fact that Gandhi withdraws his commitment to the movement by calling off the entire campaign and then substitute his original strategy with the "Constructive Program" indicates to Dutt that the Bourgeoisie was losing control of the movement and would attempt to regain it by calming the masses. Dutt is critical of Gandhi's actions that resulted in the suspension of the mass movement. Gandhi claims that he suspended the movement to end the violent outbreaks associated with it. Dutt believes that the Bardoli decision/resolution had an economic motive. Since the movement was cancelled at "the height of public enthusiasm" it is an indication to the Marxist that the interests of the Bourgeoisie were being jeopardized.

The enthusiasm and force of the masses at this time was potent enough to sweep away imperialism and might have done the same to landlordism in the process. This opinion is supported by the fact that the Ryots (peasants) had been instructed to resume the payment of taxes and rent once the mass civil disobedience movement was suspended. Dutt thinks that the resolution instituted by the Working Committee at Bardoli has little relation to the outbreak of violence. Three of its seven clauses specifically refer to the payment of rents by the peasants to the landlords. His conclusion is that this was a question of class interest and not a matter of suppressing the violence for its own sake. Non-violence is held to be disguise for class interest and to serve as a leash for the masses' activities that might have been counter productive to the interests of the propertied class. The keystone to this argument is that the payment or non-payment of taxes and rents is totally unrelated to the presence of mass hysteria, yet it was a major issue in the aftermath of this movement.

Dutt sees Gandhi as "an ascetic defender of property..." because he uses "...the most religious principles of humanity and love to disguise his support of the property class. "Gandhi is reduced to a" tool or mascot of the Bourgeoisie in every wave of the Indian struggle" It was Gandhi who was able to attracted and guide the masses when the Bourgeoisie leadership failed to do so. He was able to harness the enthusiasm of the people in order to gain concessions from the British and also keep the masses in check by preventing a class revolution in India through the use of his nonviolent philosophy. Further evidence to support Dutt's opinion that nonviolence was not a means of achieving independence but a method of maintaining leadership and bourgeois position is the salt march of March 1930. Gandhi limited this campaign to himself and his chosen disciples. It was by his instruction that the masses, including industrial workers were asked to be patient and continue the work of the "Constructive Program". In short, Dutt believes that Gandhi manipulated the masses by calling them to action when favourable to the bourgeoisie and then withdrawing his support if things got out of hand. Dutt claims this was the case in 1932, when Gandhi abandoned the movement once more to tend to the cause of the Harijans.

It is easy to discern why a Marxist would oppose Gandhian philosophy. A Marxist such as Dutt, advocates the violent over turning of society by the masses and the establishment of a state based on Marxist doctrine. Gandhi was opposed to violence in general, especially as a means of bringing about political change. To Gandhi, the only acceptable method of attaining freedom was through nonviolence and civil disobedience.

Through this method true Swaraj could be achieved. This did not mean the mere ousting of the British imperialists from India but that Indians, through Gandhi's methods, would first learn how to master themselves.

This was the purpose of the "Constructive Program" as proposed by Gandhi in the 1920's, to help the Indian people achieve independence by first creating "an atmosphere of perfect calm", unity among all Indians and to give up foreign cloth by producing their own. It was through this program that Gandhi thought people could learn how to rule themselves as individuals. To sum it up-Inward freedom must come before outward freedom. To Gandhi Swaraj was more than just political, economic and social freedom, it was a continuous movement of spiritual liberation and self-purification. This explains why Gandhi called for peaceful protest even though many others utilized violence. "If India was to achieve independence without violence and coercion that is how India would govern herself...once the British are gone."

It is no lie that Gandhi suspended the mass movement, as Dutt claimed. In light of the occurrences at Chauri Chaura, Gandhi felt that the people were not ready for mass disobedience, since a prerequisite of a movement of mass disobedience is a law abiding citizenry. This was not the case at Chauri Chaura. The murder of the constables, who were defenceless at the hands of the crowd, was a blow to Gandhi who believed that "no provocation could have justified such an act. "He believed that" India was not ready for self-government until Indians were able to restrain themselves and have succeeded in getting control over the hooligans of India."

The notion that Gandhi was a spokesman or spin doctor for the Bourgeoisie seems absurd. Gandhi was simply a spokesman for all of humanity. He sought to help the "Untouchables" as well as the wealthy Hindus. Dutt claimed that Gandhi was guilty of manipulating the Ryots but Gandhi's actions show differently-they show that he had a genuine concern for them. Farmers in the village of Champaran were required, by law to plant three out of twenty parts of land with Indigo for their landlords. One peasant asked Gandhi to travel to Champaran and to inquire into the conditions of the Ryots there. Gandhi's inquiry led to an official investigation that found in favour of the Ryots. They were refunded a portion of the money, but the greater benefit was that this tithe was abolished. Another example of Gandhi's concern for the common folk was his actions in Ahmedabad. Mill hands were discontented with the low wages they were receiving from the mill owners. Gandhi first suggested arbitration between the two groups but that did not resolve the problem. Gandhi advises the labourers to strike and provides them with further advice on how to make the strike a success. In the end, a mutual agreement was reached and the strikers returned to work.

If Gandhi did remove his support from any civil disobedience movement it was only because it became marred with acts of violence perpetrated by his fellow countrymen. Gandhi best explains his own actions by stating "if I can have nothing to do with the organized violence of the government, I can have even less to do with the unorganized violence of the people. "Nonviolent noncooperation was not just a method of achieving Swaraj but a method of resisting evil. Gandhi did not distinguish between violent acts committed by Indians or Englishmen, to him they are equally evil.

It is obvious that a Marxist would be an opponent of Gandhism, and it come as no surprise that K. Sarwar Hasan, a. Pakistani Muslim would also portray Gandhi's ideas and actions in a negative light. Gandhi's failure to attract a large Muslim following was his downfall according to Hasan. This deficiency was due to Gandhi's inability to understand and gratify the needs of the Muslim population in India.

This became evident in 1919 when the terms of the Treaty of Sevres became known to India's Muslims. This treaty proposed a dismemberment of the Ottoman Empire and caused general unrest amongst Muslims in India. Hasan's contention is that Gandhi only took action on this matter because he felt forced to do so and it was an opportunity to address issues that concerned Hindus as well. "Gandhi consolidated joint grievances and proposed that congress should launch a campaign of mass noncooperation. "Gandhi's proposal received opposition from Muslims, like Jinnah who saw Gandhi's "soul force" as a tree that would bear no fruit. The slow going pace of Gandhi's methods would only increase the divide between Muslims and Hindus since his method possessed an ideological foundation based on Hinduism. Muslims like Jinnah believed if mass support was to be gathered for the cause of independence, it had to be done quickly.

Hasan's most stalwart criticism is that Gandhi utilized the Hindu religion and traditions to guide the quest for India's independence. Gandhi's inspiration and language, that was associated with the movement, were products of Hindu scriptures like the Gita. India's independence was referred to as Ram Raj (Rule of God-Hindu god Rama) and the struggle itself was referred to as Dharma Yudh (Hindu religious war). These associations with Hinduism coupled with the fact that Gandhi was a Hindu repelled Muslims. According to Hasan it was Gandhi's desire to establish an independent India that was free of western models. This ruled out the possibility of independent India becoming a secular state. The Muslims wanted a secular state established to ensure that their religious rights would not be trampled on. Hasan believes that Gandhi could have done more to solidify Hindu-Muslim relations. He sees Gandhi's actions as futile attempts to appease Muslims and contends that nothing concrete was ever offered to Muslims.

The fact that Gandhi was unable to rally enough Muslim support is not his downfall alone. Culpability can be found with the Muslims themselves. The fact that the Muslim community disapproved of Jinnah's joining of the Indian National Congress is proof enough that the divisions were not caused by Gandhi's actions alone, not to mention the historical rivalry. Gandhi's intentions and actions illustrate that he did not just placate the Muslims but truly desired to form a united India.

Gandhi treated Muslims as his equals. This was evident in South Africa as well as India. A main provision of his Triple Program was his commitment to strengthen Hindu-Muslim unity. He was a firm believer in the philosophy of the majority having respect for the minority. He considered Hindus and Muslims "natural brothers of India" and thought that it was more surprising to see them feud than if they should unite. His entire equation of a free India was based upon the notion of a "brotherhood of man". No distinctions were made between Hindus or Muslims or any other religion or race for that matter.

On the eve of partition, Gandhi still advocated brotherhood between the two groups even though the splitting of India was the cause of severe disappointment for him. Hasan's claim that Gandhi saw the independence movement as a Hindu Holy war is a near-sighted judgement. Gandhi was simply expressing his feeling and ideas in a medium that he was most familiar with-Hinduism.

If Gandhi did disagree with Muslim opinions at times it was only because they contradicted his creed of Ahimsa and Satyagraha and his vision of an independent India. Not to mention that it was not only Muslims that Gandhi disagreed with. Hindu nationalists as well as Muslim nationalists set forth staunch opposition to Gandhi's plans and ideas.

Gandhi's actions seemed extremely unorthodox to many Hindus. V. D. Savarkar, a Hindu nationalist, saw Gandhi as a threat to the existence of Hindus in India. Savarkar believed that Gandhi's influence over Congress hurt the Hindu cause, because Gandhi gave in to Muslim demands. Gandhi supposedly jeopardized Swaraj by taking up the Khilafat issue. Muslim leaders in India tried to coerce Amir Nuillakhan of Afghanistan to invade India. Gandhi was aware of this vision to establish an Afghanistanian kingdom in India, yet did not distance himself from those that supported this invasion. In short, Gandhi's continual appeasement of the Muslims endangered the interests of Hindus according to Savarkar.

This criticism serves to calcify the previous argument that Gandhi was in favour of a united India and had no ill will towards the Muslims or their interests. Gandhi probably would not have minded if a Muslim was head of the government as long as he shared the same views on brotherhood and equality among all people as Gandhi did. Gandhi did say that "Muslims in India were once Hindus, they just accepted Islam. "Savarkar's criticisms stems from the criticisms that Gandhi made about Hindus that suggested that they were too closed minded to accept Muslims as their brothers and fellow countrymen.

Criticism directed at Gandhi seems expected from the three previous sources, criticism from an Untouchable seems surprising. B. R. Ambedkar is under the impression that Gandhi was an advocate of the caste system. Gandhi saw the caste system as the backbone of Hindu society and did nothing to put an end to this evil practice even though it was the cause of misery for the Untouchables that Gandhi was supposedly trying to help. Ambedkar attempted to support his claims by stating that Gandhi believes that "intermarriages were not necessarily for national unity, that dining together does not create peace and that the abandonment of the caste system in favour of a social system based on western ideals was a detriment to all. Ambedkar assumes that Gandhi is undemocratic in thought because he opposes a social system similar to that of western nations that made discrimination illegal. Ambedkar interprets Gandhi's views as conservative, reactionary, downright archaic and unrealistic. Gandhi's opposition to machinery and his commitment to Charka (the spinning wheel) is rejected by Ambedkar who believes that such modern devices will end economic and social ills in so far as progress will liberate the depressed classes of India not Gandhi's idealism. Gandhi's views will never be able to help the common man, so states Ambedkar. The only thing that will elevate him is culture. Culture advances and liberates humanity. It is the only thing that divorces humans from animals. But culture cannot be transmitted if people do not possess leisure time.

Leisure time will only become available if the toils of life are lessened. In Ambedkar's opinion machines would produce leisure time by reducing the labour of the common person and this leisure time could be used for a "life of culture". Gandhi was an ordinary man who had great ideas. These critics misunderstood many of Gandhi's ideas. Their lack of comprehension is the cause of their criticisms. Their lack of vision is the cause of these criticisms. Gandhi was a dreamer and these men did not share the same dreams as Gandhi. It is no secret that Gandhi's ultimate dream did not come true-an independent united India.

Does this mean that "the method" failed? Gandhi believed "the method" could never fail since it was a method of truth and love. If anything failed, he admitted "...I did." In his life long search for the truth he like any other human being made mistakes and attracted criticisms. Even if these criticisms were all true, does that negate what Gandhi did for India and humanity? Gandhi saw the caste system as a blemish to Hinduism. If he ever said that the caste system possessed positive attributes it was only because he was in search of the truth. Which means he thought it was to this end that the both the positive and negatives of the caste system should be examined.

Gandhi was a friend to the Untouchables and despised their plight. He fought against the system of Untouchability by admitting Untouchables into the Ashram. Even though he was criticized for doing this and lost monetary support from many Hindus, he stuck to his guns. Gandhi believed that "it was a sin to believe anyone else is inferior to ourselves... Sin pollutes us not another human's touch. Caste is a blot to Hinduism that must be ended". Gandhi criticizes his fellow Hindus for treating the Untouchables the same way the British treated Indians. His assumption was that, if the British were incorrect in their conduct then Hindus must be as well. Untouchables should be "treated as blood brothers as they are in fact. We (Indians) must free ourselves from this miserable condition then true Swaraj can be achieved".

Gandhi was correct in his assumption that peace and brotherhood would not be a product of intermarriages, dining together and the adoption of a social system based on a western model. In Gandhi's view all these things were useless if there was not a change in the conscience of Hindus. No law can force someone not to discriminate, only one's own convictions could do that. Ambedkar's assumption that a social system based on western ideals would bring about "civilization" in India was held in contempt by Gandhi.

To Gandhi, civilization was equated with good conduct. Western culture was plagued by various maladies such as materialism, competition and overindulgence. An assimilation in that direction would only hurt India and the depressed classes. Industrialization as advocated by Ambedkar would only cause the further exploitation of the Untouchables. Labour saving machines would result in more unemployment, further starvation, poverty and homelessness. It would provide benefits for the few and suffering for the many. Gandhi believed progress would not be thwarted by the refusal of labour saving machines because the only progress that mattered was that considered all people. To Gandhi, progress is only progress if all Indians progressed together. The only device that considered the needs of all Indians was the spinning wheel. With it people could become self sufficient and labour for their benefit.

2

AMBEDKAR VIEWS AND REVIEWS ON CASTES SYSTEM

DR. AMBEDKAR VIEW ON SALVATION

The subject of conversion is very dear to me. According to me, the whole of your future depends upon this subject. I have no hesitation in saying that you have clearly understood the gravity of this problem. Had it not been so, you would not have assembled here in such large numbers. I am very happy to see this (gathering). Since the time of the declaration of Conversion, our men have conducted several meetings at various places and expressed their views and opinions, which I hope must have reached you. But we have had no opportunity so far to gather, and to discuss and decide the problem of conversion at one place. I was much more concerned for such an opportunity. You must have come to know by now that this Conference has been purposefully called upon to brood over the declaration of Conversion which I made recently.

You will all agree that planning is very necessary for making the movement of Conversion a success. Conversion is not a children's game. It is not a subject of entertainment. It deals with how to make man's life successful. Just as a boatman has to make all necessary preparation before he starts on a voyage, so also we have to make such preparation. Without preparation, it will be impossible to reach the other shore. But just as the boatman does not collect luggage unless he gets an idea of the number of passengers boarding the boat, so also is the case with me. Unless I get an idea as to how many persons are willing to leave the Hindu fold, I cannot start preparation for conversion. When I expressed to some workers of Bombay that I would not be able to judge the public opinion unless we meet at a conference, they shouldered the responsibility of this conference voluntarily, without putting up any excuse about expenses and labour. What pains they had to take, has already been described by our revered leader and the President of the Reception Committee, Shri Rawji Dagduji Dolas, in his speech. I am extremely indebted to the Reception Committee of the Conference for arranging the meeting, after making such strenuous efforts.

Some people may raise an objection as to why the conference is called (with the participation) only of the Mahars. If the declaration of Conversion is meant for all the Untouchables, why has a meeting of all the Untouchables not been convened? Before starting the discussion on the issues before the conference, I feel it obligatory to reply to these questions. There are various reasons for convening a conference of the Mahars alone.

Firstly, neither any safeguards nor any social rights are to be demanded from the Hindus through this conference. The only question before this conference is, what should be done for the betterment of our life? How to carve out the path for our future life? This question can be solved, and needs to be solved, by the respective castes separately, discussing it through their respective conferences. This is one of the reasons why I have not called a conference of all the Untouchables.

There is another reason for convening a conference of Mahars only. About ten months have passed since the declaration of Conversion was made. During this period, sufficient efforts have been made to awaken the public conscience. I felt that this was the proper time to judge the public opinion. In my opinion, the holding of meetings of each caste separately is the simplest way to judge the opinion. In order to materialize (give substance to) the problem of conversion, it is very necessary to judge the public opinion. And I believe the public opinion judged through the meetings of each caste separately will be more representative and reliable than the opinion arrived at through a common meeting of all the Untouchable castes. In order to avert this situation, and to ensure the (knowledge of) public opinion, this meeting of Mahars alone has been called.

Although the other communities are not included, they will not be at a loss. If they do not intend to convert, they have no reason to regret their not being included in this conference. If at all they wish to leave their religion, nothing can come in their way simply because they have not participated in this conference. The other communities, like the Mahars, are free to hold meetings and express their public opinion. I would advise them to hold such meetings, and whatever help is needed from me shall be extended to them to the best of my capacity.

This much is enough as introduction. Now I turn to the main subject. For a common man, this subject of conversion is important as well as difficult to understand. It is equally difficult to grasp the subject. It is not an easy task to satisfy the common man on the subject of conversion. I realise that unless you are all satisfied, it is difficult to bring the idea of conversion into reality. I shall therefore try my level best to explain the subject as simply as possible.

GAIN THE STRENGTH

The question that follows, which you must consider, is whether you have enough strength to survive through this struggle. Three types of strength are known to man: (1) manpower; (2) finance; and (3) mental strength. Which of these do you think that you possess? So far as manpower is concerned, it is clear that you are in a minority. In Bombay Presidency, Untouchables are only one-eighth of the total population. And that too, an unorganised (one-eighth). The castes among them do not allow them to organise. They are not even compact. They are scattered through the villages. Under these circumstances, this small population is of no use to the Untouchables at their crucial hours.

Financial strength is also just the same. It is an undisputed fact that you have a little bit of manpower; but finances you have none. You have no trade, no business, no service, no land. The piece of bread thrown by the higher castes is your means of livelihood. You have no food, no clothes. What financial strength can you have? You have no capacity to get redress from the law courts. Thousands of Untouchables tolerate insult, tyranny, and oppression at the hands of Hindus without a sigh of complaint, because they have no capacity to bear the expenses of the courts.

As regards mental strength, the condition is still worse. The tolerance of insults and tyranny without grudge and complaint has killed the sense of retort and revolt. Confidence, vigour, and ambition have completely vanished from you. All of you have become helpless, unenergetic, and pale. Everywhere there is an atmosphere of defeatism and pessimism. Even the slight idea that you can do something, cannot peep (penetrate) into your minds.

WHY THIS OPPRESSION AGAINST YOU?

If whatever I have described above is correct, then you will have to agree with the conclusion that follows. The conclusion is: if you depend upon your own strength, you will never be able to face the tyranny of the Hindus. I have no doubt that you are oppressed because you have no strength. It is not that you alone are in a minority. The Muslims are equally small in number. Like Mahar-Mangs, they too have few houses in the village. But no one dares to trouble the Muslims, while you are always a victim of tyranny. Why is this so? Though there are two houses of Muslims in the village, nobody dares to harm them, while the whole village practises tyranny against you though you have about ten houses. Why does this happen? This is a very pertinent question, and you will have to find a suitable answer for this.

In my opinion, there is only one answer to this question. The Hindus realise that the strength of the whole of the Muslim population in India stands behind those two houses of Muslims living in the village; and therefore they do not dare to touch them. These two houses also enjoy a free and fearless life because they are aware that if any Hindu commits aggression against them, the whole Muslim community from Punjab to Madras will rush down to protect them at any cost.

On the contrary (by contrast), Hindus are sure that no one will come to your rescue, nobody will help you, no financial help will reach you, nor will the officers help you in any eventuality. The Tehsildar and police belong to the caste Hindus, and in cases of disputes between the Hindus and the Untouchables, they are more faithful to their caste than towards their duty. The Hindus practise injustice and tyranny against you only because you are helpless. From the above discussion, two facts are very clear.

Firstly, you cannot face the tyranny without strength. And secondly, you do not possess enough strength to face the tyranny. With these two conclusions, a third one automatically follows. That is, the strength required to face the tyranny needs to be secured from outside. How you will be able to secure this strength, is really an important question. And you will have to think this over with an unbiased mind.

STRENGTH NEEDS TO BE BROUGHT FROM OUTSIDE

Casteism and religious fanaticism, as I see it, has had a very peculiar effect on the minds and morality of the people of this country. In this country, nobody feels pain at poverty and suffering. And if at all anybody is moved, he does not try to eradicate it. People (give) help in poverty, sorrows, and suffering, only to those who belong to their caste or religion. Though this sense of morality is perverted, it cannot be forgotten that it is prevalent in this country. In the village, the Untouchables suffer at the hands of Hindus.

It is not that there are no men of other religions, and that they do not realise the oppression of Untouchables as unjust. Knowing full well that the oppression of the Untouchables by the Hindus is most unjustified, they do not rush to the rescue of the Untouchables. If you ask them why do they not help you, they would say, "What business do we have to interfere? Had you been the members of our religion, we would have helped you."

From this you will understand one thing: that unless you establish close relations with some other society, unless you join some other religion, you cannot get the strength from outside. It clearly means, you must leave your present religion and assimilate yourselves with some other society. Without that, you cannot gain the strength of that society. So long as you do not have strength, you and your future generations will have to lead a life in the same pitiable condition.

THE MATERIAL ASPECT OF CONVERSION

There are two aspects of conversion: social as well as religious, material as well as spiritual. Whatever may be the aspect or line of thinking, it is necessary to understand at the beginning the nature of Untouchability and how it is practised. Without this understanding, you will not be able to realise the real meaning underlying my declaration of Conversion. In order to have a clear understanding of the problem of Untouchability and its practice in real life, I would want you to recall the stories of atrocities perpetrated against you.

The instances of beating by the caste Hindus for the simple reason that you have claimed the right to enrol your children in the Government school, or the right to draw water from the public well, or the right to take out a marriage procession with the groom on horseback, are very common. You all know such instances, as they happen right before your eyes. But there are several other causes for which atrocities are committed on the Untouchables by the caste Hindus—causes which, if they are revealed, the foreigners will be surprised to hear.

The Untouchables are beaten for putting on clothes of superior quality. They are whipped because they used utensils made of metal like copper, etc. Their houses are burnt for having purchased land for cultivation. They are beaten for putting on the sacred thread on their body. They are beaten for refusing to carry away dead animals and eat the carrion, or for walking through the village road with socks and shoes on, or for not bowing down before a caste Hindu, or for taking water in a copper pot while going out in the field to ease (defecate). Recently, an instance has been noticed where the Untouchables were beaten for serving chapatis at a dinner party.

You must have heard of, and some of you must also have experienced, such types of atrocities. Where beating is not possible, you must be aware as to how the weapon of boycott is used against you. You all know how the caste Hindus have made your daily life unbearable by prohibiting you from labour, by disallowing your cattle from grazing through the jungle (uncultivated land), and by prohibiting your men from entering into the village. But perhaps very few of you have realised as to why all this happens! What is at the root of their tyranny? To me, it is very necessary for us to understand it.

THIS IS A MATTER OF CLASS STRUGGLE

Untouchability is a matter of class struggle. It is a struggle between caste Hindus and the Untouchables. This is not a matter of doing injustice against one man. This is a matter of injustice being done by one class against another. This class struggle has its relation with the social status. This struggle indicates how one class should keep its relations with the other class. From the instances given above, one thing is clear. This struggle starts as soon as you start claiming equal treatment with others. Had it not been so, there would have been no struggle for a simple reason like serving chapatis, wearing superior-quality clothes, putting on the sacred thread, fetching water in a metal pot, seating the bridegroom on horseback, etc. In all these cases, you lose your money.

Why then do the caste Hindus get irritated? The reason for their anger is very simple. Your behaviour with them on a par insults them. Your status is low. You are impure, you must remain at the lowest rung; then alone they will allow you to live happily. The moment you cross your level, the struggle starts. The above instances also prove one more fact. Untouchability is not a timely (transient) or temporary feature. It is a permanent one. To put it straight (plainly), it can be said that the struggle between the Hindus and the Untouchables is a permanent phenomenon. It is eternal, because the religion which has given you the lowest level in the society is itself eternal, according to the belief of the high-caste people. No change according to times and circumstances is possible. You are the lowest of the rungs today. You shall remain the lowest forever. This means the struggle between Hindus and Untouchables will continue forever. How you will survive through this struggle, is a main question. And unless you think it over, there is no escape.

Those who desire to behave in obedience to the wishes of the Hindus, those who wish to be their slaves, need not think over this problem. But those who wish to live a life with self-respect and equality, will have to think it over. How should we survive through this struggle? For me, it is not difficult to answer this question. Those who have assembled here will have to agree that in any struggle, one who holds strength becomes the victor. One who has no strength need not expect success. This has been proved by experience, and I do not need to cite examples to prove it.

THE SPIRITUAL ASPECT OF CONVERSION

Until now, we have discussed how conversion is necessary for material gains. Now I propose to put forth my thoughts as to how this conversion is equally necessary for spiritual well-being. What is religion? Why is it necessary? Let us first try to understand. Several people have tried to define religion. But amongst all of these definitions, only one is most meaningful and agreeable to all. "That which knits the people together is religion." This is the true definition of religion. This is not my definition. Mr. Tilak, the foremost leader of the Sanatani Hindus himself, is the author of this definition. So nobody can accuse me of having interpolated (invented) the definition of religion.

However, I have not accepted it (merely) for argument's sake. I accept it (as a principle). Religion means the rules imposed for the maintenance of society. Mine is also the same concept of religion. Although this definition logically appears to be correct, it does not disclose or clarify the nature of the rules which maintain the society. The question still remains as to what should be the nature of the rules which govern society. This question is more important than that of definition. Because the question of which religion is necessary for a man, does not depend on its definition but on the motive and nature of the rules that bind and govern the society. What should be the real nature of religion? While deciding this question, another question follows. What should be the relation between a man and the society?

The modern social philosophers have proposed three answers to this question. Some have proposed that the ultimate goal of the society is to achieve happiness for the individual. Some say the society exists for the development of man's inherent qualities and energies, and to help him develop his self. However, some put up (maintain) that the chief object of the social organisation is not the development or happiness of the individual, but to create an ideal society.

The concept of the Hindu religion is, however, much different from all these concepts. There is no place for an individual in Hindu society. The Hindu religion is constituted on the class concept. The Hindu religion does not teach as to how an individual should behave with another individual. A religion which does not recognize the individual is not acceptable to me personally. Although society is necessary for the individual, social welfare cannot be the ultimate goal of religion. To me, individual welfare and progress is the real aim of religion. Although the individual is a part of the society, his relation with the society is not like that of the body and its organs, or that of the cart and its wheels.

SOCIETY AND THE INDIVIDUAL

Unlike a drop of water which submerges its existence with the ocean in which it is dropped, man does not lose his identity in the society in which he lives. The man's life is independent. He is born not for the service of the society, but for the development of his self. For this reason alone, one man cannot make another a slave, in the developed countries. A religion in which the individual has no importance is not acceptable to me. Likewise, Hinduism does not recognise the importance of an individual, and hence it cannot be acceptable to me.

So also, I do not accept a religion in which one class alone has a right to gain knowledge; another has only a right to use arms; the third one, to trade; and the fourth, only to serve. Everyone needs knowledge. Everybody needs arms. Everyone wants money. The religion which forgets this, and with a view to educate a few persons keeps the rest in the dark, is not a religicn but a strategy to keep the people in mental slavery. A religion which permits some to bear the arms and prohibits the rest, is not a religion but a plan to keep the latter in perpetual slavery. A religion which opens the path of acquiring property for some, and compels others to depend on these few even for the daily necessities of life, is not a religion, but an utter selfishness.

This is what is called the Chaturvarnya of Hinduism. I have clearly stated my views about it. It is for you now to think whether this Hinduism is beneficial to you. The basic idea underlying a religion is to create an atmosphere for the spiritual development of an individual. If this is agreed upon, it is clear that you cannot develop yourself at all in Hinduism.

Three factors are required for the uplift of an individual. They are: Sympathy, Equality, and Liberty. Can you say by experience that any of these factors exist for you in Hinduism?

IS THERE ANY SYMPATHY FOR YOU IN HINDUISM?

So far as sympathy is concerned, it is nil. Wherever you go, nobody looks at you sympathetically. You all have good (ample) experience of it. Not only this, but the Hindus have no sense of brotherhood towards you. You are treated by them worse than foreigners. If one looks at the relations of the neighbouring Hindus and the Untouchables of the village, no one can say that they are brothers. They can rather be called two opposite armies in warring camps.

The Hindus have not the slightest affinity towards you, as they have towards Muslims. They consider Muslims closer than you. Hindus and Muslims are helpful to each other in local boards, in legislative councils, and in business. But is there a single instance of such sympathetic consideration shown towards you by the caste Hindus? On the contrary: they always cultivate hatred against you in their minds. What dreadful effects this hatred has produced, can be heard from those who have had occasion to go to the court for justice or to the police for help.

Does any one of you believe that the court will do justice, and the police will act rightly? And if not, what is the reason for (their) cultivating such a sense of hatred? In my opinion, there is only one reason: you do not believe that the Hindus will rightly use their authority, because they lack sympathy towards you. And if it is so, what is the use of living in the midst of such hatred?

IS THERE EQUALITY FOR YOU IN HINDUISM?

In fact, this question should not be asked. Such a living example of inequality will not be found anywhere in the world. Nowhere in the history of mankind can be seen inequality more intense than Untouchability. On account of (this) superiority-inferiority complex, one may not offer his daughter to another in marriage, or one may not dine with others. Such examples of inequality are not uncommon. But is there a system anywhere existing, except in Hindu religion and Hindu society, where a man is treated (as) so low as (for others) not to touch him? Can anybody believe that there exists an animal called man by whose touch the water is polluted, and the god becomes unworthy for worship?

Is there any difference between the treatment given to an Untouchable and to a leper? Though the people have nausea in their minds for a leper, they have at least sympathy for him. But people have nausea as well as hatred against you. Your condition is worse than (that of) a leper. Even today, if anyone hears words from the mouth of a Mahar at the time of breaking the fast, he will not touch the food. Such a filth is attached to your body and your words. Some people say that Untouchability is a stigma on Hindu religion. This statement, however, does not convey any sense at all. Nobody believes that the Hindu religion is dirty. The majority of the Hindus, however, believe that you are dirty, you are polluted.

How have you been brought to this condition? I think you have been forced to this condition because you continued to be Hindus. Those of you who have become Muslims are treated by the Hindus neither as Untouchables nor even as unequals. The same is the case with those who became Christians. An instance recently happened at Travancore (that is) worth mentioning. The Untouchables called Thiya in that region are prohibited from walking on the streets. A few days ago, some of these Untouchables embraced the Sikh religion. All of a sudden, the ban prohibiting them from walking on the street was withdrawn. What does all this show? It proves that if there is any reason for your being treated as Untouchables and unequals, it is your relation with the Hindu religion.

In such a state of inequality and injustice, some Hindus try to soothe the Untouchables. They say, "Get educated yourselves, be clean, and then we will touch you, we will treat you on par. "In fact, we all know by experience that the condition of an educated, moneyed, and clean Mahar is as bad as that of an uneducated, poor, and dirty one. Leave aside for the time being this aspect, and consider: if one is not respected because he is uneducated, poor, and not a well-dressed person, what should a common Mahar do? How can he secure equality, who cannot gain education, achieve property, or dress highly?

The principle of equality as taught in Christianity and Islam has no concern whatsoever with knowledge, wealth, or dress, as outward aspects. Both these religions consider a sense of humanity as the mean feature of religion. They preach that the sense of humanity should be respected by all; and none should disrespect others, none should treat others as unequals. These teachings are completely wanting in the Hindu religion. What is the use of such a religion, in which man's sense of humanity has no value? And what is the good in clinging to it?

In reply to this, some Hindus cite the Upanishads, and proudly say that the God is all-pervading, according to the principle enunciated in the Upanishads. It may be pointed out here that the religion and science are two different things. It is necessary to consider whether a particular theory is a principle of science, or a teaching of religion. That the God is all-pervading is the principle of science (philosophy) and not of religion. Religion has a direct relation with the behaviour of a man. The principle of the God being omnipresent is not the teaching of religion, it is a principle of science (philosophy). This statement is supported by the fact that the Hindus do not act according to the above principle. On the contrary: if Hindus insist on this very point, and say that the principle of God being omnipresent is not a principle of philosophy but is a basic principle of this religion, I would simply say that nowhere in the world such meanness would be found as exists among Hindus. The Hindus can be ranked among those cruel people whose utterances and acts are two poles asunder (poles apart). They have (as in the proverb) "Ram on their tongue, and a knife under their armpit." They speak like saints and act as butchers.

Do not keep company with those who believe that the God is omnipresent, but treat men worse than animals. They are hypocrites. Do not keep contact with those who feed ants with sugar, but kill men by prohibiting them to drink water. Are you aware what effects their company has produced upon you? You have ceased to be respected. You have no status at all. To say that the Hindus alone do not pay you any respect is only a half-truth. Not only the Hindus, but the Muslims and the Christians too, consider you the lowliest of the lowly. In fact, the teachings of Islam and Christianity do not create the sense of high and low. Then why do the followers of these two religions treat you as low? Because the Hindus consider you as the lowest of the low, the Muslims and Christians also consider you likewise. They fear that if they treat you on par, the Hindus will treat them also as low. Thus we are not low in the eyes of the Hindus alone. We are the lowest in the whole of India, because of the treatment given (us) by the Hindus. If you have to get rid of this shameful condition, if you have to cleanse this filth and make use of this precious life, there is only one way—and that is to throw away the shackles of the Hindu religion and the Hindu society in which you are groaning.

HAVE YOU HAD ANY FREEDOM IN THE HINDU RELIGION?

Some people might say that you have had a freedom of trade guaranteed by law, like any other citizen of the country. You are also said to have got the personal liberty like others. You will have to think deeply over such statements—whether they really carry any meaning. What is the good in saying, "You have freedom of trade," to a person who is deprived of any business by virtue of his birth, by the society? What is the truth in consoling with the words, "You are at liberty to enjoy your property, nobody else will touch your money," to a person to whom all the doors of means of livelihood and acquiring property are closed? To tell a person who is treated as unfit for entry into any service due to the defilement attached to him by birth, and working under whom is most contemptuous (contemptible) for others, that he has a right to serve, is making a fun of him.

The law may guarantee various rights. But those alone can be called real rights, which are permitted by the society to be exercised by you. The law guarantees to the Untouchables the right to wear decent clothes. But if the Hindus do not allow them to put on these clothes, what is the use of this right? The law guarantees to the Untouchables the right to fetch water in metal pots, the right to use metal utensils, the right to put tiles on their houses; but if the Hindu society does not allow them to exercise these rights, what is the use of such rights? Various instances of such types can be cited. In short, that which is permitted by the society to be exercised can alone be called a right. A right which is guaranteed by law but is opposed by the society is of no use at all.

The Untouchables are in need of social liberty, more than that which is guaranteed by law. So long as you do not achieve social liberty, whatever freedom is provided by law to you is of no avail. Some persons might advise you that you have physical freedom. Of course, you can go anywhere, can speak anything you wish, subject to the restrictions imposed by law. But what is the use of such freedom? Man has a body as well as a mind. He needs physical as well as mental freedom. Mere physical freedom is of no use. Freedom of the mind is of prime importance. Really speaking, what is meant to a man by physical freedom? It means he is free to act according to his own free will. A prisoner is unchained and is set free. What is the principle underlying this? The principle is, he should be free to act according to his free will, and he should be able to make the maximum use of the abilities he possesses. But what is the use of such freedom of a man whose mind is not free? The freedom of mind is the real freedom.

A person whose mind is not free, though he is not in chains, is a slave. One whose mind is not free, though he is not in jail, is a prisoner. One whose mind is not free, though he is alive, is dead. Freedom of mind is the proof of one's existence. What is the proof, then, to judge that the flame of mental freedom is not extinguished from a person? To whom can we say that his mind is free? I call him free who with consciousness awake, realises his rights, responsibilities, and duties; he who is not a slave of circumstances, and is always bent upon changing them in his favour, I call him free. One who is not a slave of usage, customs, and traditions, or of the teachings because they are brought down from the ancestors; one whose flame of reason is not extinguished—I call him a free man.

He who has not surrendered himself, who does not act on the teachings of others blindly; who does not keep faith on anything unless (it has been) examined critically in the light of the cause and effect theory; who is always prepared to protect his rights; who is not afraid of public criticism; who has enough intellect and self-respect so as not to become a doll in the hands of others—I call such a man a free man. He who does not lead his life under the direction of others, who carves out his own aim of life according to his own reason, and decides himself as to how and in what way the life should be led—I call him a free man. In short, a man who is the master of his own (life), him alone I consider a free man.

In the light of the above observations, are you free? Have you any freedom to carve out your own life and your aim? In my opinion, not only you have no freedom, but you are worse than slaves. Your slavery has no parallel. In the Hindu religion, one can(not) have freedom of speech. A Hindu must surrender his freedom of speech. He must act according to the Vedas. If the Vedas do not support the actions, instructions must be sought from the Smritis, and if the Smritis fail to provide any such instructions, he must follow in the footsteps of the great men. He is not supposed to reason. Hence, so long as you are in the Hindu religion, you cannot expect to have freedom of thought.

Some people might argue that the Hindu religion did not force you alone into mental slavery, but has snatched away the freedom of mind of all other communities. It is quite true that all the Hindus are living under a state of mental slavery. But from this nobody should conclude that the sufferings of all are alike. Everyone in the Hindu religion is not equally affected by the adverse effects this mental slavery has produced. This mental slavery is in no way detrimental to the material happiness of the caste Hindus. Though the caste Hindus are slaves of the above-mentioned trio—*viz.*, Vedas, Smritis, and the dictates of great men—they are given a high position in the Hindu social system. They are empowered to rule over others. It is an undisputed fact that the whole Hindu religion is the creation of the high-caste Hindus for the welfare and prosperity of the high-castes.

Society, which they call religion, has assigned you the role of the slave. So that you may not be able to escape from this slavery, every arrangement is made in the structure of the society. And that is why you are more in need of breaking the bondage of the mental slavery of this religion than is any other community. Hinduism has marred your progress from all sides. It has sacked (devastated) your mental freedom and made you slaves. In the outer world also, it has doomed you to the condition of a slave. If you want to be free, you must change your religion.

UNTOUCHABLES' ORGANISATION AND CONVERSION

The present movement of the Untouchables has been very severely criticised. It has been said that there are several castes among the Untouchables, and every caste practices untouchability. Mahars and Mangs do not dine together. Both these castes do not touch the scavengers, and practice untouchability against them. It is therefore asked what right these people have to expect from others the non-observance of the practice of untouchability, when they themselves practice casteism and untouchability amongst themselves. The untouchables are generally advised to abolish castes and untouchability from amongst them, and then come (to the caste Hindus) for redress.

There is a little truth in this argument. But the allegations made in this against the Untouchables are absolutely false. It cannot be denied that the castes included in the (category of) Untouchables practice untouchability. But equally, it is false to say that they are in any way responsible for this crime. Casteism and untouchability originated not from the Untouchables, but from the high-caste Hindus. And if this is true, the responsibility for this age-old tradition falls on the caste Hindus and not on the Untouchables. While practising untouchability and casteism, the Untouchables merely follow the lesson taught by the caste Hindus. If this lesson is not true, the burden of its being untruthful falls on those who taught it, and not on those who learnt it.

Though this reply may appear to be correct, it does not satisfy me. Though we are not responsible for the causes due to which castes and untouchability have taken root among us, it will be insane not to fight them but to allow them to continue as they are. Though we are not responsible for the introduction of untouchability and castes among us, we are surely responsible for their annihilation. And I am glad that all of us have realised this responsibility.

I am sure there is no leader among the Mahars who advocates the practice of casteism. If comparison is to be made, it will have to be made among the leaders. Compare the educated class of the Mahar community with that of the Brahmins, and one will have to admit that the educated Mahars are more eager to abolish castes.

This can well be proved by facts also. Not only the educated class of Mahars, but even the uneducated and illiterate Mahars, are the protagonists (advocates) of the abolition of castes. This also can be proved. Today, there is not a single person in the Mahar community who is opposed to the inter-caste dining among the Mahars and the Mangs. I feel greatly satisfied that you have realised the necessity of the abolition of castes—for which I extend my heartiest congratulations.

But have you ever thought as to how the efforts toward the abolition of castes can be made successful? Castes cannot be abolished by inter-caste dinners or stray instances of inter-caste marriages. Caste is a state of mind. It is a disease of the mind. The teachings of the Hindu religion are the root cause of this disease. We practise casteism, we observe untouchability, because we are asked to do it by the Hindu religion in which we live. A bitter thing can be made sweet. The taste of anything can be changed. But poison cannot be made Amrit (nectar). To talk of annihilating castes is like talking of changing poison into Amrit. In short, so long as we remain in a religion which teaches man to treat man as a leper, the sense of discrimination on account of caste, which is deeply rooted in our minds, cannot go. For annihilating castes and untouchability from among the Untouchables, change of religion is the only antidote.

THE DISTINCTION BETWEEN "CHANGE IN NAME" AND "CHANGE IN RELIGION"

So far, I have placed before you the points in favour of conversion. I hope this has been good food for your thoughts. Those who consider this discussion very difficult and complicated—I propose to put up (provide) simple thoughts in simple language for them.

What is there in conversion which can be called novel? Really speaking, what sort of social relations do you have with the caste Hindus at present? You are as separate from the Hindus as Muslims and Christians are. The same is (true of) their relation with you. Your society, and that of the Hindus, are two distinct groups. By (our choosing) conversion, nobody can say or feel that one society has been split up. You will remain separate from the Hindus, as you are today. Nothing new will happen on account of this conversion. If this is true, then why should some people be afraid of conversion? I, at least, do not find any reason for such fear.

Secondly, though, you undoubtedly have understood the importance of a change of name. If anybody from among you is asked about his caste, he tells it as Chokhamela, Harijan, or Walmiki, but does not say that he is a Mahar. Nobody can change a name unless certain conditions demand it. There is a very simple reason for such a change of name. An unknown (unknowing) person cannot distinguish between a touchable and an Untouchable. And so long as a Hindu does not come to know the caste of a person, he cannot have born in him the hatred of that person for being an Untouchable. The caste

Hindus and Untouchables behave in very friendly ways during journeys, so long as they are unaware of their castes. They exchange betels, bidis, cigarettes, fruits, etc. But as soon as the Hindu comes to know that the person with whom he is talking is an Untouchable, a sense of hatred germinates in his mind. He thinks that he is deceived. He gets angry, and ultimately this temporary friendship ends in abuses and quarrels.

Such experiences are not new to you. Why does all this happen? The names that depict your caste are considered so filthy that even their utterance is enough to create a vomiting sensation in the heart of Hindus. Thus by calling oneself a Chokhamela instead of a Mahar, you try to deceive the people. But you know, people are not deceived. Whether you call yourself a Chokhamela or a Harijan, people understand what you are. By your actions, you have proved the necessity of a change of name. Then what objection should there be to a change of religion? Changing a religion is like changing a name.

A change of religion, followed by a change of name, will be more beneficial to you. To call oneself a Muslim, a Christian, a Buddhist, or a Sikh, is not merely a change of religion, but is also a change of name. That is a real change of name. This new name will have no filth attached to it. It is an overall change.

No one will search for the origin of it. The change of name as Chokhamela or Harijan has no meaning at all. In this case, all the hatred, contempt, etc., attached to the original name passes to the new name. So long as you remain in the Hindu religion, you will have to change the name. (To seek change) by calling oneself a Hindu is not enough. Nobody recognises that there is a man called a Hindu. So also, calling oneself a Mahar will not serve the purpose.

As soon as you utter this name, you will not be allowed to come near. So I ask you, why should you not change your name permanently by changing your religion, instead of changing to one name today and another tomorrow, and thus remaining in the state of a pendulum?

THE ROLE OF OPPONENTS

Since the beginning of this movement of conversion, various people raised various objections to it. Let us now examine the truth, if any, in such objections. Some Hindus, pretending to be religious preachers, advise you, saying, "Religion is not a thing that can be consumed. Religion cannot be changed as we change our coat daily. You wish to leave this Hindu religion and embrace another one. Then do you think that your ancestors who clung to this religion for so long a period were fools?" Some wise men have raised this question.

I do not find any substance in this objection. A congenital idiot alone can say that one should stick to his religion because it is ancestral. No sane man will accept such a proposition. Those who advocate such an argument seem not to have read history at all. The ancient Aryan religion was called Vedic religion. It has three distinct characteristics: beef eating, drinking, and merrymaking was the religion of the day. Thousands of people followed it in India, and even now some people dream of going back to it. If the ancient religion alone is to be adhered to, then why did the people of India leave it and accept Buddhism? Why did they divorce (themselves) from the Vedic religion?

It cannot be denied that our ancestors lived in the ancient religion, but I cannot say that they remained there voluntarily. The Chaturvarnya system prevailed in this country for a pretty long time. In this system, the Brahmins were permitted to learn, the Kshatriyas to fight, the Vaishyas to earn property, and the Sudras to serve. This way of life was the rule of the day. In those days, the Sudras had no learning, no property, and no food and clothing. Your ancestors were thus forced to live in penniless and armless (disarmed) conditions.

Under these circumstances, no man with common sense can say that they accepted that religion voluntarily. Here it is also necessary to consider whether it was possible for your ancestors to revolt against this religion. Had it been possible for them to revolt, and had they still not acted upon (the possibility), only then can we say that they had accepted this religion voluntarily.

But if we try to look into the then-prevalent conditions, it will be clear that our ancestors were forced to live in that religion. Thus this Hindu religion is not the religion of our ancestors, but it was a slavery forced upon them. Our ancestors had no means to fight this slavery, and hence they could not revolt. They were compelled to live in this religion. Nobody can blame them for this helplessness. Rather, anyone will pity them. But now nobody can force any type of slavery upon the present generation. We have all sorts of freedom. If the present generation do not avail (themselves) of such freedom and free themselves, one will have to call them, most regretfully, the most mean, slavish, and dependent people who ever lived on earth.

THE DIFFERENCE BETWEEN MAN AND ANIMAL

Only a fool can say that one should cling to one's own religion only because it is ancestral. No sane person can accept such an argument. "You should live in the same circumstances in which you are living at present" may be worthy advice for the animals, but it can never be for man. The difference between an animal and a man is that the man can make progress, while the animal cannot. No progress can be made without change. Conversion is a sort of change. And if no progress can be made without change, *i.e.* conversion, obviously conversion becomes essential. The ancestral religion cannot be a hindrance in the path of a progressive man.

There is still one more argument against conversion. They say, "Conversion is a sort of escapism. Today a number of Hindus are bent upon improving the Hindu religion. Untouchability and caste can be eradicated with the help of these Hindu reformers. It is therefore not proper to change the religion at this juncture." Whatever opinion anybody may possess about the Hindu social reformers, I personally have a nausea for them. I have no regard for them. I have had very bitter experience of them. That those people, who live in their own caste, die in their own caste, marry in their own caste, should befool the people with false slogans, saying, "We will break the caste!", is really surprising. And if the Untouchables do not believe them, they get annoyed with them! Is it not astonishing?

When I hear the slogans shouted by these Hindu social reformers, I recollect the efforts made by the American white people for the emancipation of the American Negroes. Years ago, the condition of the Negroes in America was just the same as that of Untouchables in India. The difference between the two was that the slavery of Negroes had the sanction of the law; while that of your (people), by religion. So, some reformers were trying for abolition of the slavery of the Negroes. But can those white reformers be compared with their counterparts, the Hindu social reformers in India? The American white reformers fought battles in war with their kith and kin for the emancipation of the Negroes. They killed thousands of whites who defended the slavery of the Negro people, and also sacrificed their own blood for this cause.

When we read these chapters through the pages of history, the social reformers in India cut a very sorry figure before them. These so-called benefactors of the Untouchables of India called "reformers" need to be asked the following questions: Are you prepared to fight a civil war with your Hindu brethren, like the whites in America who fought with their white brothers for the cause of the coloured people? And if not, why these proclamations of reforms?

Now let us take the example of Mahatma Gandhi, the greatest of the Hindus who claim to fight for the cause of the Untouchables. To what extent can he go? Mahatma Gandhi, who pilots the nonviolent agitation against the British Government, is not prepared to hurt the feelings of the Hindus, the oppressors of the Untouchables. He is not willing to launch a peaceful Satyagraha against them. He is not even prepared to take legal action against the Hindus. What is the good of such Hindu reformers for us? I don't see any.

DOES THE FAULT LIE WITH THE UNTOUCHABLES ALONE?

Some Hindus attend the meetings of the Untouchables and rebuke the caste Hindus. Some will advise the Untouchables from their stage, preaching, "Brothers, live clean, educate yourselves, stand on your own feet, etc. etc." Really speaking, if anybody is to be blamed for the stigma of Untouchability, it is the caste Hindus alone. It is the caste Hindu class which commits this wrong. Yet no one will try to gather these caste Hindus and preach to them. Those who preach to the Untouchables to continue their agitation with the help of the Hindus and by remaining in the Hindu fold—I would like to remind them of a couple of illustrations from history.

I remember to have read a conversation between an American and an English soldier during the last World War. I find it most appropriate at this juncture. How long the war should be continued, was the subject of discussion. In reply to a question, the Englishman said with great pride, "We shall fight the war till the last Frenchman dies." When the Hindu social reformers proclaim that they shall fight to the last for the cause of the Untouchables, it means that they propose to fight till the last Untouchable dies. This is the meaning, as I understand it, of their proclamation. One who fights for a cause at the cost of the lives of others cannot be expected to win the battle.

If we are to die in our struggle for freedom, what is the use of fighting at the wrong place? To reform the Hindu society is neither our aim nor our field of action. Our aim is to gain freedom. We have nothing to do with anything else. If we can gain our freedom by conversion, why should we shoulder the responsibility for the reform of the Hindu religion? And why should we sacrifice our strength and property for that? No one should misunderstand the object of our movement as being Hindu social reform. The object of our movement is to achieve social freedom for the Untouchables. It is equally true that this freedom cannot be secured without conversion.

I do accept that the Untouchables need equality as well. And to secure equality is also one of their objectives. But nobody can say that this equality can be achieved only by remaining as Hindus and not otherwise. There are two ways of achieving equality. One, by remaining in the Hindu fold. Mere removal of the sense of being a touchable or an Untouchable will not serve the purpose: equality can be achieved only when inter-caste dinners and marriages take place. This means that the Chaturvarna must be abolished, and the Brahminic religion must be uprooted. Is it possible? And if not, will it be wise to expect equality of treatment by remaining in the Hindu religion? And can you be successful in your efforts to bring equality? Of course not. The path of conversion is far simpler than this. Hindu society gives treatment of equality to Muslims and Christians. Obviously, social equality is easily achieved by conversion. If this is true, then why should you not adopt this simple path of conversion?

According to me, this conversion of religion will bring happiness to both—the Untouchables as well as the Hindus. So long as you remain Hindus, you will have to struggle for social intercourse, for food and water, and for inter-caste marriages. And so long as this quarrel continues, relations between you and the Hindus will be strained, and you will be their perpetual enemies. By conversion, the roots of all the quarrels will vanish. Then you will have no right to claim temple entry in the Hindu temples, much less the need for the same. There will be no reason for you to struggle for the social rights—*e.g.*, inter-caste dinners, inter-caste marriages, etc. Once these quarrels cease to exist, mutual love and affection will automatically develop.

Look at the present relations between the Hindus on the one hand, and the Christians and Muslims on the other. The Hindus do not allow the Muslims and the Christians to enter their temples, just as they do not allow you. They also have no inter-caste marriages or inter-dining with them. Irrespective of this, the affinity and love which these people have with the caste Hindus, is not extended to you by the Hindus. The reason for this differential or step-motherly treatment with you is that you have to struggle with the Hindus for social and religious rights, unlike the Christians and the Muslims—only because you live as Hindus.

Secondly, although these religions have no social rights in the Hindu society, that is to say, although they have no inter-dining and intermarriage with the Hindus, the Hindus treat them on a par. Thus by conversion, if equality of treatment can be achieved and an affinity between Hindus and Untouchables can be brought about, then why should the Untouchables not adopt this simple and happy path for securing equality? Looking at the problem from this angle, it will be seen that this path of conversion is the only right path of freedom, which ultimately leads to equality. It is neither cowardice nor escapism. It is the wise step.

One more argument is put forth against Conversion. Some Hindus argue, "Conversion is worthless if you do it out of frustration with the caste system. Wherever you may go, you will face caste. Muslims have their own castes. If you become Christians, there are also castes." This is what these Hindus plead. Unfortunately, it has to be admitted that the Caste system has crept into other religions also in this country. But the burden of nurturing this great sin lies with the Hindus alone. This disease originally started from the Hindus, and thereafter infected others. Although the castes exist among Muslims and Christians alike, it will be meanness (meaningless?) to liken it with that of the Hindus.

There is a great distinction between the caste system of the Hindus and that of the Muslims and Christians. Firstly, it must be noted that though castes exist among Christians and Muslims, it is not the chief characteristic of their body social. If one asks, "Who are you?" and someone says, "I am a Hindu," one is not satisfied with this reply. He is further asked, "What is your caste?" And unless this is replied to, no one can have the idea of his social status. From this it is evident how caste has prime importance in the Hindu religion, and how minor it is in Christianity and among the Muslims.

There is one more difference between the caste system of the Hindus and that of the Muslims and Christians. The caste system among the Hindus has the foundation of religion. The castes in other religions have no sanction of their religion. If Hindus proclaim (that they intend) to disband the caste system, their religion will come in the way. On the other hand, if the Muslims and Christians start movements for abolishing the caste system in their religion, their religion will not obstruct. Hindus cannot destroy their castes without destroying their religion. Muslims and Christians need not destroy their religion for eradication of the castes. Rather, their religion will support such movements to a great extent.

Even if for the sake of argument it is admitted that castes exist everywhere, it cannot be concluded that one should remain in the Hindu fold. If the caste system is useless, then the logical conclusion is that one should accept a kind of society in which the caste system has no serious adverse effect upon the person, or wherein the castes can be abolished early and easily, in a simple manner.

Some of the Hindus say, "What can be done by conversion alone? First improve your financial and educational status." Some of our people are confused and puzzled by such questions. I therefore feel it necessary to discuss it here. Firstly, the question is, who is going to improve your financial and educational conditions? You yourself, or those who argue as above? I do not think that those who advise you will be able to do anything but showing their lip-sympathy. Nor do I find any efforts toward this direction from their side. On the contrary: every Hindu tries to improve the economic status of his own caste. His outlook is limited to his own caste alone. Brahmins are engaged in establishing maternity homes for Brahmin women, providing scholarships to Brahmin pupils, and securing jobs for the unemployed Brahmin personnel. Saraswats (one of the castes amongst the Brahmins) are also doing the same.

Everybody is for himself, and those who have no benefactor are at the mercy of God. This is the present-day condition of the society. If you yourself have to rise, if no one else is to come to your aid—if this be the situation, what is the purpose in listening to the advice of the Hindus? There is no other motive in such advice but to misguide you and kill (waste) your time. If you are to improve yourselves, then that (misguiding and time-wasting effect) is what they mean, so nobody need pay attention to their gossip. Although this may seem enough, I do not propose to leave this point here. I propose to refute this argument.

WHAT CAN BE ACHIEVED BY CONVERSION ALONE?

I am simply surprised by the question which some Hindus ask, as to what can be achieved by conversion alone. Most of the present-day Sikhs, Muslims, and Christians in India were formerly Hindus, the majority of them being from the Sudras and Untouchables. Do these critics mean to say that those who left the Hindu fold and embraced Sikhism or Christianity, have made no progress at all? And if this is not true, and if it is admitted that conversion has brought a distinct improvement in their condition, then to say that the Untouchables will not be benefited by conversion carries no meaning.

This statement that "nothing can be achieved by conversion" has another implied meaning, and that is that "religion is bogus and useless; there is neither gain nor loss from religion." If this be the case, then why do the advocates of this argument insist upon the Untouchables' remaining in the Hindu religion? I do not understand. If they do not find any meaning in religion, why should they unnecessarily argue for and against conversion?

Those Hindus who ask as to what can be achieved by conversion alone, can be accosted with the similar question: *i.e.*, what can be achieved by self-government alone? If financial and educational progress is the condition precedent (prerequisite) for freedom, what is the good of self-government?

And if the country is to be benefited by self-government alone, the Untouchables are also bound to be benefited by conversion.

After giving deep thought to the problem, everybody will have to admit that conversion is as necessary to the Untouchables as self-government is to India. The ultimate object of both is the same. There is not the slightest difference in their ultimate goal. This ultimate aim is to attain freedom. And if the freedom is necessary for the life of mankind, conversion of the Untouchables, which brings them complete freedom, cannot be called worthless by any stretch of the imagination.

PROGRESS OR CONVERSION—WHAT FIRST?

I think it necessary here to discuss the question as to what should be initiated first, whether economic progress or conversion. I do not agree with the view that economic progress should precede. This issue whether religious conversion or economic progress should precede is as dry as that which dealt with political reform versus social reform. Several methods are required to be applied for the development and progress of the society. Each of these methods has its own significance. No definite seriatum (sequence) can be applied for the application of these methods.

If however anybody insists on such a seriatum with regard to conversion and economic reform, I will place the former as the first. I fail to understand how can you achieve economic progress so long as you have the stigma of being an Untouchable. If any one of you opens a shop, as soon as it is known that the shopkeeper is an Untouchable, nobody will purchase articles from you. If any one of you applies for a job, and it is disclosed that the applicant is an Untouchable, he will not get the job. If anyone intends to sell his land, and one of you proposes to purchase it, once it has been known that the purchaser is an Untouchable, nobody will sell the land. Whatever methods you may adopt for your own economic progress, your efforts will be frustrated due to untouchability. Untouchability is a permanent handicap on your path of progress. And unless you remove it, your path cannot be safe. Without conversion, this hurdle cannot be removed.

Some of your young ones are after education, and they are collecting money for this purpose from whatever source they find proper. Due to this temptation of money, some are inclined to remain Untouchables and make their progress (as such). To these youngsters, I wish to ask one question. After the completion of your education, if you do not get a job suited to your qualifications, what will you do? What is the reason that most of our educated persons are unemployed today?

To me, the chief cause for this unemployment is untouchability. Your calibre has no scope due to your untouchability. Because of untouchability, you have been ousted from the military services. You are not employed in the police department on account of your untouchability. Due to untouchability, you cannot secure even the post of a peon. You are not promoted to the higher rank only because you are an Untouchable.

Untouchability is a curse. You have been completely ruined and all your virtues have turned into dust. Under these circumstances, what more qualifications can you add? And even if you add them, what is the use? So, if you sincerely desire that your qualifications should be valued, that your education should be of some use to you, you must throw away the shackles of untouchability, which means that you must change your religion.

DOUBTS ABOUT CONVERSION

So far, the arguments put forth by the critics have been discussed. Now I propose to clarify the doubts expressed by the sympathisers of conversion. In the first place, it has reached my ears that some of the Mahars are worried as to what will be the fate of their Watan (hereditary rights of a village servant).

The high-caste Hindus are also reported to have threatened the Mahars that they will be deprived of their services as village servants, if they leave the Hindu religion.

All of you are aware that I am least worried if the Mahar Watan is abolished. During the last ten years, I have been advocating that if there is anything that dooms the fate of Mahars, it is the Mahar Watan alone. And the day on which you will be freed from these chains of Maharness (Maharki), I think your path of liberation will be open to you.

However, for those who need this Mahar Watan, I can assure them that their Watan will not come in trouble (be endangered) by their conversion. In this regard, the Act of 1850 can be referred to. Under the provisions of this Act, no rights of a person or his successors with respect to his property are affected by virtue of his conversion.

As for those who feel this reference of law to be insufficient, their attention is drawn to the circumstances prevalent in Nagar District. A number of persons from the Mahar community in this District have become Christians. At some places, we find that in one family, some are Christians while others still remain as Mahars. However, the Watan rights of these converted Christians have not been vanquished (removed). This may be confirmed from the Mahars of Nagar. So no one should fear that their Watan will come in peril by conversion.

A second doubt is about political rights. Some people express (concern) as to what will happen to our political safeguards if we convert. Nobody can say that I do not realise the importance of the political safeguards the Untouchables have achieved. Nobody else has taken so much pains and has made so much effort for securing political rights for the Untouchables as I have done. But I feel it is not proper to depend solely on political rights. These political safeguards are not granted on the condition that they shall be everlasting. They are bound to be ended sometime. According to the Communal Award of the British Government, our political safeguards were limited for twenty years. Although no such limitation has been fixed by the Poona Pact, nobody can say they are everlasting.

Those who depend upon these political safeguards must think about what will happen after these safeguards are withdrawn. On the day on which our political rights cease to exist, we will have to depend upon our social strength. I have already told you that this social strength is wanting in us. So also I have proved in the beginning, that this strength cannot be achieved without conversion. No one should think only of the present. To forget what is eternally beneficial, and to be lured by temporary gains, is bound to lead to suffering. Under these circumstances, one must think what is permanently beneficial. In my opinion, conversion is the only remedy, for eternal bliss. Nobody should hesitate, even if political rights are required to be sacrificed for this purpose.

Conversion brings no harm to political safeguards. I do not understand why political safeguards should at all come in trouble (be endangered) by conversion. Wherever you may go, your political rights and safeguards will accompany you. I have no doubt about it. If you become Muslims, you will get political rights as Muslims. If you become Christians, you will get your political rights as Christians. If you become Sikhs, you will have your political safeguards as Sikhs. Political rights are based on population. The political safeguards of any society (group) will increase with the increase of its population.

Nobody should misunderstand (wrongly think) that if we leave the Hindu society, all the fifteen seats allotted to us will go back to Hindus. If we become Muslims, our fifteen seats will be added to the seats reserved for Muslims. Likewise, if we become Christians, our seats will be added to the seats reserved for Christians. In short, our political rights will accompany us. So nobody should be afraid of it.

On the other hand, if we remain Hindus and do not convert, (think about) whether our rights will be safe. This you must think carefully about. Suppose the Hindus have passed a law whereby untouchability is prohibited and its practice is made punishable. Then they ask you, "We have abolished untouchability by law. Now you are no longer Untouchables. At the most, you are simply poor and backward. But other castes are equally backward. We have not provided any political safeguards for these backward communities. Then why should you be given such political safeguards?" What will be your reply to these questions?

The reply of the Muslims and the Christians will be very simple. They will say, "We are not granted political safeguards and rights because we are poor, illiterate, or backward, but because our religion is different, our society is different, and so on. And so long as our religion is different from yours, we must get our share in the political rights." This will be their appropriate reply. As long as you are Hindus, you cannot take this stand—that you are entitled to political safeguards because your society, your religion, is altogether different. You will be able to take this stand on the day on which you liberate yourselves from the serfdom of Hindu society. And unless you stand on such a sound footing and claim political safeguards, your political rights and safeguards cannot be considered to be permanent and free from danger.

Looking from this perspective, conversion becomes a means for strengthening political safeguards, rather than becoming a hindrance. If you remain Hindus, you are sure to lose your political safeguards. If you want to save them, leave this religion. Political safeguards will be permanent only through conversion.

CONCLUSION

I have decided for myself. My conversion is sure as anything. My conversion is not for any material gain. There is nothing which I cannot achieve by remaining an Untouchable. My conversion is purely out of my spiritual attitude. The Hindu religion does not appeal to my conscience. It does not appeal to my self-respect. However, your conversion will be both for material as well as for spiritual gains. Some persons mock and laugh at the idea of conversion for material gain. I do not feel hesitant in calling such persons stupid.

The religion which preaches what will happen to your soul after death may be useful for the rich. They may entertain themselves in such religion at their own leisure (by dreaming the future of their soul after death). It is quite natural that those who have enjoyed all sorts of pleasures in their lifetime may consider such religion as a real religion, which promises to them these pleasures even after death.

But what of those who by remaining in a particular religion have been reduced to the state of dust, who have been denied the basic necessities of life such as food and clothing, who have not been treated even as human beings, and have since (thus) completely lost the sense of being human? Are these people not supposed to think of religion from a material point of view? Are they expected to look at the sky and merely pray? What good is this superfluous Vedanta of the easy-going, self-satisfied, rich people, to the poor ones?

RELIGION IS FOR MAN

I tell you all very specifically, religion is for man and not man for religion. For getting human treatment, convert yourselves. Convert for getting organised. Convert for becoming strong. Convert for securing equality. Convert for getting liberty. Convert so that your domestic life should be happy. Why do you remain in a religion which does not treat you as human beings? Why do you remain in a religion which prohibits you from entering temples? Why do you remain in a religion which prohibits you from securing drinking water from the public well? Why do you remain in a religion which comes in your way for getting a job? Why do you remain in a religion which insults you at every step?

A religion in which man's human behaviour with man is prohibited, is not religion, but a display of force. A religion which does not recognise a man as man, is not a religion but a disease. A religion in which the touch of animals is permitted, but the touch of human beings is prohibited, is not a religion but a mockery. A religion which precludes some classes from education, forbids them to accumulate wealth and to bear arms, is not a religion but a mockery of human beings. A religion that compels the ignorant to be ignorant, and the poor to be poor, is not a religion but a punishment.

I have tried here, with the best of my knowledge, to analyse and explain all the probable problems arising out of conversion. This discourse might have become a lengthy one, but I had decided to be elaborate from the beginning. It was imperative for me to discuss and reply to the points raised by the opponents of conversion. Nobody should leave the Hindu religion unless he fully realises the utility of this declaration. So as to clear up all doubts, I had to discuss this problem so much in detail.

How far you will agree with my views, I cannot say. But I hope you will give deep thought to them. To speak that which pleases the audience and earn goodwill, may be a convenient principle for the man in the street. But it does not befit the leader. I consider him a leader who, without fear or favour, tells the people what is good and what is bad for them. It is my duty to tell you what is good for you, even if you don't like it. I must do my duty. And now I have done it. It is now for you to decide and discharge your responsibility.

I have deliberately divided this problem of conversion into two parts. Whether to leave the Hindu religion or to remain in it is the first part of the problem. If the Hindu religion is to be abandoned, what other religion should be adopted, or whether a new religion should be established—this is the second part of the problem. Today, I wish to know your decision on the first part. Unless the first aspect is decided, it is futile to discuss or prepare for the latter. Therefore you must decide the first point. You will have no other opportunity. Whatever decision you will arrive at in this conference, it will be of the utmost use for me, to chalk out my future programme.

If you decide against conversion, this question will be closed forever. Then whatever is to be done for myself, I will do. If at all you decide in favour of conversion, then you will have to promise me organised and enmasse conversion. If the decision is taken in favour of conversion, and the people start embracing any religion they like individually, I will not dabble in your conversion. I wish you all to join me. Whatever religion we may accept, I am prepared to put all my sincere efforts and labour for the welfare of our people in that religion.

You should not, however, be led away by emotion, and follow me only because I say so. You should consent only if it appeals to your reason. I will not at all feel (angry?) if you decide not to join me. Rather, I will feel relieved of the responsibility. This is therefore a crucial occasion. You must bear in mind that your today's decision will carve out a path for posterity, for future generations. But if you decide to remain slaves, your future generations will also be slaves. Hence yours is the most difficult task.

BE THY OWN LIGHT

What message should I give you on this occasion? While I thought over it, I recollected the message given by the Lord Bhagwan Buddha to his Bhikkhu Sangh (Congregation of Monks) just before his Mahaparinirvan (death), and which has been quoted in "Mahaparinibban Sutta." Once the Bhagwan, after having recovered from an illness, was resting on a seat under a tree. His disciple the Venerable Anand approached the Buddha and, having saluted, sat beside him. Then he said to the Buddha, "I have seen the Lord in his illness as well as in his happiness. But from the beginning of the present illness, my body has become heavy like lead. My mind is not in peace. I can't concentrate on the Dhamma. However, I feel consolation and satisfaction that the Lord will not attain the Parinibban until he gives a message to the Sangh."

Then the Lord replied thus: "Ananda! What does the Sangh expect from me? Ananda, I have preached the Dhamma with an open heart, without concealing anything. The Tathagata (Buddha) has not kept anything concealed, as some other teachers do. So Ananda, what more can I tell to the Bhikkhu Sangh? So Ananda, be self-illuminating like the lamp. Don't be dependent for light, like the Earth. Don't be a satellite. Be a light unto thyself. Believe in Self. Don't be dependent on Others.

Be truthful. Always take refuge in the Truth, and do not surrender to anybody!"

I also take your leave in the words of the Buddha. "Be your own guide. Take refuge in reason. Do not listen to the advice of others. Do not succumb to others. Be truthful. Take refuge in truth. Never surrender to anybody!" If you keep in mind this message of Lord Buddha at this juncture, I am sure your decision will not be wrong.

WHY GO FOR CONVERSION?

In 1935 at Nasik district, Maharashtra, Dr. Babasaheb Ambedkar had declared his firm resolve to change his religion. He had declared that he was born as a Hindu but will not die as Hindu. About a year later, a massive Mahar conference was held on May 30 and 31, 1936, in Mumbai, to access the impact of that declaration on Mahar masses. In his address to the conference, Dr. Ambedkar expressed his views on conversion in an elaborate, well-prepared and written speech in Marathi. Here is an English translation of that speech by Mr. Vasant Moon, OSD to the committee of Govt. of Maharashtra for publication of Writings & speeches of Dr. B. R. Ambedkar.

Conversion is not a game of children. It is not a subject of entertainment. It deals with how to make man's life successful. Just as a boatman has to make all necessary preparations before he starts for voyage, so also we have to make preparations. Unless I get an idea as to how many persons are willing to leave the Hindu fold, I cannot start preparations for conversion.

For a common man this subject of conversion is very important but also very difficult to understand.

CLASS STRUGGLE

There are two aspects of conversion; social as well as religious; material as well as spiritual. Whatever may be the aspect, or line of thinking, it is necessary to understand the beginning, the nature of Untouchability and how it is practiced. Without this understanding, you will not be able to realize the real meaning underlying my declaration of conversion. In order to have a clear understanding of untouchability and its practice in real life, I want you to recall the stories of the atrocities perpetrated against you. But very few of you might have realized as to why all this happens! What is at the root cause of their tyranny? To me it is very necessary, that we understand it.

This is not a feud between rival men. The problem of untouchability is a matter of class struggle. It is the struggle between caste Hindus and the Untouchables. That is not a matter of doing injustice against one man. This is a matter of injustice being done by one class against another. This "class struggle" has a relation with the social status. This struggle indicates, how one class should keep its relation with another class. This struggle starts as soon as you start claiming equal treatment with others.

CONVERSION NOT FOR SLAVES

The reason for their anger is very simple. Your behaving on par with them insults them. The untouchability is not a short or temporary feature; it is a permanent one. To put it straight, it can be said that the struggle between the Hindus and the Untouchables is a permanent phenomena. It is eternal, because the religion which has placed you at the lowest level of the society is itself eternal, according to the belief of the Hindu caste people. No change, according to time and circumstances is possible. You are at the lowest rung of the ladder today. You shall remain lowest forever. This means the struggle between Hindus and Untouchables shall continue forever. How will you survive through this struggle is the main question. And unless you think over it, there is no way out. Those who desire to live in obedience to the dictates of the Hindus, those who wish to remain their slaves, they do not need to think over this problem.

But those who wish to live a life of self-respect, and equality, will have to think over this. How should we survive through this struggle? For me, it is not difficult to answer this question.

Those who have assembled here will have to agree that in any struggle one who holds strength becomes the victor. One, who has no strength, need not expect success. This has been proved by experience, and I do not need to cite illustration to prove it.

THREE TYPES OF STRENGTH

The question that follows, which you must now consider, is whether you have enough strength to survive through this struggle? Three types of strength are known to man: (i) Manpower, (ii) Finance and (iii) Mental Strength. Which of these, you think that you possess? So far as manpower is concerned, it is clear, that you are in a minority. In Mumbai Presidency, the untouchables are only one-eighth of the total population. That too unorganized. The castes within themselves do not allow them to organize. They are not even compact. They are scattered through the villages. Under these circumstances, this small population is of no use as a fighting force to the untouchables at their critical moments.

Financial strength is also just the same. It is an undisputed fact that you at least have a little bit of manpower, but finances you have none. You have no trade, no business, no service, no land. The piece of bread thrown out by the higher castes, are your means of livelihood. You have no food, no clothes. What financial strength can you have? You have no capacity to get redress from the law courts. Thousands of untouchables tolerate insult, tyranny and oppression at the hands of Hindus without a sigh of complaint, because they have no capacity to bear the expenses of the courts. As regards mental strength, the condition is still worst.

The tolerance of insults and tyranny without grudge and complaint has killed the sense of retort and revolt. Confidence, vigour and ambition have been completely vanished from you. All of you have been become helpless, unenergetic and pale. Everywhere, there is an atmosphere of defeatism and pessimism. Even the slight idea, that you can do something does not enter your mind.

MUSLIM EXAMPLE

If, whatever I have described above is correct then you will have to agree with the conclusion that follows. The conclusion is, if you depend only upon your own strength, you will never be able to face the tyranny of the Hindus. I have no doubt that you are oppressed because you have no strength. It is not that you alone are in minority. The Muslims are equally small in number. Like Mahar-Mangs, they too have few houses in the village. But no one dares to trouble the Muslims while you are always a victim of tyranny. Why is this so? Though there may be two houses of Muslims in the village, nobody dares to harm them, while the whole village practices tyranny against you though you have ten houses. Why does this happen? This is a very pertinent question and you will have to find out a suitable answer to this. In my opinion, there is only one answer to this question.

The Hindus realize that the strength of the whole of the Muslim population in India stands behind those two houses of Muslims living in a village and, therefore, they do not dare to touch them. Those two houses also enjoy free and fearless life because they are aware that if any Hindu commits aggression against them, the whole Muslim community from Punjab to Madras will rush to their protection at any cost. On the other hand, the Hindus are sure that none will come to your rescue, nobody will help you, no financial help will reach you. Tahsildar and police belong to caste Hindus and in case of disputes between Hindus and Untouchables, they are more faithful to their caste than to their duty. The Hindus practice injustice and tyranny against you only because you are helpless.

OUTSIDE SUPPORT

From the above discussion, two facts are very clear. Firstly, you can not face tyranny without strength. And secondly, you do not possess enough strength to face the tyranny. With these two conclusions, a third one automatically follows. That is, the strength required to face this tyranny needs to be secured from outside. How are you to gain this strength is really an important question? And you will have to think over this with an unbiased mind.

From this, you will realize one thing, that unless you establish close relations with some other society, unless you join some other religion, you cannot get the strength from outside. It clearly means, you must leave your present religion and assimilate yourselves with some other society. Without that, you cannot gain the strength of that society. So long as you do not have strength, you and your future generations will have to lead your lives in the same pitiable condition.

SPIRITUAL ASPECT OF CONVERSION

Uptil now, we have discussed why conversion is necessary for material gains. Now, I propose to put forth my thoughts as to why conversion is as much necessary for spiritual wellbeing. What is Religion? Why is it necessary?... 'That which govern people is religion'. That is the true definition of Religion. There is no place for an individual in Hindu society. The Hindu religion is constituted on a class-concept. Hindu religion does nct teach how an individual should behave with another individual. A religion, which does not recognize the individual, is not personally acceptable to me. Three factors are required for the uplift of an individual. They are: Sympathy, Equality and Liberty. Can you say by experience that any of these factors exist for you in Hinduism?

NO EQUALITY IN HINDUISM

Such a living example of inequality is not to be found anywhere in the world. Not at anytime in the history of mankind can we find such inequality, which is more intense than untouchability... I think, you have been thrust into this condition because you have continued to be Hindus. Those of you who have become Muslims, are treated by the Hindus neither as Untouchables nor as unequals. The same can be said of those who have become Christians. That God is all pervading is a principle of science and not of religion, because religion has a direct relation with the behaviour of man. Hindus can be ranked among those cruel people whose utterances and acts are two poles apart. They have this Ram on their tongues and a knife under their armpits. They speak like saints but act like butchers.

Thus we are not low in the eyes of the Hindus alone, but we are the lowest in the whole of India, because of the treatment given to us by the Hindus. If you have to get rid of this same shameful condition, if you have to cleanse this filth and make use of this precious life; there is only one way and that is to throw off the shackles of Hindu religion and the Hindu society in which you are bound.

The taste of a thing can be changed. But the poison cannot be made amrit. To talk of annihilating castes is like talking of changing the poison into amrit. In short, so long as we remain in a religion, which teaches a man to treat another man like a leper, the sense of discrimination on account of caste, which is deeply rooted in our minds, can not go. For annihilating caste and untouchables, change of religion is the only antidote.

UNTOUCHABLES ARE NOT HINDUS

What is there in conversion, which can be called novel? Really speaking what sort of social relations have you with the caste Hindus at present? You are as separate from the Hindus as Muslims and Christians are. So is their relation with you. Your society and that of the Hindus are two distinct groups. By conversion, nobody can say or feel that one society has been split up. You will remain as separate from the Hindus as you are today. Nothing new will happen on account of this conversion. If this is true, then why should people be afraid of conversion? At least, I do not find any reason for such a fear.

REVOLUTION-NOT REFORM

Changing a religion is like changing a name. Change of religion followed by the change of name will be more beneficial to you. To call oneself a Muslim, a Christian, a Buddhist or a

Sikh is not merely a change of religion but also a change of name. . Since the beginning of this movement of conversion, various people have raised various objections to it. Let us now examine the truth, if any, in such objections.

A congenital idiot alone will say that one has to adhere to one's religion because it is that of our ancestors. No sane man will accept such a proposition. Those who advocate such an argument, seem not to have read the history at all. The ancient Aryan religion was called Vedic religion. It has three distinct characteristic (features). Beef-eating, drinking and merrymaking was part of the religion of the day. Thousands of people followed it in India and even now some people dream of going back to it. If the ancient religion alone is to be adhered to why did the people of India leave Hinduism and accept Buddhism? Why did they divorce themselves from the Vedic religion?... Thus this Hindu religion is not the religion of our ancestors, but it was a slavery forced upon them.

To reform the Hindu society is neither our aim nor our field of action. Our aim is to gain freedom. We have nothing to do with anything else.

If we can gain freedom by conversion, why should we shoulder the responsibility of reforming the Hindu religion? And why should we sacrifice our strength and property for that? None should misunderstand the object of our movement as being Hindu social reform. The object of our movement is to achieve social freedom for the untouchables. It is equally true that this freedom cannot be secured without conversion.

CASTE CAN'T BE DESTROYED

I do accept that the untouchables need equality as well. And to secure equality is also one of our objectives. But nobody can say that this equality can be achieved only by remaining as Hindu and not otherwise. There are two ways of achieving equality. One, by remaining in the Hindu fold and another by leaving it by conversion. If equality is to be achieved by remaining in the Hindu fold, mere removal of the sense of being a touchable or an untouchable will not serve the purpose. Equality can be achieved only when inter-caste dinners and marriages take place. This means that the Chaturvarnya must be abolished and the Brahminic religion must be uprooted. Is it possible? And if not, will it be wise to expect equality of treatment by remaining in the Hindu religion? And can you be successful in your efforts to bring equality?

Of course not. The path of conversion is far simpler than this. The Hindu society does not give equality of treatment, but the same is easily achieved by conversion. If this is true, then why should you not adopt this simple path of conversion?

CONVERSION IS A SIMPLEST PATH

According to me, this conversion of religion will bring happiness to both the Untouchables as well as the Hindus. So long as you remain Hindus, you will have to struggle for social intercourse, for food and water, and for inter-caste marriages. And so long as this quarrel continues, relations between you and the Hindus will be of perpetual enemies.

By conversion, the roots of all the quarrels will vanish... thus by conversion, if equality of treatment can be achieved and the affinity between the Hindus and the Untouchables can be brought about then why should the Untouchables not adopt the simple and happy path of securing equality? Looking at this problem through this angle, it will be seen that this path of conversion is the only right path of freedom, which ultimately leads to equality. It is neither cowardice nor escapism.

SANCTIFIED RACISM

Although the castes exist in Muslims and the Christians alike, it will be meanness to liken it to that of the Hindus. There is a great distinction between the caste-system of the Hindus and that of the Muslims and Christians. Firstly, it must be noted that though the castes exist amongst the Christians and the Muslims, it is not the chief characteristic of their body social.

There is one more difference between the caste system of the Hindus and that of the Muslims and Christians. The caste system in the Hindus has the foundation of religion. The castes in other religions have no sanction in their religion... Hindus cannot destroy their castes without destroying their religion. Muslims and Christians need not destroy their religions for eradication of their castes. Rather their religion will support such movements to a great extent.

CONVERSION ALONE LIBERATES US

I am simply surprised by the question, which some Hindus ask us as to what can be achieved by conversion alone? Most of the present day Sikhs, Muslims and Christians were formerly Hindus, majority of them being from the Sudras and Untouchables. Do these critics mean to say that those, who left the Hindu fold and embraced Sikhism or Christianity, have made no progress at all? And if this is not true, and if it is admitted that the conversion has brought a distinct improvement in their condition, then to say that the untouchables will not be benefited by conversion, carries no meaning.

After giving deep thought to the problem, everybody will have to admit that conversion is necessary to the Untouchables as self-government is to India. The ultimate object of both is the same. There is not the slightest difference in their ultimate goal. This ultimate aim is to attain freedom. And if the freedom is necessary for the life of mankind, conversion of Untouchables which brings them complete freedom cannot be called worthless by any stretch of imagination.

3

POVERTY AND THE STATE IN MODERN INDIA

INTRODUCTION TO GANDHI

Mohandas Karamchand Gandhi was born Oct. 2, 1869 in the Gujarat province of India. His father was the Dewan ("Prime Minister") of the princely state of Porbandar, population about 72,000. "My father was a lover of his clan, truthful, brave and generous, but short-tempered. To a certain extent he might have been given to carnal pleasures... The outstanding impression my mother has left on my memory is that of saintliness. She was deeply religious. She would take the hardest vows and keep them without flinching." The family belonged to the Banya (merchant) caste, known for their frugality. Thus a disciple said of Gandhi: "He wrote on the backs of letters he'd received, or even on the envelopes. What a Banya he was! He didn't believe in wasting anything." In the same century that proved forever that the human capacity for cruelty is boundless, one man took it upon himself to free his country of a foreign oppressor by the unlikely method of nonviolence. Stranger still, it worked.

Mohan was married at the age of 13 to a local girl named Kasturbai. "Kasturbai was illiterate. I was very anxious to teach her, but lustful love left me no time. I am sure that, had my love for her been absolutely untainted with lust, she would be a learned lady today; for I could then have conquered her dislike for studies. I know that nothing is impossible for pure love." Mohandas was in bed with his wife when a servant brought him the news that his father had just died. "The shame to which I have referred... was this shame of my carnal desire even at the critical hour of my father's death, which demanded wakeful service. It is a blot I have never been able to efface or forget."

In 1888, the upwardly mobile Gandhi clan sent Mohandas to England to become a barrister. There he began his lifelong experiments with diet. He learned to like English cooking, on the grounds that it discouraged sensuality. "I now relished the boiled spinach which in Richmond tasted insipid, cooked without condiments." Gandhi never liked school, and took more interest in promoting vegetarianism. He passed his bar examinations in 1890, and returned to India, where he discovered that his mother had died in his absence. "My grief was even greater than over my father's death."

Gandhi was unhappy as a lawyer in India, and in 1893 his family sent him to South Africa (at the time, like India, part of the British Empire.) There, "I discovered that as a man and as an Indian I had no rights", so Gandhi found his true vocation as an activist and moral reformer. He developed three rules which were to shape the rest of his life: satyagraha or truth-force ("The term denotes the method of securing rights by personal suffering; it is the reverse of resistance by arms"); Ahimsa or nonviolence ("He who injures others, is jealous of others, is not fit to live in the world"); and brahmacharya or sexual abstinence ("A man or woman completely practising Brahmacharya is absolutely free from passion. Such a one therefore lives nigh unto God, is Godlike").

After twenty-one years in South Africa, Gandhi returned to India. He founded an Ashram, intended to be a model community, where he eroded the barriers of caste by inviting a family of untouchables to live alongside the caste Hindus. Untouchables were thought to be a source of spiritual pollution: one reason for Hindu resentment of Muslims in India is that many Muslims are the descendants of untouchable converts.

Untouchables lived apart and were barred from schools, temples, and certain roads and wells. They did work that would defile a caste Hindu, for instance, cleaning up human excrement. An unfortunate result of this system was that human excrement generally didn't get cleaned up, causing cholera, typhoid, and dysentery. Gandhi was appalled. Sanitation became a main theme of his reforms. "If we approach any village, the very first thing we encounter is the dunghill. If a traveller who is unfamiliar with these parts comes across this state of affairs, he will not be able to differentiate between the dunghill and the residential part. As a matter of fact, there is not much of a difference between the two." One of Gandhi's favourite object-lessons was to publicly clean a latrine (he had no sense of smell, which must have been a help).

Rabindranath Tagore called Gandhi Mahatma ("Great Soul") and the title stuck in spite of Gandhi's resistance to it. "I shall gladly subscribe to a bill to make it criminal for anybody to call me Mahatma and to touch my feet."

Gandhi did not separate religion and politics. "Politics bereft of religion are absolute dirt, ever to be shunned." He took the term Swaraj ("self-rule") to mean both "self-control" and "home rule for India." To promote Swaraj, he joined the Indian National Congress, India's largest political party, which in 1920 consisted of Anglicized lawyers, all talk and no action. "Of the prominent Congress leaders only one, Motilal Nehru, supported Gandhi in the early stages" (reported Motilal's son, Jawaharlal). With Motilal Nehru's help, Gandhi persuaded the Congress to adopt his plan of noncooperation, a total boycott of all things British; so Indian lawyers quit their practice in the British-run courts, students stopped attending British-run universities, and everyone gave up their British-made clothes. Khadi ("homespun") became the uniform of the Congress Party, and the spinning wheel its emblem. "Spinning was the cottage industry years ago and if the millions are to be saved from starvation they must be enabled to reintroduce spinning in their homes and every village must repossess its own weaver."

Noncooperation was called to a halt by Gandhi himself after rioting broke out in the village of Chauri Chaura. Nehru wrote, "The sudden suspension of our movement after the Chauri Chaura incident was resented, I think, by almost all the prominent Congress leaders."

Gandhi's next campaign, in 1930, was a brilliant symbolic gesture. Salt is a staple in India's climate; but the government held a monopoly on its production and imposed a tax on its sale. Gandhi planned to march to the sea and make salt in defiance of the government monopoly, setting off a nationwide campaign. He began the march at his Ashram, with a few satyagrahis ("truth warriors"); as his progress continued, the procession picked up more people, including, not coincidentally, foreign newsmen. Day after day Westerners saw on their newsreels what Nehru saw: "He was at Jambusar with his pilgrim band, and we spent a few hours with him there and then saw him stride away with his party to the next stage in the journey to the salt sea. That was my last glimpse of him then as I saw him, staff in hand, marching along at the head of his followers, with firm step and a peaceful but undaunted look."

The Salt Campaign was Gandhi's most successful, resulting in civil disobedience throughout India. Nehru recalled: "It seemed as though a spring had been suddenly released; all over the country, in town and village, salt manufacture was the topic of the day... we collected pots and pans and ultimately succeeded in producing some unwholesome stuff, which we waved about in triumph and often auctioned for fancy prices." Within a few months the British had jailed thousands of satyagrahis and most of the Congress leadership, including Gandhi and Nehru.

Jawaharlal Nehru was born in 1889 to a wealthy clan of the self-satisfied Kashmiri Brahmin caste; he was handsome, charming, highly intelligent, and completely secular ("The spectacle of what is called religion... has filled me with horror.") The vital and complex Nehru-Gandhi partnership was to shape modern India. Nehru wrote of Gandhi: "he was a very difficult person to understand, sometimes his language was almost incomprehensible to an average modern", but also: "(he was) a tremendous personality, drawing people to himself like a magnet, and calling out fierce loyalties and attachments."

In 1931 the British released Gandhi from jail long enough for him to negotiate with the Viceroy, Lord Irwin, and then attend a Round Table Conference in London. Gandhi seized the opportunity as a public relations windfall. He spoke on the radio: "The world is sick unto death of blood-spilling. The world is seeking a way out, and I flatter myself with the belief that perhaps it will be the privilege of the ancient land of India to show the way out to the hungering world." When the conference overlapped his evening prayer time, he sat on the floor of the House of Commons and chanted the Bhagavad Gita, to the amazement of the British. He took tea with the King at Buckingham Palace wearing nothing but loincloth and sandals, explaining later, "the King was wearing enough for both of us." Little was accomplished by the Conference itself, and within a week of Gandhi's return to India he was back in prison again.

The British had proposed a new Constitution for India which included a separate electorate for untouchables. Gandhi saw this as one more barrier, and he began a "fast to the death" in protest. "Untouchability poisons Hinduism as a drop of arsenic poisons milk." Nehru wrote, "I felt angry with him at his religious and sentimental approach to a political question, and his frequent references to God in connection with it... What a terrible example to set!" The government brought in the leaders of the various factions to negotiate with Gandhi while he lay on an iron cot in the jail yard, and new legislation was worked out. The fast was over. Nehru sent him a telegram: "news that some settlement reached filled me with relief and joy... Am unable to judge from religious viewpoint. Danger your methods being exploited by others but how can I presume to advise a magician. Love."

In 1942 Gandhi mounted his final independence campaign, "Quit India." He was jailed almost immediately, along with

Kasturba. When Kasturbai became seriously ill with acute bronchitis, the British had a precious shipment of penicillin flown in to the prison for her. But Gandhi felt that the injection of penicillin would be an act of violence; he insisted on nursing her himself using natural methods. Kasturba died. "I cannot imagine life without Ba ("Mother")... her passing has left a vacuum which never will be filled."

With the end of World War II, the British realized they would have to let India go. They could not afford the manpower and material to continue suppressing the Indian independence movement. At the same time Muhammed Ali Jinnah and his Muslim League were lobbying hard for a separate Islamic nation. In August of 1946 the Muslim League proclaimed a "direct action day" which set off a wave of Hindu-Muslim violence. Gandhi was in despair. "I would love to attempt an answer to a question which has been addressed to me from more than one quarter of the globe... Does your message of nonviolence still hold? In reply I must confess my bankruptcy, not that of nonviolence." The partitioning of India into Hindu India and Muslim Pakistan would result in the deaths of about five hundred thousand people through sectarian violence.

In Birla House in Delhi Gandhi began a fast to bring peace. He was met with hostility; a crowd of refugees gathered outside Birla House and chanted, "Let Gandhi die." Two days into the fast, Gandhi's doctor, realizing that his kidneys had ceased to function, told him he was dying. "If I have acetone in my urine, it is because my faith in Rama (loosely, "God") is incomplete", he told her. Finally, the city of Delhi came around. The leaders of all the major factions signed pledges to end the violence, and Gandhi ended his fast. "In the name of God we have indulged in lies, massacres of people, without caring whether they were innocent or guilty, men or women, children or infants. We have indulged in abductions, forcible conversions, and we have done all this shamelessly. I am not aware if anybody has done these things in the name of Truth. With that same name on my lips I have broken the fast."

On January 30, 1948, Gandhi was walking toward his evening prayer meeting in front of a congregation of about five hundred people when he was approached by a Hindu extremist named Nathuram Godse. Gandhi put his palms together in a traditional gesture of greeting. Godse pulled out a pistol and shot three bullets into Gandhi's chest at point-blank range. For a moment Gandhi continued to move forward; then he crumpled and died. It was left to Nehru, now India's Prime Minister, to announce Gandhi's death on All-India radio: "Friends and comrades, the light has gone out of our lives and there is darkness everywhere. I do not know what to tell you and how to say it. Our beloved leader, Bapu ("Father") as we called him, the father of the nation, is no more."

GANDHI AND THE BLACK UNTOUCHABLES

As opposed to the popular perceptions, here you will see Gandhi's image from the eyes of a very famous untouchable leader, named, Dr. B. R. Ambedkar (1893-1956). Born and raised as an untouchable, Dr. Ambedkar received his masters and Ph. D. from Columbia University, which later on also conferred upon him the Doctor of Law. Dr. Ambedkar also received a D. Sc. degree from London School of Economics, and the Bar-at-Law from the Grays Inn, London. Suffice to say, Dr. Ambedkar's sharp intellect has provided us an insight into Gandhi, some of which we will like to share with you all. We recommend the following:

1. Nichols, Beverley. Verdict on India. New York: Harcourt, Brace and Company, 1944.

A book we highly recommend. Beverley Nichols, a famous novelist, musician, playwright, essayist, reporter, and a journalist visited British India. During this visit, he met Dr. Ambedkar, who told him:

> "*Gandhi is the greatest enemy the untouchables have ever had in India.*"

So what did Ambedkar mean? Mr. Nichols explained it as follows:

We can best explain it by a parallel. Take Ambedkar's remark, and for the word "untouchable" substitute the word "peace." Now imagine that a great champion of peace, like Lord Cecil, said, "Gandhi is the greatest enemy of peace the world has ever had." What would he mean, using these words of the most spectacular pacifist of modern times? He would mean that passive resistance—which is Gandhi's form of pacifism—could only lead to chaos and the eventual triumph of brute force; that to lie down and let people trample on you (which was Gandhi's recipe for dealing with the Japanese) is a temptation to the aggressor rather than an example to the aggressed; and that in order to have peace you must organize, you must be strong, and that you must be prepared to use force. Mutatis mutandis, that is precisely what Ambedkar meant about the untouchables. He wanted them to be recognized and he wanted them to be strong. He rightly considered that the best way of gaining his object was by granting them separate electorates; a solid block of 60 million would be in a position to dictate terms to its oppressors. Gandhi fiercely opposed this scheme. "Give the untouchables separate electorates," he cried, "and you only perpetuate their status for all time." It was a queer argument, and those who were not bemused by the Mahatma's charm considered it a phoney one. They suspected that Gandhi was a little afraid that 60 million untouchables might join up with the 100 million Muslims—(as they nearly did)—and challenge the dictatorship of the 180 million orthodox Hindus. With such irreverent criticisms were made to him, Gandhi resorted to his usual tactics: he began to fast unto death. (As if that altered the situation by a comma or proved anything but his own obstinacy!) There was a frenzy of excitement, ending in a compromise on the seventh day of the fast. The untouchables still vote in the same constituencies as the caste Hindus, but a substantial number of seats are now reserved for them in the provincial legislatures. It is better than nothing, but it is not nearly so good as it would have been if Gandhi had not interfered. That is what Doctor Ambedkar meant. And I think that he was right.

2. Ambedkar, B. R. What Congress and Gandhi Have Done to the Untouchables. Bombay: Thacker & Co., Ltd, 2nd edition, 1946. Excerpts from this book were published in: Gandhi: Maker of Modern India? Edited by Martin Deming Lewis. Boston: D. C. Heath and Co., 1965. Here is the report which you must read in its entirety:

Mr. Gandhi's views on the caste system—which constitutes the main social problem in India—were fully elaborated by him in 1921-22 in a Gujrati journal called Nava-Jivan. The article is written in Gujrati. I give below an English translation of his views as near as possible in his own words. Says Mr. Gandhi:

(1) I believe that if Hindu Society has been able to stand it is because it is founded on the caste system.

(2) The seeds of Swaraj are to be found in the caste system. Different castes are like different sections of miliary division. Each division is working for the good of the whole.

(3) A community which can create the caste system must be said to possess unique power of organization.

(4) Caste has a ready made means for spreading primary education. Each caste can take the responsibility for the education of the children of the caste. Caste has a political basis. It can work as an electorate for a representative body. Caste can perform judicial functions by electing persons to act as judges to decide disputes among members of the same caste. With castes it is easy to raise a defense force by requiring each caste to raise a brigade.

(5) I believe that interdining or intermarriage are not necessary for promoting national unity. That dining together creates friendship is contrary to experience. If this was true there would have been no war in Europe.... Taking food is as dirty an act as answering the call of nature. The only difference is that after answering call

of nature we get peace while after eating food we get discomfort. Just as we perform the act of answering the call of nature in seclusion so also the act of taking food must also be done in seclusion.

(6) In India children of brothers do not intermarry. Do they cease to love because they do not intermarry? Among the Vaishnavas many women are so orthodox that they will not eat with members of the family nor will they drink water from a common water pot. Have they no love? The caste system cannot be said to be bad because it does not allow interdining or intermarriage between different castes.

(7) Caste is another name for control. Caste puts a limit on enjoyment. Caste does not allow a person to transgress caste limits in pursuit of his enjoyment. That is the meaning of such caste restrictions as interdining and intermarriage.

(8) To destroy caste system and adopt Western European social system means that Hindus must give up the principle of hereditary occupation which is the soul of the caste system. Hereditary principle is an eternal principle. To change it is to create disorder. I have no use for a Brahmin if I cannot call him a Brahmin for my life. It will be a chaos if every day a Brahmin is to be changed into a Sudra and a Sudra is to be changed into a Brahmin.

(9) The caste system is a natural order of society. In India it has been given a religious coating. Other countries not having understood the utility of the caste system, it existed only in a loose condition and consequently those countries have not derived from caste system the same degree of advantage which India has derived. These being my views I am opposed to all those who are out to destroy the caste system.

In 1922, Mr. Gandhi was a defender of the caste system. Pursuing the inquiry, one comes across a somewhat critical view of the caste system by Mr. Gandhi in the year 1925. This is what Mr. Gandhi said on 3rd February 1925:

> I gave support to caste because it stands for restraint. But at present caste does not mean restraint, it means limitations. Restraint is glorious and helps to achieve freedom. But limitation is like chain. It binds. There is nothing commendable in castes as they exist today. They are contrary to the tenets of the Shastras. The number of castes is infinite and there is a bar against intermarriage. This is not a condition of elevation. It is a state of fall.

In reply to the question: What is the way out? Mr. Gandhi said:

> The best remedy is that small castes should fuse themselves into one big caste. There should be four big castes so that we may reproduce the old system of four Varnas.

In short, in 1925 Mr. Gandhi became an upholder of the Varna system.

The old Varna system prevalent in ancient India had the society divided into four orders: (1) Brahmins, whose occupation was learning; (2) Kshatriyas, whose occupation was warfare; (3) Vaishyas, whose occupation was trade and (4) Sudras, whose occupation was service of the other classes. Is Mr. Gandhi's Varna system the same as this old Varna system of the orthodox Hindus? Mr. Gandhi explained his Varna system in the following terms:

(1) I believe that the divisions into Varna is based on birth.

(2) There is nothing in the Varna system which stands in the way of the Sudra acquiring learning or studying military art of offence or defence. Contra it is open to a Kshatriya to serve. The Varna system is no bar to him. What the Varna system enjoins is that a Sudra will not make learning a way of earning a living. Nor will a Kshatriya adopt service as a way of learning a living. (Similarly a Brahmin may learn the art of war

or trade. But he must not make them a way of earning his living. Contra a Vaishya may acquire learning or may cultivate the art of war. But he must not make them a way of learning his living.)

(3) The Varna system is connected with the way of earning a living. There is no harm if a person belonging to one Varna acquires the knowledge or science and art specialized in by persons belonging to other Varnas. But as far as the way of earning his living is concerned he must follow the occupation of the Varna to which he belongs which means he must follow the hereditary profession of his forefathers.

(4) The object of the Varna is to prevent competition and class struggle and class war. I believe in the Varna system because it fixes the duties and occupations of persons.

(5) Varna means the determination of a man's occupation before he is born.

(6) In the Varna system no man has any liberty to choose his occupation. His occupation is determined for him by heredity.

The social life of Gandhism is either caste or Varna. Though it may be difficult to say which, there can be no doubt that the social ideal of Gandhism is not democracy. For, whether one takes for comparison caste or Varnaboth are fundamentally opposed to democracy.

That Mr. Gandhi changed over from the caste system to the Varna system does not make the slightest difference to the charge that Gandhism is opposed to democracy. In the first place, the idea of Varna is the parent of the idea of caste. If the idea of caste is a pernicious idea it is entirely because of the viciousness of the idea of Varna. Both are evil ideas and it matters very little whether one believes in Varna or in caste.

Turning to the field of economic life, Mr. Gandhi stands for two ideals. One of these is the opposition to machinery...

evidenced by his idolization of Charkha (the spinning wheel) and by insistence upon hand-spinning and hand-weaving. His opposition to machinery and his love for Charkha are not matter of accident. They are a matter of his philosophy of life.

The second ideal of Mr. Gandhi is the elimination of class war and even class struggle in the relationship between employers and employees and between landlords and tenants.... Mr. Gandhi does not wish to hurt the propertied class. He is even opposed to a campaign against them. He has no passion for economic equality. Referring to the propertied class Mr. Gandhi said quite recently that he does not wish to destroy the hen that lays the golden egg. His solution for the economic conflict between the owners and the workers, between the rich and the poor, between the landlords and the tenants and between the employers and the employees is very simple. The owners need not deprive themselves of their property. All they need do is to declare themselves trustees for the poor. Of course, the trust is to be a voluntary one carrying only a spiritual obligation.

Is there anything new in the Gandhian analysis of economic ills? Are the economics of Gandhism sound? What hope does Gandhism hold out to the common man, to the down and out? Does it promise him a better life, a life of joy and culture, a life of freedom, not merely freedom from want but freedom to rise, to grow to the full stature which his capacities can reach?

There is nothing new in the Gandhian analysis of economic ills, insofar as it attributes them to machinery and the civilization that is built upon it. That machinery and modern civilization help to concentrate management and control into relatively few hands, and with the aid of banking and credit facilitate the transfer into still fewer hands of all materials and factories and mills in which millions are bled white in order to support huge industries thousands of miles away from their cottages, maimings and cripplings far in excess of the corresponding injuries by war, and are responsible for disease and physical deterioration due directly and indirectly to the development of large cities with their smoke, dirt, noise, foul air, lack of sunshine and outdoor life, slums, prostitution and unnatural living which they bring about, are all old and worn-out arguments. There is nothing new in them. Gandhism is merely repeating the views of Rousseau, Ruskin, Tolstoy and their school.

The ideas which go to make up Gandhism are just primitive. It is a return to nature, to animal life. The only merit is their simplicity. As there is always a large corps of simple people who are attracted by them, such simple ideas do not die, and there is always some simpleton to preach them. There is, however, no doubt that the practical instincts of men—which seldom go wrong—have found them unfruitful and which society in search of progress has thought it best to reject.

The economics of Gandhism are hopelessly fallacious. The fact that machinery and modern civilization have produced many evils may be admitted. But these evils are no argument against them. For the evils are not due to machinery and modern civilization. They are due to wrong social organization, which has made private property and pursuit of personal gain, matters of absolute sanctity. If machinery and civilization have not benefited everybody, the remedy is not to condemn machinery and civilization but to alter the organization of society so that the benefits will not be usurped by the few but will accrue to all.

In Gandhism, the common man has no hope. It treats man as an animal and no more. It is true that man shares the constitution and functions of animals, nutritive, reproductive, etc. But these are not distinctively human functions. The distinctively human function is reason, the purpose of which is to enable man to observe, meditate, cogitate, study and discover the beauties of the Universe and enrich his life and control the animal elements in his life. Man thus occupies the highest place in the scheme of animate existence. If this is true what is the conclusion that follows: The conclusion that follows is that while the ultimate goal of a brute's life is reached once his physical appetites are satisfied, the ultimate goal of man's existence is not reached unless and until he has fully cultivated his mind. In short, what divides the brute from man is culture. Culture is not possible for the brute, but it is essential for man. That being so, the aim of human society must be to enable every person to lead a life of culture, which means the cultivation of mind as distinguished from the satisfaction of mere physical wants. How can this happen?

Both for society as well as for individual(s) there is always a gulf between merely living and living worthily. In order that one may live worthily one must first live. The time and energy spent upon mere life, upon gaining of subsistence detracts from that available for activities of a distinctively human nature and which go to make up a life of culture. How then can a life of culture be made possible? It is not possible unless there is sufficient leisure. For, it is only when there is leisure that a person is free to devote himself to a life of culture.

The problem of all problems, which human society has to face, is how to provide leisure to every individual. What does leisure mean? Leisure means the lessening of the toil and effort necessary for satisfying the physical wants of life. How can leisure be made possible? Leisure is quite impossible unless some means are found whereby the toil required for producing goods necessary to satisfy human needs is lessened. What can lessen such toil? Only when machine takes the place of man. There is no other means of producing leisure. Machinery and modern civilization are thus indispensable for emancipating man from leading the life of a brute, and for providing him with leisure and for making a life of culture possible. The man who condemns machinery and modern civilization simply does not understand their purpose and the ultimate aim which human society must strive to achieve.

Gandhism may well be well suited to a society which does not accept democracy as its ideal. A society which does not believe in democracy may be indifferent to machinery and the civilization based upon it. But a democratic society cannot. The former may well content itself with a life of leisure and culture for the few and a life of toil and drudgery for the many. But a democratic society must assure a life of leisure and culture to each one of its citizens. If the above analysis is correct then the slogan of a democratic society must be machinery, and more machinery, civilization and more civilization. Under Gandhism the common man must keep on toiling ceaselessly for a pittance and remain a brute. In short, Gandhism with its call of back to nature, means back to nakedness, back to squalor, back to poverty and back to ignorance for the vast mass of the people.

Gandhism insists upon class structure. It regards the class structure of society and also the income structure as sacrosanct with the consequent distinctions of rich and poor, high and low, owners and workers, as permanent parts of social organization. From the point of view of social consequences, nothing can be more pernicious.... It is not enough to say that Gandhism believes in a class structure. Gandhism stands for more than that. A class structure which is a faded, jejune, effete thing—a mere sentimentality, a mere skeleton is not what Gandhism wants. It wants class structure to function as a living faith. In this there is nothing to be surprised at. For, class structure in Gandhism is not a mere accident. It is its official doctrine.

The idea of trusteeship, which Gandhism proposes as a panacea and by which the moneyed classes will hold their properties in trust for the poor, is the most ridiculous part of it. All that one can say about it is that if anybody else had propounded it the author would have been laughed at as a silly fool, who had not known the hard realities of life and was deceiving the servile classes by telling them that a little dose of moral rearmament to the propertied classes—those who by their insatiable cupidity and indomitable arrogance have made and will always make this world a vale of tears for the toiling millions—will recondition them to such an extent that they will be able to withstand the temptation to misuse the tremendous powers which the class structure gives them over servile classes.

Mr. Gandhi sometimes speaks on social and economic subjects as though he was a blushing Red. Those who will study

Gandhism will not be deceived by the occasional aberrations of Mr. Gandhi in favour of democracy and against capitalism. For, Gandhism is in no sense a revolutionary creed. It is conservatism in excelsis. So far as India is concerned, it is a reactionary creed blazoning on its banner the call of Return to Antiquity. Gandhism aims at the resuscitation and reanimating of India's dread, dying past.

Gandhism is a paradox. It stands for freedom from foreign domination, which means the destruction of the existing political structure of the country. At the same time, it seeks to maintain intact a social structure which permits the domination of one class by another on a hereditary basis which means a perpetual domination of one class by another... .

The first special feature of Gandhism is that its philosophy helps those who want to keep what they have and to prevent those who have not from getting what they have a right to get. No one who examines the Gandhian attitude to strikes, the Gandhian reverence for caste and the Gandhian doctrine of Trusteeship by the rich for the benefit of the poor can deny that this is an upshot of Gandhism. Whether this is the calculated result of a deliberate design or whether it is a matter of accident may be open to argument. But the fact remains that Gandhism is the philosophy of the well-to-do and the leisure class.

The second special feature of Gandhism is to delude people into accepting their misfortunes by presenting them as best of good fortunes. One or two illustrations will suffice to bring out the truth of this statement.

The Hindu sacred law penalized the Sudras (Hindus of the fourth class) from acquiring wealth. It is a law of enforced poverty unknown in any other part of thc world. What does Gandhism do? It does not lift the ban. It blesses the Sudra for his moral courage to give up property. It is well worth quoting Mr. Gandhi's own words. Here they are:

The Sudra who only serves (the higher caste) as a matter of religious duty, and who will never own any property, who indeed has not even the ambition to own anything, is deserving of thousand obeisance... The very Gods will shower flowers on him.

Another illustration in support is the attitude of Gandhism towards the scavenger. The sacred law of the Hindus lays down that a scavenger's progeny shall live by scavenging. Under Hinduism scavenging was not a matter of choice, it was a matter of force. What does Gandhism do? It seeks to perpetuate this system by praising scavenging as the noblest service to society! Let me quote Mr. Gandhi: As a President of a Conference of the Untouchables, Mr. Gandhi said:

I do not want to attain Moksha. I do not want to be reborn. But if I have to be reborn, I should be born an untouchable, so that I may share their sorrows, sufferings and the affronts levelled at them, in order that I endeavour to free myself and them from that miserable condition. I, therefore prayed that if I should be born again, I should do so not as a Brahmin, Kshatriya, Vaishya, or Sudra, but as an Atishudra.... I love scavenging. In my Ashram, an eighteen-years-old Brahmin lad is doing the scavenger's work in order to teach the Ashram scavenger cleanliness. The lad is no reformer. He was born and bred in orthodoxy.... But he felt that his accomplishments were incomplete until he had become also a perfect sweeper, and that, if he wanted the Ashram sweeper to do his work well, he must do it himself and set an example. You should realize that you are cleaning Hindu Society.

Can there be a worse example of false propaganda than this attempt of Gandhism to perpetuate evils which have been deliberately imposed by one class over another? If Gandhism preached the rule of poverty for all and not merely for the Sudra the worst that could be said about it is that it is mistaken idea. But why preach it as good for one class only?... In India a man is not a scavenger because of his work. He is a scavenger because of his birth irrespective of the question whether he does scavenging or not. If Gandhism preached that scavenging is a noble profession with the object of inducing those who refuse to engage in it, one could understand it. But why appeal to the scavenger's pride and vanity in order to induce him and him only to keep on to scavenging by telling him that scavenging is a noble profession and that he need not be ashamed of it? To preach that poverty is good for the Sudra and for none else, to preach that scavenging is good for the Untouchables and for none else and to make them accept these onerous impositions as voluntary purposes of life, by appeal to their failings is an outrage and a cruel joke on the helpless classes which none but Mr. Gandhi can perpetrate with equanimity and impunity.

Criticism apart, this is the technique of Gandhism to make wrongs done appear to the very victim as though they were his privileges. If there is an "ism" which has made full use of religion as an opium to lull the people into false beliefs and false security, it is Gandhism. Following Shakespeare, one can well say: Plausibility! Ingenuity! Thy name is Gandhism. Such is Gandhism. Having known what is Gandhism the answer to the question, "Should Gandhism become the law of the land what would be the lot of the Untouchables under it?" cannot require much scratching of the brain.... In India even the lowest man among the caste Hindus—why even the aboriginal and the Hill Tribe man—though educationally and economically not very much above the Untouchables. The Hindu society accepts him claim to superiority over the Untouchables. The Untouchable will therefore continue to suffer the worst fate as he does now namely, in prosperity he will be the last to be employed and in depression the first to be fired.

What does Gandhism do to relieve the Untouchables from this fate? Gandhism professes to abolish Untouchability. That is hailed as the greatest virtue of Gandhism. But what does this virtue amount to in actual life? To assess the value of this anti-Untouchability which is regarded as a very big element in Gandhism, it is necessary to understand fully the scope of Mr. Gandhi's programme for the removal of Untouchability. Does it mean anything more than that the Hindus will not mind touching the Untouchables? Does it mean the removal of the ban on the right of the Untouchables to education? It would be better to take the two questions separately.

To start wit the first question. Mr. Gandhi does not say that a Hindu should not take a bath after touching the Untouchables. If Mr. Gandhi does not object to it as a purification of pollution then it is difficult to see how Untouchability can be said to vanish by touching the Untouchables. Untouchability centres round the idea of pollution by contact and purification by bath to remove the pollution. Does it mean social assimilation of the Untouchables with the Hindus? Mr. Gandhi has most categorically stated that removal of Untouchability does not mean interdining or intermarriage between the Hindus and the Untouchables. Mr. Gandhi's anti-Untouchability means that the Untouchables will be classes as Sudras instead of being classed as Atishudras (*i.e.,* "beyond Sudras").

There is nothing more in it. Mr. Gandhi has not considered whether the old Sudras will accept the new Sudras into their fold. If they don't then the removal of Untouchability is a senseless proposition for it will still keep the Untouchables as a separate social category. Mr. Gandhi probably knows that the abolition of Untouchability will not bring about the assimilation of the Untouchables by the Sudras. That seems to be the reason why Mr. Gandhi himself has given a new and a different name to the Untouchables. The new name registers by anticipation what is likely to be the fact. By calling the Untouchables Harijans, Mr. Gandhi has killed two birds with one stone. He has shown that assimilation of the Untouchables by the Sudras is not possible. He has also by his new name counteracted assimilation and made it impossible.

Regarding the second question, it is true that Gandhism is prepared to remove the old ban placed by the Hindu Shastras on the right of the Untouchables to education and permit them to acquire knowledge and learning. Under Gandhism the Untouchables may study law, they may study medicine, they may study engineering or anything else they may fancy. So far so good. But will the Untouchables be free to make use of their knowledge and learning? Will they have the right to choose their profession? Can they adopt the career of lawyer, doctor or engineer? To these questions the answer which Gandhism gives is an emphatic "no." The untouchables must follow their hereditary professions. That those occupations are unclean is no excuse. That before the occupation became hereditary it was the result of force and not volition does not matter.

The argument of Gandhism is that what is once settled is settled forever even it was wrongly settled. Under Gandhism the Untouchables are to be eternal scavengers. There is no doubt that the Untouchables would much prefer the orthodox system of Untouchability. A compulsory state of ignorance imposed upon the Untouchables by the Hindu Shastras made scavenging bearable. But Gandhism which compels an educated Untouchable to do scavenging is nothing short of cruelty. The grace in Gandhism is a curse in its worst form. The virtue of the anti-Untouchability plant in Gandhism is quite illusory. There is no substance in it.

What else is there in Gandhism which the Untouchables can accept as opening a way for their ultimate salvation? Barring this illusory campaign against Untouchability, Gandhism is simply another form of Sanatanism which is the ancient name for militant orthodox Hinduism. What is there in Gandhism which is not to be found in orthodox Hinduism? There is caste in Hinduism, there is caste in Gandhism. Hinduism believes in the law of hereditary profession, so does Gandhism. Hinduism enjoins cow-worship. So does Gandhism. Hinduism upholds the law of karma, predestination of man's condition in this world, so does Gandhism. Hinduism accepts the authority of the Shastras. So does Gandhism. Hinduism believes in idols. So does Gandhism. All that Gandhism has done is to find a philosophic justification for Hinduism and its dogmas. Hinduism is bald in the sense that it is just a set of rules which bear on their face the appearance of a crude and cruel system. Gandhism supplies the philosophy which smoothens its surface and gives it the appearance of decency and respectability and so alters it and embellishes it as to make it even more attractive.

What hope can Gandhism offer to the Untouchables? To the Untouchables, Hinduism is a veritable chamber of horrors. The sanctity and infallibility of the Vedas, Smritis and Shastras, the iron law of caste, the heartless law of karma and the senseless law of status by birth are to the Untouchables veritable instruments of torture which Hinduism has forged against the Untouchables. These very instruments which have mutilated, blasted and blighted the life of the Untouchables are to be found intact and untarnished in the bosom of Gandhism. How can the Untouchables say that Gandhism is a heaven and not a chamber of horrors as Hinduism has been? The only reaction and a very natural reaction of the Untouchables would be to run away from Gandhism.

Gandhists may say that what I have stated applies to the old type of Gandhism. There is a new Gandhism, Gandhism without caste. This has reference to the recent statement of Mr. Gandhi that caste is an anachronism. Reformers were naturally gladdened by this declaration of Mr. Gandhi. And who would not be glad to see that a man like Mr. Gandhi having such terrible influence over the Hindus, after having played the most mischievous part of a social reactionary, after having stood out as the protagonist of the caste system, after having beguiled and befooled the unthinking Hindus with arguments which made no distinction between what is fair and foul should have come out with this recantation? But is this really a matter for jubilation? Does it change the nature of Gandhism? Does it make Gandhism a new and a better "ism" than it was before? Those who are carried away by this recantation of Mr. Gandhi, forget two things. In the first place, all that Mr. Gandhi has said is that caste is an anachronism. He does not say it is an evil. He does not say it is anathema. Mr. Gandhi may be taken to be not in favour of caste, but Mr. Gandhi does not say that he is against the Varna system. And what is Mr. Gandhi's Varna system? It is simply a new name for the caste system and retains all the worst features of the caste system.

The declaration of Mr. Gandhi cannot be taken to mean any fundamental change in Gandhism. It cannot make Gandhism acceptable to the Untouchables. The untouchables will still have ground to say: "Good God! Is this man Gandhi our Saviour?"

GANDHI AND RACISM

Summary: To understand Gandhi's role towards the blacks, one requires a knowledge of Hinduism. Within the constraints, a few words on Hinduism will suffice: The caste is the bedrock of Hinduism. The Hindu term for caste is varna; which means arranging the society on a four-level hierarchy based on the skin colour: The darker-skinned relegated to the lowest level, the lighter-skinned to the top three levels of the apartheid scale called the Caste System. The race factor underlies the intricate workings of Hinduism, not to mention the countless evil practices embedded within. Have no doubt, Gandhi loved the Caste system.

Gandhi lived in South Africa for roughly twenty one years from 1893 to 1914. In 1906, he joined the military with a rank of Sergeant-Major and actively participated in the war against the blacks. Gandhi's racist ideas are also evident in his writings of these periods. One should ask a question: Were our American Black leaders including Dr. King aware of Gandhi's anti-black activities? Painfully, we have researched the literature and the answer is, no. For this lapse, the blame lies on the Afro-American newspapers which portrayed Gandhi in ever glowing terms, setting the stage for African-American leaders Howard Thurman, Sue Baily Thurman, Reverend Edward Carroll, Benjamin E. Mays, Channing H. Tobias, and William Stuart Nelson to visit India at different time periods to meet Gandhi in person. None of these leaders had any deeper understanding of Hinduism, British India, or the complexities of Gandhi's convoluted multilayered Hindu mind.

Frankly speaking, these leaders were no match to Gandhi's deceit; Gandhi hoodwinked them all, and that too, with great ease. Understanding of Hindu India with our black leaders never really improved even considering years later in March 1959, much after Gandhi's death, Dr. Martin Luther King, Jr., his wife, and Professor Lawrence D. Reddick visited India and to our way of analysis, they fared no better than their predecessors. We are certain, had Dr. King known Gandhi's anti-black and other criminal activities, he would have distanced his civil-rights movement away from the name of Gandhi. We recommend the following:

1. Grenier, Richard. The Gandhi Nobody Knows published in Commentary March 1983; pages 59 to 72. This is the best article on Gandhi briefly outlining his war activities against the blacks.
2. Kapur, Sudarshan. Raising up a Prophet: The African-American Encounter with Gandhi; Boston: Beacon Press, 1992 Excellent research book into the perspective of distant American blacks with respect to their new hero, Gandhi. However, this book has one major flaw: The author seems to be unaware of Gandhi's anti-black activities in South Africa.
3. Huq, Fazlul. Gandhi: Saint or Sinner? Bangalore: Dalit Sahitya Akademy, 1992.

Superb book. Really gets into the Gandhi's anti-black ideology with a sense of history setting intact.

This book's second chapter-Gandhi's Anti-African Racismóis a superb analysis of Gandhi's anti-black thinking. We bring to you the whole chapter for your review:

Gandhi was not a whit less racist than the white racists of South Africa. When Gandhi formed the Natal Indian Congress on August 22, 1894, the no. 1 objective he declared was: "To promote concord and harmony among the Indians and Europeans in the Colony." (Collected Works (CW)1 pp. 132-33)

He launched his Indian Opinion on June 4 1904: "The object of Indian Opinion was to bring the European and the Indian subjects of the King Edward closer together." (CW. IV P. 320)

What was the harm in making an effort to bring understanding among all people, irrespective of colour, creed or religion? Did not Gandhi know that a huge population of blacks and coloured lived there? Perhaps to Gandhi they were less than human beings.

Addressing a public meeting in Bombay on Sept. 26 1896 (CW II p. 74), Gandhi said:

Ours is one continued struggle against degradation sought to be inflicted upon us by the European, who desire to degrade us to the level of the raw Kaffir, whose occupation is hunting and whose sole ambition is to collect a certain number of cattle to buy a wife with, and then pass his life in indolence and nakedness.

In 1904, he wrote (CW. IV p. 193): It is one thing to register natives who would not work, and whom it is very difficult to find out if they absent themselves, but it is another thing-and most insulting-to expect decent, hard-working, and respectable Indians, whose only fault is that they work too much, to have themselves registered and carry with them registration badges.

In its editorial on the Natal Municipal Corporation Bill, the Indian Opinion of March 18 1905 wrote:

Clause 200 makes provision for registration of persons belonging to uncivilized races (meaning the local Africans), resident and employed within the Borough. One can understand the necessity of registration of Kaffirs who will not work, but why should registration be required for indentured Indians who have become free, and for their descendants about whom the general complaint is that they work too much? (Italic portion is added)

The Indian Opinion published an editorial on September 9 1905 under the heading, "The relative Value of the Natives and the Indians in Natal". In it Gandhi referred to a speech made by Rev. Dube, a most accomplished African, who said that an African had the capacity for improvement, if only the Colonials would look upon him as better than dirt, and give him a chance to develop self-respect. Gandhi suggested that "A little judicious extra taxation would do no harm; in the majority of cases it compels the native to work for at least a few days a year." Then he added:

Now let us turn our attention to another and entirely unrepresented community-the Indian. He is in striking contrast with the native. While the native has been of little benefit to the State, it owes its prosperity largely to the Indians. While native loafers abound on every side, that species of humanity is almost unknown among Indians here.

Nothing could be further from the truth, that Gandhi fought against Apartheid, which many propagandists in later years wanted people to believe. He was all in favour of continuation of white domination and oppression of the blacks in South Africa.

In the Government Gazette of Natal for Feb. 28 1905, a Bill was published regulating the use of firearms by the natives and Asiatics. Commenting on the Bill, the Indian Opinion of March 25 1905 stated:

> *In this instance of the firearms, the Asiatic has been most improperly bracketed with the natives. The British Indian does not need any such restrictions as are imposed by the Bill on the natives regarding the carrying of firearms. The prominent race can remain so by preventing the native from arming himself. Is there a slightest vestige of justification for so preventing the British Indian?*

Here is the budding Mahatma telling the white racists how they can perpetuate their Nazi domination over the vast majority of Africans.

In the British imperialist scheme, one important strategy was to divide and rule. Gandhi advised Indians not to align with other political groups in either coloured or African communities. In 1906 the coloured people in the colonies of Good Hope, the Transvaal and the Orange River colony, addressed a petition to the King Emperor demanding franchise rights. The petitioners showed clearly that, in one part of South Africa, namely the Cape of Good Hope, they had enjoyed the franchise ever since the introduction of representative institutions. Commenting on the petition, the Indian Opinion of March 24 1906, declaring that "British Indians have, in order that they may never be misunderstood, made it clear that they do not aspire to any political power," added:

It seems that the petition is being widely circulated, and signatures are being taken of all coloured people in the three colonies named. The petition is non-Indian in character, although British Indians, being coloured people, are very largely affected by it. We consider that it was a wise policy on the part of the British Indians throughout South Africa, to have kept themselves apart and distinct from the other coloured communities in this country.

In a statement made in 1906 to the Constitution Committee, the British Indian Association led by Gandhi (CW. V p. 335) said:

The British Indian Association has always admitted the principle of white domination and has, therefore, no desire, on behalf of the community it represents, for any political rights just for the sake of them. Commenting on a court case, the Indian Opinion of 2, June 1906, in its Gujrati section, stated:

> *You say that the magistrate's decision is unsatisfactory because it would enable a person, however unclean, to travel by a tram, and that even the Kaffirs would be able to do so. But the magistrate's decision is quite different. The Court declared that the Kaffirs have no legal right to travel by tram. And according to tram regulations, those in an unclean dress or in a drunken state are prohibited from boarding a tram. Thanks to the Court's decision, only clean Indians (meaning upper caste Hindu Indians) or coloured people other than Kaffirs, can now travel in the trams. (Italic portion is added)*

Apartheid defended: Gandhi accepted racial segregation, not only because it was politically expedient as his Imperial masters had already drawn such a blueprint, it also conformed with his own attitude to the caste system. In his own mind he fitted Apartheid into the caste system: whites in the position of Brahmins, Indian merchants and professionals as Sudras, and all other non-whites as Untouchables. Though Gandhi was strongly opposed to the comingling of races, the working-class

Indians did not share his distaste. There were many areas where Indians, Chinese, Coloured, Africans and poor whites lived together. On February 15 1905, Gandhi wrote to Dr. Porter, the Medical Officer of Health, Johannesburg (CW. IV p. 244, and "Indian Opinion" 9 April 1904):

Why, of all places in Johannesburg, the Indian location should be chosen for dumping down all kaffirs of the town, passes my comprehension.

Of course, under my suggestion, the Town Council must withdraw the Kaffirs from the Location. About this mixing of the Kaffirs with the Indians I must confess I feel most strongly. I think it is very unfair to the Indian population, and it is an undue tax on even the proverbial patience of my countrymen.

Dr. Porter replied that it was the Indians who sub-let to Africans.

Commenting on the White League's agitation, Gandhi wrote in his Indian Opinion of September 24 1903:

We believe as much in the purity of race as we think they do, only we believe that they would best serve these interests, which are as dear to us as to them, by advocating the purity of all races, and not one alone. We believe also that the white race of South Africa should be the predominating race.

Again, on December 24 1903, Indian Opinion stated:

The petition dwells upon `the comingling of the coloured and white races'. May we inform the members of the Conference that so far as British Indians are concerned, such a thing is particularly unknown. If there is one thing which the Indian cherishes more than any other, it is the purity of type.

In his farewell speech at a meeting held in the house of Dr. Gool in Capetown, which was reported in the Indian Opinion of July 1 1914, Gandhi said:

The Indians knew perfectly well which was the dominant and governing race. They aspired to no social equality with

Europeans. They felt that the path of their development was separate. They did not even aspire to the franchise, or, if the aspiration exists, it was with no idea of its having a present effect.

Gandhi joined in the orgy of Zulu slaughter when the Bambata Rebellion broke out. It is essential to discuss the background of the Bambata Rebellion, to place Gandhi's Nazi war crime in its proper perspective.

THE BAMBATTA REBELLION—BACKGROUND

The spiritual foundation of Nazism was the superiority of the Aryan race or its modern version, the Anglo-Saxon race. When Disraeli was Prime Minister, Britain enunciated a doctrine, like the Monroe Doctrine, warning other European powers that Africa would be a British preserve, and that from the Cape to the Limpopo, if not to Cairo, only white people would have local political power. Successive British Governments pursued this policy.

In the 1870s, the Zulu Kingdom was by far the most powerful African State of the Limpopo. Cetewayo, who succeeded his father in 1872, was an able and popular ruler. He united the kingdom and built up a most efficient army. He followed a policy of alliance with the British Colony of Natal. The Zulu Kingdom and the Boer Republic of the Transvaal had been feuding for a long time. The Zulus were defeated twice by the Boers; in 1838 and 1840. By 1877 Cetewayo was ready to invade the Transvaal. But the British stepped in and annexed the Transvaal in 1877, only to prevent Cetewayo from doing it first and becoming powerful and a challenge to white supremacy.

Some contemporary reports throw light on the relative strength of the Zulus and their Boer enemies. Colonel A. W. Durnford wrote in a memorandum on July 5 ("The Secret History of South Africa" by Abercrombe. The Central News Agency Ltd., Johannesburg South Africa. 1951 p. 6):

About this time (April 10th) Cetewayo had massed his forces in three corps on the borders, and would undoubtedly have swept the Transvaal, at least up to the Vaal River if not to Pretoria itself, had the country not been taken over by the English. In my opinion he would have cleared the country to Pretoria.

Shepstone, the British Administrator, himself wrote concerning the reality of the danger on Dec. 25 1877:

The Boers are still flying, and I think by this time there must be a belt of more than a hundred miles long and thirty broad in which, with three insignificant exceptions, there is nothing but absolute desolation. This will give some idea of the mischief which Cetewayo's conduct has caused. (Ibid p.7).

The above facts explode the myth that the British protected the Zulus from the Boers.

British barbarity on Blacks: After annexing the Transvaal, Shepstone turned his attention to destroying all the independent African states in that region, particularly the Zulu Kingdom. Before annexation of the Transvaal, Shepstone sided with the Zulus in their border disputes with the Transvaal. After annexation he made a volte-face and used those disputes as excuses to invade Zululand. The British public was told that the Zulu War was to liberate the Zulu people from a tyrannical ruler, and South Africa from a menace to "Christianity and civilisation".

In 1879, the British invaded the Zulu Kingdom and defeated Cetawayo. Then they started their complete subjugation. First the army was broken, thus destroying their ability to defend themselves. The country was then split into thirteen separate units under the nominal control of the chiefs, salaried by the Government. The white magistrates supplanted the chiefs as the most powerful men in their districts. Most important of all, the land was partitioned. Before the war, Shepstone had expressed the hope that Cetewayo's warriors would be "changed to labourers working for wages". It makes a sad story, how this was accomplished. In 1902-4, the Land Commission delineated a number of locations for the Zulus, and threw open the rest of the country to white settlement. Out of a total acreage of more than 12 million acres, the Africans held some 2 million acres. They numbered, at the lowest reckoning, over three hundred thousand.

The Europeans, who were less than 20, 000, owned most of the best land. A large proportion of the African population was forced to live upon land to which it had no legal claim. Where the Africans lived upon private or crown lands, they lived there entirely upon sufferance and without legal title. By this time, other independent African states in that region were also destroyed by the British army. Wheresoever, they marched, in Basutoland, Zululand or Bechuanaland, the Queen's horses and the Queen's men were like unto a "Salvation Army" ministering to the welfare of the colonists. The sufferers were the Africans.

Gandhi wrote in his Satyagraha in South Africa (p. 15):

The Boers are simple, frank and religious. They settle in the midst of extensive farms. We can have no idea of the extent of these farms. A farm with us means generally an acre or two, and sometimes even less. In South Africa, a single farmer has hundreds or thousands of acres of land in his possession. He is not anxious to put all this under cultivation at once, and if any one argues with him he will say, `Let it lie fallow; lands which are now fallow will be cultivated by our children'.

Also in his Indian Opinion (March 15 1913), he wrote:

General Botha has thousands of acres of land.... (there is) a big company in Natal which has hundreds of thousands of acres of land.

Thou shalt not steal but rob.

It did not seem to occur to Gandhi how these people came into possession of thousands of acres of land, whereas Africans were cooped in locations like chicken in pens.

Grabbing the land was not enough: it needed manpower to cultivate that land. The cry of the farmers was for labour. Naturally it found a favourite response from Shepstone, whose dream it was to convert Cetewayo's warriors into labourers for white men. His native policy was to meet the demands of the European farmers. He agreed that Europeans could not expand or grow in wealth unless they could draw more fully upon the reservoirs of labour in the African reserves.

In the process of European colonisation, the swiftly expanding land-hungry Europeans turned the bulk of the African population into a proletariat. Due to the congestion and landlessness in the reserves, created deliberately by the white rulers, their agricultural return was not sufficient for bare existence. Then there were the taxes on huts, cattle and what not. On the other hand, working for white men did not provide them with adequate sustenance. In Natal, the sugar farmers of the coast relied upon the Indian indentured labour, whereas the stock farmers of the interior relied exclusively on Africans, and regarded the failure of Africans to work for them as a criminal offence.

In a report to the Chief Commissioner of Police in 1903, the Police Inspector W. F. Fairley wrote: "With regard to crime, the principal complaints made by Dutch farmers to patrols was of the refusal to work on the part of the natives." (Department Reports 1903 p. 67 cited "Reluctant Rebellion" by Marks p. 17. Clarendon Press, Oxford 1970). Complaints about the shortage of African labour were voiced in all parts of the country. The farmers were later joined by the mining industries. The most obvious change was the broadening of the economic base from being entirely agricultural to one in which mining played a more and more important part. Diamond, gold, coal became major industries, and with this development, the deeper involvement of the big finance houses, particularly Rothschilds. So the fate of the Africans as the source of cheap labour, and the fat dividends derived from mining by the British ruling class, became interlinked. This still continues in a modified form. Now it is Anglo-American corporations.

Cheap labour from India: Europeans assumed that Africans lived only to meet their requirements of cheap labour, and as such they had no right to establish themselves as self-sufficient and independent farmers because this conflicted with European interests. Famines in India facilitates the recruitment of indentured Indian labourers for white employers in the Colonies. It was no different in relation to Africans. In a Report of the Native Affairs Commission, (Native Affairs Commission Report 1939-40 cited "Oxford History of South Africa" p. 182. Clarendon Press, Oxford, 1969) it was admitted that "African reserves were regarded by whites as reservoirs of labour, and congestion, landlessness and crop failure were welcomed as stimulants to the labour supply".

Similar situations among whites were viewed as national calamities. The Government lent millions of pounds to white farmers, gave them tax relief in times of famine, paid subsidies, facilitated the export of their produce, and wrote off their debts. But what about Africans? Famine would be rampant, crops ruined, food exhausted, thousands of Africans and their cattle would starve to death, but the government would not raise a finger.

The whites not only stole the land from the Africans, and used them as cheap labour, but also looked to them for revenue. They drew a relatively large and growing income from the Africans. "The Native population of Natal", Shepstone admitted ("Imperial Factor" by De Kieweit p. 193. Clarendon Press, Oxford 1970), "contribute to the revenue annually a sum equal, at least, to that necessary to maintain the whole fixed establishment of the Colony for the government of the whites as well as themselves." Taxation is a financial measure to gather revenue to meet the expenditure of the state. But in South Africa it was used to reduce Africans to slavery. The sole motive behind the extra taxation imposed on Africans was to force the Africans to work on terms dictated by the whites.

Always there was resentment against any measure which would allow the Africans to settle in locations instead of keeping them as labourers. It was not only the farmers' conferences, the press owned by the mining magnates joined the outcry of the farmers to enact special laws to compel the Africans to come out of their locations and work for the whites. The press was in the forefront to arouse the sentiments that Africans not in European service were necessarily living in idleness. Gandhi's Indian Opinion played second fiddle to the white press in this respect. To Gandhi, the imposition of taxes upon the Africans to compel them to work for the white employers was "gentle persuasion".

By a stroke of the pen, the major part of the available land was taken away from the Zulus and given to Europeans. Some of the dispossessed Zulus were allotted locations and others remained on the land of European landlords on sufferance. Bambata was one of these unfortunate chiefs. He became Chief in 1890 and he and his people were placed in private locations on very high rents. The land was useless for any agricultural purpose. To make things worse, the Boer farmers suspected Bambata of informing the British about their pro-Boer activities, and naturally they tried to victimise him and his people. But after the war, the British rulers leaned backwards and went out of their way to kiss and hug the Boers. So Bambata was caught in a cleft stick. By 1905 the tension between Bambata and his white landlords reached crisis point. The Assistant Magistrate of Greytown, H. Von Gerard, wrote to the Under Secretary of Native Affairs recommending the allocation of a location for his people. Gerard described how people were being oppressed and squeezed by the landlords, what useless land it was for agricultural purposes, and how summons after summons was being issued against people who were unable to pay high rents. Finally he remarked ("Reluctant Rebellion" by Marks. P. 201):

> A most desperate state of affairs, the more so as there seems no remedy for it.... My sympathies with Bambata's people... but I see no way out of the difficulty.

The military and civilian leaders of Natal were consciously developing a picture as if an uprising was imminent. Not that they could foresee one, but they wanted to foresee one because that would give them a golden opportunity to inflict severe punishments on Zulus who, according to the colonists, were growing insolent. They drew up a plan to deal with this imaginary uprising swiftly, and all agreed that was the way they could save not only Natal but North Africa from the "barbarities which only the savage mind can conceive." (Ibid p. xvii)

Zulu Revolt: But outside Natal, people were not so sure. Styne, President of the Orange Free State, called it "hysteria". Smuts, Botha and Merriman expressed concern as to whether the whites of Natal would spur a rebellion. Some churchmen and many radical humanitarians in Natal, as well as England, produced volumes of irrefutable evidence proving that it was a conspiracy to goad the Zulus into rebellion and then massacre them. In this, Hariette Colenso, the famous daughter of a famous father, Bishop Colenso, made the most outstanding contribution. There was a cry of imminent native revolt in the press long before active rebellion broke out.

As far back as 1902, Lieu. G. A. Mills in his report (GH18/02. Cited "Reluctant Rebellion" p. 158) to the Chief of Staff, Natal, on July 1 informed him:

> *Every Boer expresses the most bitter hatred of the Zulus. They all express a wish that the Zulus would rise now while the British troops are in the country so that they may be practically wiped out. The Boers all say that in the event of the rising, every one of them would join the British troops in order to have a chance of paying off old scores against the Zulus. When I first came here, I visited farms and asked the Boers what they thought of the advisability of keeping troops here. They all said it was most necessary, as they were afraid of the Kaffirs and it would not be safe to stay on their farms if the troops withdrew.... Taking everything into consideration, I cannot help being forced to the opinion*

that many Boers intend to provoke a Zulu rising if they can do so.

It was Colonel Mackenzie, the military supremo before the rebellion, who was prophesying a native uprising and cleaning the barrels of his guns to use the "golden opportunity" to inflict "the most drastic punishment" on leading natives he found guilty of treason, and to "instill a proper respect for the white man". (C. O. 179/233/12460. Dispatch 9. 3. 06 cited "Reluctant Rebellion" p. 188).

On June 14, Charles Saunders, Chief Magistrate and Civil Commissioner in Zululand (1899-1909) wrote to C. J. Hignet, the magistrate of Nqutu ("Reluctant Rebellion" p. 241):

I quite agree with your conclusions as to our men trying to goad the whole population into rebellion, and you have no idea of the difficulties we had in Nkandha in trying to protect people one knew perfectly well were faithful to us.

In his communication of July 10 1906 to the Prime Minister, (PM 61/15/66 Governor to PM 10. 7. 06) the Governor described the "sweeping actions and the mopping-up operations as continued slaughter. Fred Graham, a permanent civil servant in the Colonial Office, in his Minute of July 10, described it as "massacre".

Nazism & racism: The most revealing was the long letter of July 24 1906 (CO 179/236/24787 minute 10-7-06) sent by the Anglican Archdeacon, Charles Johnson, from St. Augustine's in Nqutu division, to the Society for the Propagation of the Gospels in London. He was a man of the British establishment and not known to have excessive zeal for standing up for the rights of the Africans. He wrote (cited "Reluctant Rebellion" p. 241):

Many thinking people have been asking themselves, what are we going to do with his teeming population? Some strong-handed men have thought the time was ripe for solving the great question. They knew that there was a general widespread spirit of disaffection among the natives

> *of Natal, the Free State and the Transvaal, but specially in Natal, and they commenced the suppression of the rebellion in the fierce hope that the rebellion might so spread throughout the land and engender a war of practical extermination. I fully believe that they were imbued with the conviction that this was the only safe way of dealing with the native question, and they are greatly disappointed that the spirit of rebellion was not strong enough to bring more than a moiety of the native peoples under the influence of the rifle. Over and over again it was said, `They are only sitting on the fence, it shall be our endeavour to bring them over'; and again, speaking of the big chiefs, `We must endeavour to bring them in if possible! Yes, they have been honest and outspoken enough-the wish being father to the thought-they prophesied the rebellion would spread throughout South Africa; had they been true prophets, no doubt the necessity of solving the native question would have been solved for this generation at least.*

John Merriman was a veteran Cape politician. He was one of those so-called liberals who accepted Nazism as a doctrine, or in other words Anglo-Saxon superiority, but regretted its consequent atrocities and thus fumigated their consciences. He wrote to Goldwin Smith (Merriman papers NHo. 202, 16. 9. 06 cited "Reluctant Rebellion" p. 246) in September 1906:

> *We have had a horrible business in Natal with the natives. I suppose the whole truth will never be known, but enough comes out to make us see how thin the crust is that keeps our Christian civilisation from the old-fashioned savagery-machine-guns and modern rifles against knobsticks and assagais are heavy odds and do not add much to the glory of the superior race.*

In the letter of the Archdeacon the expression "practical extermination", and in a letter of Lieutenant Mills "practically wiped out", have been used. This was what the German Nazis wanted to do to the Jews: to exterminate them. Does it make any difference whether the victims of racial slaughter are Jews or blacks?

Conspiracy to massacre Blacks: Gandhi was well aware of the conspiracy to massacre the Africans. When there was war hysteria in the colonial press, this prophet of nonviolence did not apply his mind as to how to stop such a conflict. On the contrary, he did not want Indians to be left behind, but wanted them to take a full part in this genocide.

In his editorial in the Indian Opinion of Nov. 18 1905, long before the actual rebellion broke out, Gandhi complained that the Government simply did not wish to give Indians an opportunity of showing that they were as capable as any other community of taking their share in the defence of the colony. He suggested that a volunteer corps should be formed from colonial-born Indians, which would be useful in actual service.

Indentured Indians lived in conditions worse than slavery. Gandhi during his 20 years' stay in South Africa, did not raise a finger to ease their sufferings. But he was quick to suggest using them as cannon fodder for racists against Africans. In his Indian Opinion in Dec. 2 1905 he referred to Law 25 of 1875 which was specially passed to increase "the maximum strength of the volunteer force in the colony adding thereto a force of Indian immigrant volunteer infantry". To assure the Europeans that such Indians would only kill Africans, he pointed out that "section 83 of the Militia Act states that no ordinary member of the coloured contingent shall be armed with weapons of precision, unless such contingent is called to operate against other than Europeans".

Gandhi defends massacre: Many years later, he wrote (p. 233) in his autobiography:

> *The Boer War had not brought home to me the horrors of war with anything like the vividness that the 'rebellion' did. This was no war but a man-hunt, not only in my opinion but also in that of many Englishmen with whom I had occasion to talk. To hear every morning reports of the soldiers' rifles exploding like crackers in innocent hamlets, and to live in the midst of them, was a trial.*

Then to justify his participation in this massacre, he went on (Autobiography p. 231):

> *I bore no grudge against the Zulus, they had harmed no Indian. I had doubts about the 'rebellion' itself, but I then believed that the British Empire existed for the welfare of the world. A genuine sense of loyalty prevented me from even wishing ill to the Empire. The righteness or otherwise of the 'rebellion' was therefore not likely to affect my decision.*

What about the Nazi war criminals? Did they not have a genuine sense of loyalty to Hitler and Nazism?

In Great Britain another storm of protest was raised against the atrocities perpetrated in Natal. The only time Gandhi mentioned the Zulu suppression was on August 4 1906, when he wrote in his Indian Opinion:

> *A controversy is going on in England about what the Natal Army did during the Kaffir rebellion. The people here believe that the whites of Natal perpetrated great atrocities on the Kaffirs. In reply to such critics, the Star has pointed to the doings of the Imperial Army in Egypt. Those among the Egyptian rebels who had been captured were ordered to be flogged. The flogging was continued to the limits of the victim's endurance; it took place in public and was watched by thousands of people. Those sentenced to death were also hanged at the same time. While those sentenced to death were hanging, the flogging of others was taken up. While the sentences were being executed, the relatives of the victims cried and wept until many of them swooned. If this is true, there is no reason why there should be such an outcry in England against Natal outrages.*

One may notice that the article was very cleverly written. First Gandhi stated that people in England believed that the whites of Natal perpetrated great atrocities on Africans, as if he himself did not know what happened, and also gave the impression that it was the local Natal Army and not the Imperial

Army which was involved in the atrocities, which is not true. Even at this stage, he was not willing to tell the simple truth, that atrocities were committed. Then he borrowed the description of hanging and flogging in Egypt from the Star as if he did not know about that either. Did or did not Gandhi know that those Egyptians were not common criminals to be flogged and hanged-that they were the patriots, the flowers of the Egyptian nation?

If Gandhi unequivocally accepted or found out that the Imperial Army committed those atrocities, then he could not claim that he believed the British Empire existed for the welfare of mankind. The last and the vilest of all was the subtle suggestion that if the Imperial Army did what they were accused of doing, then there was no reason why there should be such an outcry in England against the Natal outrage. Why could this Imperialist-manufactured Mahatma not say clearly that both were crimes against humanity?

THE GANDHI NOBODY KNOWS

I had the singular honour of attending an early private screening of Gandhi with an audience of invited guests from the National Council of Churches. At the end of the three-hour movie there was hardly, as they say, a dry eye in the house.

When the lights came up I fell into conversation with a young woman who observed, reverently, that Gandhi's last words were "Oh, God," causing me to remark regretfully that the real Gandhi had not spoken in English, but had cried, Hai Rama! ("Oh, Rama"). Well, Rama was just Indian for God, she replied, at which I felt compelled to explain that, alas, Rama, collectively with his three half-brothers, represented the seventh reincarnation of Vishnu. The young woman, who seemed to have been under the impression that Hinduism was Christianity under another name, sensed somehow that she had fallen on an uncongenial spirit, and the conversation ended.

At a dinner party shortly afterward, a friend of mine, who had visited India many times and even gone to the trouble of learning Hindi, objected strenuously that the picture of Gandhi that emerges in the movie is grossly inaccurate, omitting, as one of many examples, that when Gandhi's wife lay dying of pneumonia and British doctors insisted that a shot of penicillin would save her, Gandhi refused to have this alien medicine injected in her body and simply let her die. (It must be noted that when Gandhi contracted malaria shortly afterward he accepted for himself the alien medicine quinine, and that when he had appendicitis he allowed British doctors to perform on him the alien outrage of an appendectomy.) All of this produced a wistful mooing from an editor of a major newspaper and a recalcitrant, "But still.... " I would prefer to explicate things more substantial than a wistful mooing, but there is little doubt it meant the editor in question felt that even if the real Mohandas K. Gandhi had been different from the Gandhi of the movie it would have been nice if he had been like the movie-Gandhi, and that presenting him in this admittedly false manner was beautiful, stirring, and perhaps socially beneficial.

An important step in the canonization of this movie-Gandhi was taken by the New York Film Critics Circle, which not only awarded the picture its prize as best film of 1982, but awarded Ben Kingsley, who played Gandhi (a remarkably good performance), its prize as best actor of the year. But I cannot believe for one second that these awards were made independently of the film's content—which, not to put too fine a point on it, is an all-out appeal for pacifism—or in anything but the most shameful ignorance of the historical Gandhi.

Now it does not bother me that Shakespeare omitted from his 'King John' the signing of the Magna Charta—by far the most important event in John's reign. All Shakespeare's "histories" are strewn with errors and inventions. Shifting to the cinema and to more recent times, it is hard for me to work up much indignation over the fact that neither Eisenstein's 'Battleship Potemkin' nor his 'October' recounts historical episodes in anything like the manner in which they actually occurred (the famous march of the White Guards down the steps at Odessa—artistically one of the greatest sequences in film history—simply did not take place). As we draw closer to the present, however, the problem becomes much more difficult.

If the Soviet Union were to make an artistically wondrous film about the entry of Russian tanks into Prague in 1968 (an event I happened to witness), and show them being greeted with flowers by a grateful populace, the Czechs dancing in the streets with joy, I do not guarantee that I would maintain my serene aloofness. A great deal depends on whether the historical events represented in a movie are intended to be taken as substantially true, and also on whether—separated from us by some decades or occurring yesterday—they are seen as having a direct bearing on courses of action now open to us.

On my second viewing of 'Gandhi, ' this time at a public showing at the end of the Christmas season, I happened to leave the theatre behind three teenage girls, apparently from one of Manhattan's fashionable private schools. "Gandhi was pretty much an FDR," one opined, astonishing me almost as much by her breezy use of initials to invoke a President who died almost a quarter-century before her birth as by the stupefying nature of the comparison. "But he was a religious figure, too," corrected one of her friends, adding somewhat smugly, "It's not in our historical tradition to honour spiritual leaders." Since her schoolteachers had clearly not led her to consider Jonathan Edwards and Roger Williams as spiritual leaders, let alone Joseph Smith and William Jennings Bryan, the intimation seemed to be that we are a society with poorer spiritual values than, let's say, India.

There can be no question, in any event, that the girls felt they had just been shown the historical Gandhi—an attitude shared by Ralph Nader, who at last account had seen the film three times. Nader has conceived the most extraordinary notion that Gandhi's symbolic flouting of the British salt tax was a "consumer issue" which he later expanded into the wider one of Indian independence. A modern parallel to Gandhi's program of home-spinning and home-weaving, another "consumer issue" says Nader, might be the use of solar energy to free us from the "giant multinational oil corporations."

As it happens, the government of India openly admits to having provided one-third of the financing of 'Gandhi' out of state funds, straight out of the national treasury—and after close study of the finished product I would not be a bit surprised to hear that it was 100 percent. If Pandit Nehru is portrayed flatteringly in the film, one must remember that Nehru himself took part in the initial story conferences (he originally wanted Gandhi to be played by Alec Guinness) and that his daughter Indira Gandhi is, after all, Prime Minister of India (though no relation to Mohandas Gandhi).

The screenplay was checked and rechecked by Indian officials at every stage, often by the Prime Minister herself, with close consultations on plot and even casting. If the movie contains a particularly poisonous portrait of Mohammed Ali Jinnah, the founder of Pakistan, the Indian reply, I suppose, would be that if the Pakistanis want an attractive portrayal of Jinnah let them pay for their own movie. A friend of mine, highly sophisticated in political matters but innocent about film-making, declared that 'Gandhi' should be preceded by the legend: The following film is a paid political advertisement by the government of India.

"Gandhi", then, is a large, pious, historical morality tale centred on a saintly, sanitized Mahatma Gandhi cleansed of anything too embarrassingly Hindu (the word "caste" is not mentioned from one end of the film to the other) and, indeed, of most of the rest of Gandhi's life, much of which would drastically diminish his saintliness in Western eyes. There is little to indicate that the India of today has followed Gandhi's precepts in almost nothing. There is little, in fact, to indicate that India is even India. The spectator realizes the scene is the Indian subcontinent because there are thousands of extras dressed in dhotis and saris. The characters go about talking in these quaint Peter Sellers accents.

We have occasional shots of India's holy poverty, holy hovels, some landscapes, many of them photographed quite beautifully, for those who like travelogues. We have a character called Lord Mountbatten (India's last Viceroy); a composite American journalist (assembled from Vincent Sheehan, William L. Shirer, Louis Fischer, and straight fiction); a character called simply "Viceroy" (presumably another composite); an assemblage of Gandhi's Indian followers under the name of one of them (Patel); and of course Nehru. I sorely missed the fabulous Annie Besant, that English clergyman's wife, turned atheist, turned Theosophist, turned Indian nationalist, who actually became president of the Indian National Congress and had a terrific falling out with Gandhi, becoming his fierce opponent.

And if the producers felt they had to work in a cameo role for an American star to add to the film's appeal in the United States, it is positively embarrassing that they should have brought in the photographer Margaret Bourke-White, a person of no importance whatever in Gandhi's life and a role Candice Bergen plays with a repellent unctuousness.

If the film-makers had been interested in drama and not hagiography, it is hard to see how they could have resisted the awesome confrontation between Gandhi and, yes, Margaret Sanger. For the two did meet. Now there was a meeting of East and West, and *may the better person win! (She did. Margaret Sanger argued her views on birth control with such vigour that Gandhi had a nervous breakdown.) I cannot honestly say I had any reasonable expectation that the film would show scenes of Gandhi's pretty teenage girl followers fighting "hysterically" (the word was used) for the honour of sleeping naked with the Mahatma and cuddling the nude septuagenarian in their arms. (Gandhi was "testing" his vow of chastity in order to gain moral strength for his mighty struggle with Jinnah.)

When told there was a man named Freud who said that, despite his declared intention, Gandhi might actually be enjoying the caresses of the naked girls, Gandhi continued, unperturbed.

Nor, frankly, did I expect to see Gandhi giving daily enemas to all the young girls in his Ashrams (his daily greeting was, "Have you had a good bowel movement this morning, sisters?"), nor see the girls giving him *his* daily enema. Although Gandhi seems to have written less about home rule for India than he did about enemas, and excrement, and latrine cleaning ("The bathroom is a temple. It should be so clean and inviting that anyone would enjoy eating there"), I confess such scenes might pose problems for a Western director.

'Gandhi, 'therefore, the film, this paid political advertisement for the government of India, is organized around three axes: (1) Anti-racism—all men are equal regardless of race, colour, creed, etc.; (2) anti-colonialism, which in present terms translates as support for the Third World, including, most eminently, India; (3) nonviolence, presented as an absolutist pacifism. There are other, secondary precepts and subheadings. Gandhi is portrayed as the quintessence of tolerance ("I am a Hindu and a Muslim and a Christian and a Jew"), of basic friendliness to Britain ("The British have been with us for a long time and when they leave we want them to leave as friends"), of devotion to his wife and family. His vow of chastity is represented as something selfless and holy, rather like the celibacy of the Catholic clergy. But, above all, Gandhi's life and teachings are presented as having great import for us today.

We must learn from Gandhi.

I propose to demonstrate that the film grotesquely distorts both Gandhi's life and character to the point that it is nothing more than a pious fraud, and a fraud of the most egregious kind. Hackneyed Indian falsehoods such as that "the British keep trying to break India up" (as if Britain didn't give India a unity it had never enjoyed in history), or that the British *created* Indian poverty (a poverty which had not only existed since time immemorial but had been considered holy), almost pass unnoticed in the tide of adulation for our fictional saint. Gandhi, admittedly, being a devout Hindu, was far more self-contradictory than most public men. Sanskrit scholars tell me that flat self-contradiction is even considered an element of "Sanskrit rhetoric." Perhaps it is thought to show profundity.

Gandhi rose early, usually at three-thirty, and before his first bowel movement (during which he received visitors, although possibly not Margaret Bourke-White) he spent two hours in meditation, listening to his "inner voice." Now Gandhi was an extremely vocal individual, and in addition to spending an hour each day in vigorous walking, another hour spinning at his primitive spinning wheel, another hour at further prayers, another hour being massaged nude by teenage girls, and many hours deciding such things as affairs of state, he produced a quite unconscionable number of articles and speeches and wrote an average of sixty letters a day. All considered, it is not really surprising that his inner voice said different things to him at different times. Despising consistency and never checking his earlier statements, and yet inhumanly obstinate about his position at any given moment, Gandhi is thought by some Indians today (according to V. S. Naipaul) to have been so erratic and unpredictable that he may have delayed Indian independence for twenty-five years.

For Gandhi was an extremely difficult man to work with. He had no partners, only disciples. For members of his Ashrams, he dictated every minute of their days, and not only every morsel of food they should eat but when they should eat it. Without ever having heard of a protein or a vitamin, he considered himself an expert on diet, as on most things, and was constantly experimenting. Once when he fell ill, he was found to have been living on a diet of groundnut butter and lemon juice; British doctors called it malnutrition. And Gandhi had even greater confidence in his abilities as a "nature doctor," prescribing obligatory cures for his ashramites, such as dried cow-dung powder and various concoctions containing cow dung (the cow, of course, being sacred to the Hindu). And to those he really loved he gave enemas—but again, alas, not to Margaret Bourke-White. Which is too bad, really. For admiring Candice

Bergen's work as I do, I would have been most interested in seeing how she would have experienced this beatitude. The scene might have lived in film history.

There are 400 biographies of Gandhi, and his writings run to 80 volumes, and since he lived to be seventy-nine, and rarely fell silent, there are, as I have indicated, quite a few inconsistencies. The authors of the present movie even acknowledge in a little-noticed opening title that they have made a film only true to Gandhi's spirit. For my part, I do not intend to pick through Gandhi's writings to make him look like Attila the Hun (although the thought is tempting), but to give a fair, weighted balance of his views, laying stress above all on his actions, and on what he told other men to do when the time for action had come.

Anti-racism: the reader will have noticed that in the present-day community of nations South Africa is a pariah. So it is an absolutely amazing piece of good fortune that Gandhi, born the son of the Prime Minister of a tiny Indian principality and received as an attorney at the bar of the Middle Temple in London, should have begun his climb to greatness as a member of the small Indian community in, precisely, South Africa. Natal, then a separate colony, wanted to limit Indian immigration and, as part of the government program, ordered Indians to carry identity papers (an action not without similarities to measures under consideration in the U. S. today to control illegal immigration). The film's lengthy opening sequences are devoted to Gandhi's leadership in the fight against Indians carrying their identity papers (burning their registration cards), with for good measure Gandhi being expelled from the first-class section of a railway train, and Gandhi being asked by whites to step off the sidewalk. This inspired young Indian leader calls, in the film, for interracial harmony, for people to "live together. "

Now the time is 1893, and Gandhi is a "caste" Hindu, and from one of the higher castes. Although, later, he was to call for improving the lot of India's Untouchables, he was not to have any serious misgivings about the fundamentals of the caste system for about another thirty years, and even then his doubts, to my way of thinking, were rather minor. In the India in which Gandhi grew up, and had only recently left, some castes could enter the courtyards of certain Hindu temples, while others could not. Some castes were forbidden to use the village well. Others were compelled to live outside the village, still others to leave the road at the approach of a person of higher caste and perpetually to call out, giving warning, so that no one would be polluted by their proximity.

The endless intricacies of Hindu caste by-laws varied somewhat region by region, but in Madras, where most South African Indians were from, while a Nayar could pollute a man of higher caste only by touching him, Kammalans polluted at a distance of 24 feet, toddy drawers at 36 feet, Pulayans and Cherumans at 48 feet, and beef-eating Paraiyans at 64 feet. All castes and the thousands of sub-castes were forbidden, needless to say, to marry, eat, or engage in social activity with any but members of their own group. In Gandhi's native Gujarat a caste Hindu who had been polluted by touch had to perform extensive ritual ablutions or purify himself by drinking a holy beverage composed of milk, whey, and (what else?) cow dung.

Low-caste Hindus, in short, suffered humiliations in their native India compared to which the carrying of identity cards in South Africa was almost trivial In fact, Gandhi, to his credit, was to campaign strenuously in his later life for the reduction of caste barriers in India—a campaign almost invisible in the movie, of course, conveyed in only two glancing references, leaving the audience with the officially sponsored if historically astonishing notion that racism was introduced into India by the British.

To present the Gandhi of 1893, a conventional caste Hindu, fresh from caste-ridden India where a Paraiyan could pollute at 64 feet, as the champion of interracial equalitarianism is one of the most brazen hypocrisies I have ever encountered in a serious movie.

The film, moreover, does not give the slightest hint as to Gandhi's attitude toward blacks, and the viewers of 'Gandhi' would naturally suppose that, since the future Great Soul opposed South African discrimination against Indians, he would also oppose South African discrimination against black people. But this is not so. While Gandhi, in South Africa, fought furiously to have Indians recognized as loyal subjects of the British empire, and to have them enjoy the full rights of Englishmen, he had no concern for blacks whatever. In fact, during one of the "Kaffir Wars" he volunteered to organize a brigade of Indians to put down a Zulu rising, and was decorated himself for valour under fire. For, yes, Gandhi (Sergeant Major Gandhi) was awarded Victoria's coveted War Medal. Throughout most of his life Gandhi had the most inordinate admiration for British soldiers, their sense of duty, their discipline and stoicism in defeat (a trait he emulated himself). He marvelled that they retreated with heads high, like victors. There was even a time in his life when Gandhi, hardly to be distinguished from Kipling's Gunga Din, wanted nothing much as to be a Soldier of the Queen. Since this is not in keeping with the "spirit" of Gandhi, as decided by Pandit Nehru and Indira Gandhi, it is naturally omitted from he movie.

Anti-colonialism: as almost always with historical films, even those more honest than 'Gandhi, ' the historical personage on which the movie is based is not only more complex but more interesting than the character shown on the screen. During his entire South African period, and for some time after, until he was about fifty, Gandhi was nothing more or less than an imperial loyalist, claiming for Indians the rights of Englishmen but unshakably loyal to the crown. He supported the empire ardently in no fewer than three wars: the Boer War, the "Kaffir War," and, with the most extreme zeal, World War I. If Gandhi's mind were of the modern European sort, this would seam to suggest that his later attitude toward Britain was the product of unrequited love: he had wanted to be an Englishman; Britain had rejected him and his people; very well then, they would have their own country. But this would imply a point of "agonizing reappraisal," a moment when Gandhi's most fundamental political beliefs were re-examined and, after the most bitter soul-searching, repudiated. But I have studied the literature and cannot find this moment of bitter soul-searching. Instead, listening to his "inner voice" (which in the case of divines of all countries often speaks in the tones of holy opportunism), Gandhi simply, tranquilly, without announcing any sharp break, set off in a new direction.

It should be understood that it is unlikely Gandhi ever truly conceived of "becoming" an Englishman, first, because he was a Hindu to the marrow of his bones, and also, perhaps, because his democratic instincts were really quite weak. He was a man of the most extreme, autocratic temperament, tyrannical, unyielding even regarding things he knew nothing about, totally intolerant of all opinions but his own. He was, furthermore, in the highest degree reactionary, permitting in India no change in the relationship between the feudal lord and his peasants or servants, the rich and the poor. In his 'The Life and Death of Mahatma Gandhi, ' the best and least hagiographic of the full-length studies, Robert Payne, although admiring Gandhi greatly, explains Gandhi's "new direction" on his return to India from South Africa as follows:

He spoke in generalities, but he was searching for a single cause, a single hard-edged task to which he would devote the remaining years of his life. He wanted to repeat his triumph in South Africa on Indian soil. He dreamed of assembling a small army of dedicated men around him, issuing stern commands and leading them to some almost unobtainable goal.

Gandhi, in short, was a leader looking for a cause. He found it, of course, in home rule for India and, ultimately, in independence.

We are therefore presented with the seeming anomaly of a Gandhi who, in Britain when war broke out in August 1914, instantly contacted the War Office, swore that he would stand by England in its hour of need, and created the Indian Volunteer

Corps, which he might have commanded if he hadn't fallen ill with pleurisy. In 1915, back in India, he made a memorable speech in Madras in which he proclaimed, "I discovered that the British empire had certain ideals with which I have fallen in love.... " In early 1918, as the war in Europe entered its final crisis, he wrote to the Viceroy of India, "I have an idea that if I become your recruiting agent-in-chief, I might rain men upon you," and he proclaimed in a speech in Kheda that the British "love justice; they have shielded men against oppression." Again, he wrote to the Viceroy, "I would make India offer all her able-bodied sons as a sacrifice to the empire at this critical moment To some of his pacifist friends, who were horrified, Gandhi replied by appealing to the 'Bhagavad Gita' and to the endless wars recounted in the Hindu epics, the 'Ramayana' and the 'Mahabharata, ' adding further to the pacifists' honour by declaring that Indians "have always been warlike, and the finest hymn composed by Tulsidas in praise of Rama gives the first place to his ability to strike down the enemy."

This was in contradiction to the interpretation of sacred Hindu scriptures Gandhi had offered on earlier occasions (and would offer later), which was that they did not recount military struggles but spiritual struggles; but, unusual for him, he strove to find some kind of synthesis. "I do not say, `Let us go and kill the Germans, '" Gandhi explained. "I say, `Let us go and die for the sake of India and the empire. '" And yet within two years, the time having come for Swaraj (home rule), Gandhi's inner voice spoke again, and, the leader having found his cause, Gandhi proclaimed resoundingly: "The British empire today represents Satanism, and they who love God can afford to have no love for Satan."

The idea of Swaraj, originated by others, crept into Gandhi's mind gradually. With a fair amount of winding about, Gandhi, roughly, passed through three phases. First, he was entirely pro-British, and merely wanted for Indians the rights of Englishmen (as he understood them). Second, he was still pro-

British, but with the belief that, having proved their loyalty to the empire, Indians would be granted some degree of Swaraj. Third, as the home-rule movement gathered momentum, it was the Swaraj, the whole Swaraj, and nothing but the Swaraj, and he turned relentlessly against the crown. The movie to the contrary, he caused the British no end of trouble in their struggles during World War II.

But it should not be thought for one second that Gandhi's finally full-blown desire to detach India from the British empire gave him the slightest sympathy with other colonial peoples pursuing similar objectives. Throughout his entire life Gandhi displayed the most spectacular inability to understand or even really take in people unlike himself—a trait which V. S. Naipaul considers specifically Hindu, and I am inclined to agree. Just as Gandhi had been totally unconcerned with the situation of South Africa's blacks (he hardly noticed they were there until they rebelled), so now he was totally unconcerned with other Asians or Africans. In fact, he was adamantly opposed to certain Arab movements within the Ottoman empire for reasons of internal Indian politics.

At the close of World War I, the Muslims of India were deeply absorbed in what they called the "khilafat" movement—"khilafat" being their corruption of "Caliphate," the Caliph in question being the Ottoman Sultan. In addition to his temporal powers, the Sultan of the Ottoman empire held the spiritual position of Caliph, supreme leader of the world's Muslims and successor to the Prophet Muhammad. At the defeat of the Central Powers (Germany, Austria, Turkey), the Sultan was a prisoner in his palace in Constantinople, shorn of his religious as well as his political authority, and the Muslims of India were incensed. It so happened that the former subject peoples of the Ottoman empire, principally Arabs, were perfectly happy to be rid of this Caliph, and even the Turks were glad to be rid of him, but this made no impression at all on the Muslims of India, for whom the issue was essentially a club with which to beat the British. Until this odd historical moment, Indian

Muslims had felt little real allegiance to the Ottoman Sultan either, but now that he had fallen, the British had done it! The British had taken away their khilafat! And one of the most ardent supporters of this Indian Muslim movement was the new Hindu leader, Gandhi.

No one questions that the formative period for Gandhi as a political leader was his time in South Africa. Throughout history Indians, divided into 1, 500 language and dialect groups (India today has 15 official languages), had little sense of themselves as a nation. Muslim Indians and Hindu Indians felt about as close as Christians and Moors during their 700 years of cohabitation in Spain. In addition to which, the Hindus were divided into thousands of castes and sub-castes, and there were also Parsees, Sikhs, Jains. But in South Africa officials had thrown them all in together, and in the mind of Gandhi (another one of those examples of nationalism being born in exile) grew the idea of India as a nation, and Muslim-Hindu friendship became one of the few positions on which he never really reversed himself. So Gandhi ignoring Arabs and Turks—became an adamant supporter of the Khilafat movement out of strident Indian nationalism. He had become a national figure in India for having unified 13, 000 Indians of all faiths in South Africa, and now he was determined to reach new heights by unifying hundreds of millions of Indians of all faiths in India itself. But this nationalism did not please everyone, particularly Tolstoy, who in his last years carried on a curious correspondence with the new Indian leader. For Tolstoy, Gandhi's Indian nationalism "spoils everything."

As for the "anti-colonialism" of the nationalist Indian state since independence, Indira Gandhi, India's present Prime Minister, hears an inner voice of her own, it would appear, and this inner voice told her to justify the Soviet invasion of Afghanistan as produced by provocative maneuvers on the part of the U. S. and China, as well as to be the first country outside the Soviet bloc to recognize the Hanoi puppet regime in Cambodia. So everything plainly depends on who is colonizing whom, and Mrs. Gandhi's voice perhaps tells her that the subjection of Afghanistan and Cambodia to foreign rule is "defensive" colonialism. And the movie's message that Mahatma Gandhi, and by plain implication India (the country for which he plays the role of Joan of Arc), have taken a holy, unchanging stance against the colonization of nation by nation is just another of its hypocrisies. For India, when it comes to colonialism or anti-colonialism, it has been Realpolitik all the way.

Nonviolence: but the real centre and raison d'etre of 'Gandhi' is Ahimsa, nonviolence, which principle when incorporated into vast campaigns of noncooperation with British rule the Mahatma called by an odd name he made up himself, satyagraha, which means something like "truth-striving." During the key part of his life, Gandhi devoted a great deal of time explaining the moral and philosophical meanings of both Ahimsa and satyagraha. But much as the film sanitizes Gandhi to the point where one would mistake him for a Christian saint, and sanitizes India to the point where one would take it for Shangri-la, it quite sweeps away Gandhi's ethical and religious ponderings, his complexities, his qualifications, and certainly his vacillations, which simplifying process leaves us with our old European friend: pacifism.

It is true that Gandhi was much impressed by the Sermon on the Mount, his favourite passage in the Bible, which he read over and over again. But for all the Sermon's inspirational value, and its service as an ideal in relations among individual human beings, no Christian state which survived has ever based its policies on the Sermon on the Mount since Constantine declared Christianity the official religion of the Roman empire. And no modern Western state which survives can ever base its policies on pacifism. And no Hindu state will ever base its policies on Ahimsa.

Gandhi himself—although the film dishonestly conceals this from us—many times conceded that in dire circumstances "war may have to be resorted to as a necessary evil." It is something of an anomaly that Gandhi, held in popular myth to be a pure pacifist (a myth which governments of India have always been at great pains to sustain in the belief that it will reflect credit on India itself, and to which the present movie adheres slavishly), was until fifty not ill-disposed to war at all. As I have already noted, in three wars, no sooner had the bugles sounded than Gandhi not only gave his support, but was clamouring for arms. To form new regiments! To fight! To destroy the enemies of the empire! Regular Indian army units fought in both the Boer War and World War I, but this was not enough for Gandhi. He wanted to raise new troops, even, in the case of the Boer and Kaffir Wars, from the tiny Indian colony in South Africa.

British military authorities thought it not really worth the trouble to train such a small body of Indians as soldiers, and were even resistant to training them as an auxiliary medical corps ("stretcher bearers"), but finally yielded to Gandhi's relentless importuning. As first instructed, the Indian Volunteer Corps was not supposed actually to go into combat, but Gandhi, adamant, led his Indian volunteers into the thick of battle. When the British commanding officer was mortally wounded during an engagement in the Kaffir War, Gandhi—though his corps' deputy commander—carried the officer's stretcher himself from the battlefield and for miles over the sun-baked veldt. The British empire's War Medal did not have its name for nothing, and it was generally earned.

Anyone who wants to wade through Gandhi's endless ruminations about Himsa and Ahimsa (violence and nonviolence) is welcome to do so, but it is impossible for the skeptical reader to avoid the conclusion—let us say in 1920, when Swaraj (home rule) was all the rage and Gandhi's inner voice started telling him that Ahimsa was the thing—that this inner voice knew what it was talking about. By this I mean that, though Gandhi talked with the tongue of Hindu gods and sacred scriptures, his inner voice had a strong sense of expediency. Britain, if only comparatively speaking, was a moral nation, and nonviolent civil disobedience was plainly the best and most effective way of achieving Indian independence. Skeptics might also not be surprised to learn that as independence approached, Gandhi's inner voice began to change its tune. It has been reported that Gandhi "half-welcomed" the civil war that broke out in the last days. Even a fratricidal "bloodbath" (Gandhi's word) would be preferable to the British.

And suddenly Gandhi began endorsing violence left, right, and centre. During the fearsome rioting in Calcutta he gave his approval to men "using violence in a moral cause." How could he tell them that violence was wrong, he asked, "unless I demonstrate that nonviolence is more effective?" He blessed the Nawab of Maler Kotla when he gave orders to shoot ten Muslims for every Hindu killed in his state. He sang the praises of Subhas Chandra Bose, who, sponsored by first the Nazis and then the Japanese, organized in Singapore an Indian National Army with which he hoped to conquer India with Japanese support, establishing a totalitarian dictatorship. Meanwhile, after independence in 1947, the armies of the India that Gandhi had created immediately marched into battle, incorporating the state of Hyderabad by force and making war in Kashmir on secessionist Pakistan. When Gandhi was assassinated by a Hindu extremist in January 1948 he was honoured by the new state with a vast military funeral—in my view by no means inapposite.

BUT it is not widely realized (nor will this film tell you) how much violence was associated with Gandhi's so-called "nonviolent" movement from the very beginning. India's Nobel Prize-winning poet, Rabindranath Tagore, had sensed a strong current of nihilism in Gandhi almost from his first days, and as early as 1920 wrote of Gandhi's "fierce joy of annihilation," which Tagore feared would lead India into hideous orgies of devastation—which ultimately proved to be the case. Robert Payne has said that there was unquestionably an "unhealthy atmosphere" among many of Gandhi's fanatic followers, and that Gandhi's habit of going to the edge of violence and then suddenly retreating was fraught with danger. "In matters of conscience I am uncompromising," proclaimed Gandhi proudly. "Nobody can make me yield." The judgment of Tagore was categorical. Much as he might revere Gandhi as a holy man, he quite detested him as a politician and considered that his campaigns were almost always so close to violence that it was utterly disingenuous to call them nonviolent.

For every satyagraha true believer, moreover, sworn not to harm the adversary or even to lift a finger in his own defence, there were sometimes thousands of incensed freebooters and skirmishers bound by no such vow. Gandhi, to be fair, was aware of this, and nominally deplored it—but with nothing like the consistency shown in the movie. The film leads the audience to believe that Gandhi's first "fast unto death," for example, was in protest against an act of barbarous violence, the slaughter by an Indian crowd of a detachment of police constables. But in actual fact Gandhi reserved this "ultimate weapon" of his to interdict a 1931 British proposal to grant Untouchables a "separate electorate" in the Indian national legislature—in effect a kind of affirmative-action program for Untouchables. For reasons I have not been able to decrypt, Gandhi was dead set against the project, but I confess it is another scene I would like to have seen in the movie: Gandhi almost starving himself to death to block affirmative action for Untouchables.

From what I have been able to decipher, Gandhi's main preoccupation in this particular struggle was not even the British. Benefiting from the immense publicity, he wanted to induce Hindus, overnight, ecstatically, and without any of these British legalisms, to "open their hearts" to Untouchables. For a whole week Hindu India was caught up in a joyous delirium. No more would the Untouchables be scavengers and sweepers! No more would they be banned from Hindu temples! No more would they pollute at 64 feet! It lasted just a week. Then the temple doors swung shut again, and all was as before. Meanwhile, on the passionate subject of Swaraj Gandhi was crying, "I would not flinch from sacrificing a million lives for India's liberty!" The million Indian lives were indeed sacrificed, and in full. They fell, however, not to the bullets of British soldiers but to he knives and clubs of their fellow Indians in savage butcheries when he British finally withdrew.

Although the movie sneers at his reasoning as being the flimsiest of pretexts, I cannot imagine an impartial person studying the subject without concluding that concern for Indian religious minorities was one of the principal reasons Britain stayed in India as long as it did. When it finally withdrew, blood-maddened mobs surged through the streets from one end of India to the other, the majority group in each area, Hindu or Muslim, slaughtering the defenceless minority without mercy in one of the most hideous periods of carnage of modern history.

A comparison is in order. At the famous Amritsar massacre of 1919, shot in elaborate and loving detail in the present movie and treated by post-independence Indian historians as if it were Auschwitz, Ghurka troops under the command of a British officer, General Dyer, fired into an unarmed crowd of Indians defying a ban and demonstrating for Indian independence. The crowd contained women and children; 379 persons died; it was all quite horrible. Dyer was court-martialed and cashiered, but the incident lay heavily on British consciences for the next three decades, producing a severe inhibiting effect. Never again would the British empire commit another Amritsar, anywhere.

As soon as the oppressive British were gone, however, the Indians—gentle, tolerant people that they are gave themselves over to an orgy of blood-letting. Trained troops did not pick off targets at a distance with Enfield rifles. Blood-crazed Hindus, or Muslims, ran through the streets with knives, beheading babies, stabbing women, old people. Interestingly, our movie shows none of this on camera (the oldest way of stacking the deck in Hollywood). All we see is the aged Gandhi, grieving, and of course fasting, at these terrible reports of riots. And, naturally, the film doesn't whisper a clue as to the total number of dead, which might spoil the mood somehow.

The fact is that we will never know how many Indians were murdered by other Indians during the country's Independence Massacres, but almost all serious studies place the figure over a million, and some, such as Payne's sources, go to 4 million. So, for those who like round numbers, the British killed some 400 seditious colonials at Amritsar and the name Amritsar lives in infamy, while Indians may have killed some 4 million of their own countrymen for no other reason than that they were of a different religious faith and people think their great leader would make an inspirational subject for a movie. Ahimsa, as can be seen, then, had an absolutely tremendous moral effect when used against Britain, but not only would it not have worked against Nazi Germany (the most obvious reproach, and of course quite true), but, the crowning irony, it had virtually no effect whatever when Gandhi tried to bring it into play against violent Indians.

Despite this at best patchy record, the film-makers have gone to great lengths to imply that this same principle of Ahimsa—presented in the movie as the purest form of pacifism—is universally effective, yesterday, today, here, there, everywhere. We hear no talk from Gandhi of war sometimes being a "necessary evil," but only him announcing—and more than once—"An eye for an eye makes the whole world blind." In a scene very near the end of the movie, we hear Gandhi say, as if after deep reflection: "Tyrants and murderers can seem invincible at the time, but in the end they always fall. Think of it. Always."

During the last scene of the movie, following the assassination, Margaret Bourke-White is keening over the death of the Great Soul with an English admiral's daughter named Madeleine Slade, in whose bowel movements Gandhi took the deepest interest, and Miss Slade remarks incredulously that Gandhi felt that he had failed. They are then both incredulous for a moment, after which Miss Slade observes mournfully, "When we most needed it (presumably meaning during World

War II), he offered the world a way out of madness. But the world didn't see it." Then we hear once again the assassin's shots, Gandhi's "Oh, God," and last, in case we missed them the first time, Gandhi's words (over the shimmering waters of the Ganges?): "Tyrants and murderers can seem invincible at the time, but in the end they always fall. Think of it. Always." This is the end of the picture.

Now, as it happens, I have been thinking about tyrants and murderers for some time. But the fact that in the end they always fall has never given me much comfort, partly because, not being a Hindu and not expecting reincarnation after reincarnation, I am simply not prepared to wait them out. It always occurs to me that, while I am waiting around for them to fall, they might do something mean to me, like fling me into a gas oven or send me off to a Gulag. Unlike a Hindu and not worshipping stasis, I am also given to wondering who is to bring these murderers and tyrants down, it being all too risky a process to wait for them and the regimes they establish simply to die of old age. The fact that a few reincarnations from now they will all have turned to dust somehow does not seem to suggest a rational strategy for dealing with the problem.

Since the movie's Madeleine Slade specifically invites us to revere the "way out of madness" that Gandhi offered the world at the time of World War II, I am under the embarrassing obligation of recording exactly what courses of action the Great Soul recommended to the various parties involved in that crisis. For Gandhi was never stinting in his advice. Indeed, the less he knew about a subject, the less he stinted.

I am aware that for many not privileged to have visited the former British Raj, the names Gujarat, Rajasthan, and Deccan are simply words. But other names, such as Germany, Poland, Czechoslovakia, somehow have a harder profile. The term "Jew," also, has a reasonably hard profile, and I feel all Jews sitting emotionally at the movie 'Gandhi' should be apprised of the advice that the Mahatma offered their coreligionists when faced with the Nazi peril: they should commit collective suicide. If only the Jews of Germany had the good sense to offer their throats willingly to the Nazi butchers' knives and throw themselves into the sea from cliffs they would arouse world public opinion, Gandhi was convinced, and their moral triumph would be remembered for "ages to come." If they would only pray for Hitler (as their throats were cut, presumably), they would leave a "rich heritage to mankind." Although Gandhi had known Jews from his earliest days in South Africa—where his three staunchest white supporters were Jews, every one—he disapproved of how rarely they loved their enemies. And he never repented of his recommendation of collective suicide. Even after the war, when the full extent of the Holocaust was revealed, Gandhi told Louis Fischer, one of his biographers, that the Jews died anyway, didn't they? They might as well have died significantly.

Gandhi's views on the European crisis were not entirely consistent. He vigorously opposed Munich, distrusting Chamberlain. "Europe has sold her soul for the sake of a seven days' earthly existence," he declared. "The peace that Europe gained at Munich is a triumph of violence." But when the Germans moved into the Bohemian heartland, he was back to urging nonviolent resistance, exhorting the Czechs to go forth, unarmed, against the Wehrmacht, perishing gloriously—collective suicide again. He had Madeleine Slade draw up two letters to President Eduard Benes of Czechoslovakia, instructing him on the proper conduct of Czechoslovak satyagrahi when facing the Nazis.

When Hitler attacked Poland, however, Gandhi suddenly endorsed the Polish army's military resistance, calling it "almost nonviolent." (If this sounds like double-talk, I can only urge readers to read Gandhi.) He seemed at this point to have a rather low opinion of Hitler, but when Germany's panzer divisions turned west, Allied armies collapsed under the ferocious onslaught, and British ships were streaming across the Straits of Dover from Dunkirk, he wrote furiously to the

Viceroy of India: "This manslaughter must be stopped. You are losing; if you persist, it will only result in greater bloodshed. Hitler is not a bad man.... "

Gandhi also wrote an open letter to the British people, passionately urging them to surrender and accept whatever fate Hitler' had prepared for them. "Let them take possession of your beautiful island with your many beautiful buildings. You will give all these, but neither your souls, nor your minds." Since none of this had the intended effect, Gandhi, the following year, addressed an open letter to the prince of darkness himself, Adolf Hitler.

The scene must be pictured. In late December 1941, Hitler stood at the pinnacle of his might. His armies, undefeated anywhere ruled Europe from the English Channel to the Volga. Rommel had entered Egypt. The Japanese had reached Singapore. The U. S. Pacific Fleet lay at the bottom of Pearl Harbour. At this superbly chosen moment, Mahatma Gandhi attempted to convert Adolf Hitler to the ways of nonviolence. "Dear Friend," the letter begins, and proceeds to a heartfelt appeal to the Fuhrer to embrace all mankind "irrespective of race, colour, or creed." Every admirer of the film 'Gandhi' should be compelled to read this letter. Surprisingly, it is not known to have had any deep impact on Hitler. Gandhi was no doubt disappointed. He moped about, really quite depressed, but still knew he was right. When the Japanese, having cut their way through Burma, threatened India, Gandhi's strategy was to let them occupy as much of India as they liked and then to "make them feel unwanted." His way of helping his British "friends" was, at one of the worst points of the war, to launch massive civil-disobedience campaigns against them, paralyzing some of their efforts to defend India from the Japanese.

Here, then, is your leader, the followers of Gandhi: a man who thought Hitler's heart would be melted by an appeal to forget race, colour, and creed, and who was sure the feelings of the Japanese would be hurt if they sensed themselves unwanted. As world-class statesmen go, it is not a very good record. Madeleine Slade was right, I suppose. The world certainly didn't listen to Gandhi. Nor, for that matter, has the modern government of India listened to Gandhi. Although all Indian politicians of all political parties claim to be Gandhians, India has blithely fought three wars against Pakistan, one against China, and even invaded and seized tiny, helpless Goa, and all without a whisper of a shadow of a thought of Ahimsa. And of course India now has atomic weapons, a satyagraha technique if ever there was one.

I am sure that almost everyone who sees the movie 'Gandhi' is aware that, from a religious point if view, the Mahatma was something called a "Hindu"—but I do not think one in a thousand has the dimmest notion of the fundamental beliefs of the Hindu religion. The simplest example is Gandhi's use of the word "God," which, for members of the great Western religions—Christianity, Judaism, and Islam, all interrelated—means a personal god, a godhead. But when Gandhi said "God" in speaking English, he was merely translating from Gujarati or Hindi, and from the Hindu culture. Gandhi, in fact, simply did not believe in a personal God, and wrote in so many words, "God is not a person... but a force; the undefinable mysterious Power that pervades everything; a living Power that is Love.... " And Gandhi's very favourite definition of God, repeated many thousands of times, was, "God is Truth," which reduces God to some kind of abstract principle.

Like all Hindus, Gandhi also believed in the "Great Oneness," according to which everything is part of God, meaning not just you and me and everyone else, but every living creature, every dead creature, every plant, the pitcher of milk, the milk in the pitcher, the tumbler into which the milk is poured.... After all of which, he could suddenly pop up with a declaration that God is "the Maker, the Law-Giver, a jealous Lord," phrases he had probably picked up in the Bible and, with Hindu fluidity, felt he could throw in so as to embrace even more of the Great Oneness. So when Gandhi said, "I am a Hindu and a Muslim and a Christian and a Jew," it was (from a Western standpoint) Hindu double-talk. Hindu holy men, some of them reformers lik Gandhi, have actually even "converted" to Islam, then Christianity, or whatever, to worship different "aspects" of the Great Oneness, before reconverting to Hinduism. Now for Christians, fastidious in matters of doctrine, a man who converts to Islam is an apostate (or vice versa), but a Hindu is a Hindu is a Hindu. The better to experience the Great Oneness, many Hindu holy men feel they should be women as well as men, and one quite famous one even claimed he could menstruate (I will spare the reader the details).

In this ecumenical age, it is extremely hard to shake Westerners loose from the notion that the devout of all religions, after all, worship "the one God." But Gandhi did not worship the one God. He did not worship the God of mercy. He did not worship the God of forgiveness. And this for the simple reason that the concepts of mercy and forgiveness are absent from Hinduism. In Hinduism, men do not pray to God for forgiveness, and a man's sins are never forgiven—indeed, there is no one out there to do the forgiving. In your next life you may be born someone higher up the caste scale, but in this life there is no hope. For Gandhi, a true Hindu, did not believe in man's immortal soul. He believed with every ounce of his being in karma, a series, perhaps a long series, of reincarnations, and at the end, with great good fortune: mukti, liberation from suffering and the necessity of rebirth, nothingness. Gandhi once wrote to Tolstoy (of all people) that reincarnation explained "reasonably the many mysteries of life." So if Hindus today still treat an Untouchable as barely human, this is thought to be perfectly right and fitting because of his actions in earlier lives. As can be seen, Hinduism, by its very theology, with its sacred triad of karma, reincarnation, and caste (with caste an absolutely indispensable part of the system) offers the most complacent justification of inhumanity of any of the world's great religious faiths.

Gandhi, needless to say, was a Hindu reformer, one of many. Until well into his fifties, however, he accepted the caste system in toto as the "natural order of society," promoting control and discipline and sanctioned by his religion. Later, in bursts of zeal, he favoured moderating it in a number of ways. But he stuck by the basic varna system (the four main caste groupings plus the Untouchables) until the end of his days, insisting that a man's position and occupation should be determined essentially by birth. Gandhi favoured milder treatment of Untouchables, renaming them Harijans, "children of God," but a Harijan was still a Harijan. Perhaps because his frenzies of compassion were so extreme (no, no, he would clean the Harijan's latrine), Hindu reverence for him as a holy man became immense, but his prescriptions were rarely followed.

Industrialization and modernization have introduced new occupations and sizable social and political changes in India, but the caste system has dexterously adapted and remains largely intact today. The Sudras still labour. The sweepers still sweep. Max Weber, in his 'The Religion of India,' after quoting the last line of the 'Communist Manifesto, ' suggests somewhat sardonically that low-caste Hindus, too, have "nothing to lose but their chains," that they, too, have "a world to win"—the only problem being that they have to die first and get born again, higher, it is to be hoped, in the immutable system of caste. Hinduism in general, wrote Weber, "is characterized by a dread of the magical evil of innovation." Its very essence is to guarantee stasis.

In addition to its literally thousands of castes and sub-castes, Hinduism has countless sects, with discordant rites and beliefs. It has no clear ecclesiastical organization and no universal body of doctrine. What I have described above is your standard, no-frills Hindu, of which in many ways Gandhi was an excellent example. With the reader's permission I will skip over the Upanishads, Vedanta, Yoga, the Puranas, Tantra, Bhakti, the 'Bhagavad-Gita' (which contains theistic elements), Brahma, Vishnu, Shiva, and the terrible Kali or Durga, to concentrate on those central beliefs that most motivated Gandhi's behaviour as a public figure.

It should be plain by now that here is much in the Hindu culture that is distasteful to the Western mind, and consequently is largely—unknown in the West—not because Hindus do not go on and on about these subjects, but because a Western squeamishness usually prevents these preoccupations from reaching print (not to mention film). When Gandhi attended his first Indian National Congress he was most distressed at seeing the Hindus—not labourers but high-caste Hindus, civic leaders—defecating all over the place, as if to pay attention to where the feces fell was somehow unclean. (For, as V. S. Naipaul puts it, in a twisted Hindu way it is unclean to clean.

It is unclean even to notice. "It was the business of the sweepers to remove excrement, and until the sweepers came, people were content to live in the midst of their own excrement.") Gandhi exhorted Indians endlessly on the subject, saying that sanitation was the first need of India, but he retained an obvious obsession with excreta, gleefully designing latrines and latrine drills for all hands at the Ashram, and, all in all what with giving and taking enemas, and his public bowel movements, and his deep concern with everyone else's bowel movements (much correspondence), and endless dietary experiments as a function of bowel movements, he devoted a rather large share of his life to the matter. Despite his constant campaigning for sanitation, it is hard to believe that Gandhi was not permanently marked by what Arthur Koestler terms the Hindu "morbid infatuation with filth," and what V. S. Naipaul goes as far as to call Indian "deification of filth." (Decades later, Krishna Menon, a Gandhian and one-time Indian Defence Minister, was still fortifying sanctity by drinking a daily 1 of urine.)

But even more important, because it is dealt with in the movie directly—if of course dishonestly—is Gandhi's parallel obsession with brahmacharya, or sexual chastity. There is a scene late in the film in which Margaret Bourke-White (again!) asks Gandhi's wife if he has ever broken his vow of chastity, taken, at that time, about forty years before. Gandhi's wife, by now a sweet old lady, answers wistfully, with a pathetic little note of hope, "Not yet." What lies behind this adorable scene is the following: Gandhi held as one of his most profound beliefs (a fundamental doctrine of Hindu medicine) that a man, as a matter of the utmost importance, must conserve his bindu, or seminal fluid. Koestler (in 'The Lotus and the Robot') gives a succinct account of this belief, widespread among orthodox Hindus: "A man's vital energy is concentrated in his seminal fluid, and this is stored in a cavity in the skull.

It is the most precious substance in the body... an elixir of life both in the physical and mystical sense, distilled from the blood.... A large store of bindu of pure quality guarantees health, longevity, and supernatural powers.... Conversely, every loss of it is a physical and spiritual impoverishment." Gandhi himself said in so many words, "A man who is unchaste loses stamina, becomes emasculated and cowardly, while in the chaste man secretions (semen) are sublimated into a vital force pervading his whole being." And again, still Gandhi: "Ability to retain and assimilate the vital liquid is a matter of long training. When properly conserved it is transmuted into matchless energy and strength." Most male Hindus go ahead and have sexual relations anyway, of course, but the belief in the value of bindu leaves the whole culture in what many observers have called a permanent state of "semen anxiety." When Gandhi once had a nocturnal emission he almost had a nervous breakdown.

Gandhi was a truly fanatical opponent of sex for pleasure, and worked it out carefully that a married couple should be allowed to have sex three or four times *in a lifetime*, merely to have children and favoured embodying this restriction in the law of the land. The sexual-gratification wing of the present-day feminist movement would find little to attract them in Gandhi's doctrine, since in all his seventy-nine years it never crossed his mind once that there could be anything enjoyable in sex for women, and he was constantly enjoining Indian women to deny themselves to men, to refuse to let their husbands "abuse" them. Gandhi had been married at thirteen, and when he took his vow of chastity, after twenty-four years of sexual activity, he ordered his two oldest sons, both young men, to be totally chaste as well.

But Gandhi's monstrous behaviour to his own family is notorious. He denied his sons education—to which he was bitterly hostile. His wife remained illiterate. Once when she was very sick, hemorrhaging badly, and seemed to be dying, he wrote to her from jail icily: "My struggle is not merely political. It is religious and therefore quite pure. It does not matter much whether one dies in it or lives. I hope and expect that you will also think likewise and not be unhappy." To die, that is. On another occasion he wrote, speaking about her: "I simply cannot bear to look at Ba's face.

The expression is often like that on the face of a meek cow and gives one the feeling, as a cow occasionally does, that in her own dumb manner she is saying something. I see, too, that there is selfishness in this suffering of hers.... " And in the end he let her die, as I have said, rather than allow British doctors to give her a shot of penicillin (while his inner voice told him that it would be all right for him to take quinine). He disowned his oldest son, Harilal, for wishing to marry. He banished his second son for giving his struggling older brother a small sum of money. Harilal grew quite wild with rage against his father, attacked him in print, converted to Islam, took to women, drink, and died an alcoholic in 1948. The Mahatma attacked him right back in his pious way, proclaiming modestly in an open letter in "Young India," "Men may be good, not necessarily their children."

If the reader thinks I have delivered unduly harsh judgments on India and Hindu civilization, I can refer him to 'An Area of Darkness' and 'India: A Wounded Civilization, ' two quite brilliant books on India by V. S. Naipaul, a Hindu, and a Brahmin, born in Trinidad. In the second, the more discursive, Naipaul writes that India "has little to offer the world except its Gandhian concept of holy poverty and the recurring crooked comedy of its holy men, and... is now dependent in every practical way on other, imperfectly understood civilizations."

Hinduism, Naipaul writes, "has given men no idea of a contract with other men, no idea of the state. It has enslaved one quarter of the population (the Untouchables) and always has left the whole fragmented and vulnerable. Its philosophy of withdrawal has diminished men intellectually and not equipped them to respond to challenge; it has stifled growth. So that again and again in India history has repeated itself: vulnerability, defeat, withdrawal." Indians, Naipaul says, have no historical notion of the past. "Through centuries of conquest the civilization declined into an apparatus for survival, turning away from the mind... and creativity... stripping itself down, like all decaying civilizations, to its magical practices and imprisoning social forms." He adds later, "No government can survive on Gandhian fantasy; and the spirituality, the solace of a conquered people, which Gandhi turned into a form of national assertion, has soured more obviously into the nihilism that it always was." Naipaul condemns India again and again for its "intellectual parasitism," its "intellectual vacuum," its "emptiness," the "blankness of its decayed civilization." "Indian poverty is more dehumanizing than any machine; and, more than in any machine civilization, men in India are units, locked up in the straitest obedience by their idea of their Dharma.

"The blight of caste is not only untouchability and the consequent deification in India of filth; the blight, in an India that tries to grow, is also the overall obedience it imposes, the diminishing of adventurousness, the pushing away from men of individuality and the possibility of excellence." Although Naipaul blames Gandhi as well as India itself for the country's failure to develop an "ideology" adequate for the modern world, he grants him one or two magnificent moments—always, it should be noted, when responding to "other civilizations." For Gandhi, Naipaul remarks pointedly, had matured in alien societies: Britain and South Africa. With age, back in India, he seemed from his autobiography to be headed for "lunacy," says Naipaul, and was only rescued by external events, his reactions to which were determined in part by "his experience of the democratic ways of South Africa" (my emphasis). For it is one of the enduring ironies of Gandhi's story that it was in South Africa—"South Africa"—a country in which he became far more deeply involved than he had been in Britain, that Gandhi caught a warped glimmer of that strange institution of which he would never have seen even a reflection within Hindu society: democracy.

Another of Gandhi's most powerful obsessions (to which the movie alludes in such a syrupy and misleading manner that it would be quite impossible for the audience to understand it) was his visceral hatred of the modern, industrial world. He even said, more than once, that he actually wouldn't mind if the British remained in India, to police it, conduct foreign policy, and such trivia, if it would only take away its factories and railways. And Gandhi hated, not just factories and railways, but also the telegraph, the telephone, the radio, the airplane. He happened to be in England when Louis Bleriot, the great French aviation pioneer, first flew the English Channel—an event which at the time stirred as much excitement as Lindbergh's later flight across the Atlantic and Gandhi was in a positive fury that giant crowds were acclaiming such an insignificant event. He used the telegraph extensively himself, of course, and later would broadcast daily over All-India Radio during his highly publicized fasts, but consistency was never Gandhi's strong suit.

Gandhi's view of the good society, about which he wrote ad nauseam, was an Arcadian vision set far in India's past. It was the pristine Indian village, where, with all diabolical machinery and technology abolished—and with them all unhappiness—contented villagers would hand-spin their own yarn, hand-weave their own cloth, serenely follow their bullocks in the fields, tranquilly prodding them in the anus in the time-hallowed Hindu way. This was why Gandhi taught himself to spin, and why all the devout Gandhians, like monkeys, spun also. This was Gandhi's program. Since he said it several thousand times, we have no choice but to believe that he sincerely desired the destruction of modern technology and industry and the return of India to the way of life of an idyllic (and quite likely nonexistent) past. And yet this same "Mahatma Gandhi handpicked as the first Prime Minister of an independent India Pandit Nehru, who was committed to a policy of industrialization and for whom the last word in the politico-economic organization of the state was (and remained) Beatrice Webb.

What are we to make of this Gandhi? We are dealing with two strangenesses here, Indians and Gandhi himself. The plain fact is that both Indian leaders and the Indian people ignored Gandhi's precepts almost as thoroughly as did Hitler. They ignored him on sexual abstinence. They ignored his modifications of the caste system. They ignored him on the evils of modern industry, the radio, the telephone. They ignored him on education. They ignored his appeals for national union, the former British Raj splitting into a Muslim Pakistan and a Hindu India. No one sought a return to the Arcadian Indian village of antiquity.

They ignored him, above all, in Ahimsa, nonviolence. There was always a small number of exalted Satyagrahi who, martyrs, would march into the constables' truncheons, but one of the things that alarmed the British—as Tagore indicated—was the explosions of violence that accompanied all this alleged nonviolence. Naipaul writes that with independence India discovered again that it was "cruel and horribly violent." Jaya Prakash Narayan, the late opposition leader, once admitted, "We often behave like animals.... We are more likely than not to become aggressive, wild, violent. We kill and burn and loot.

Why, then, did the Hindu masses so honour this Mahatma, almost all of whose most cherished beliefs they so pointedly ignored, even during his lifetime? For Hindus, the question is not really so puzzling. Gandhi, for them, after all, was a Mahatma, a holy man. He was a symbol of sanctity, not a guide to conduct. Hinduism has a long history of holy men who, traditionally, do not offer themselves up to the public as models of general behaviour but withdraw from the world, often into an Ashram, to pursue their sanctity in private, a practice which all Hindus honour, if few emulate.

The true oddity is that Gandhi, this holy man, having drawn from British sources his notions of nationalism and democracy, also absorbed from the British his model of virtue in public life. He was a historical original, a Hindu holy man that a British model of public service and dazzling advances in mass communications thrust out into the world, to become a great moral leader and the "father of his country."

Some Indians feel that after the early 1930's, Gandhi, although by now world-famous, was in fact in sharp decline. Did he at least "get British out of India"? Some say no. India, in the last days of British Raj, was already largely governed by Indians (a fact one would never suspect from this movie), and it is a common view that without this irrational, wildly erratic holy man the transition to full independence might have gone both more smoothly and more swiftly. There is much evidence that in his last years Gandhi was in a kind of spiritual retreat and, with all his endless praying and fasting, was no longer pursuing (the very words seem strange in a Hindu context) "the public good." What he was pursuing, in a strict reversion to Hindu tradition, was his personal holiness. In earlier days he had scoffed at the title accorded him, Mahatma (literally "great soul"). But toward the end, during the hideous paroxysms that accompanied independence, with some of the most unspeakable massacres taking place in Calcutta, he declared, "And if the whole of Calcutta swims in blood, it will not dismay me. For it will be a willing offering of innocent blood." And in his last days, after there had already been one attempt on his life, he was heard to say, "I am a true Mahatma."

We can only wonder, furthermore, at a public figure who lectures half his life about the necessity of abolishing modern industry and returning India to its ancient primitiveness, and then picks a Fabian socialist, already drawing up Five-Year Plans, as the country's first Prime Minister. Audacious as it may seem to contest the views of such heavy thinkers as Margaret Bourke-White, Ralph Nader, and J. K. Galbraith (who found the film's Gandhi "true to the original" and endorsed the movie wholeheartedly), we have a right to reservations about such a figure as a public man.

I should not be surprised if Gandhi's greatest real humanitarian achievement was an improvement in the treatment of Untouchables—an area where his efforts were not only assiduous, but actually bore fruit. In this, of course, he ranks well behind the British, who abolished suttee over ferocious Hindu opposition—in 1829. The ritual immolation by fire of widows on their husbands' funeral pyres, suttee had the full sanction of the Hindu religion, although it might perhaps be wrong to overrate its importance. Scholars remind us that it was never universal, only "usual."

And there was, after all, a rather extensive range of choice. In southern India the widow was flung into her husband's fire-pit. In the valley of the Ganges she was placed on the pyre when it was already aflame. In western India, she supported the head of the corpse with her right hand, while, torch in her left, she was allowed the honour of setting the whole thing on fire herself.

In the north, where perhaps women were more impious, the widow's body was constrained on the burning pyre by long poles pressed down by her relatives, just in case, screaming in terror and choking and burning to death, she might forget her Dharma. So, yes, ladies, members of the National Council of Churches, believers in the one God, mourners for that holy India before it was despoiled by those brutish British, remember suttee, that interesting, exotic practice in which Hindus, over the centuries, burned to death countless millions of helpless women in a spirit of pious devotion, crying for all I know, Hai Rama! Hai Rama!

I would like to conclude with some observations on two Englishmen, Madeleine Slade, the daughter of a British admiral, and Sir Richard Attenborough, the producer, director, and spiritual godfather of the film, 'Gandhi. ' Miss Slade was a jewel in Gandhi's crown—a member of the British ruling class, as she was, turned fervent disciple of this Indian Mahatma. She is played in the film by Geraldine James with nobility, dignity, and a beatific manner quite up to the level of Candice Bergen, and perhaps even the Virgin Mary. I learn from Ved Mehta's 'Mahatma Gandhi and his Apostles, ' however, that Miss Slade had another master before Gandhi. In about 1917, when she was fifteen, she made contact with the spirit of Beethoven by listening to his sonatas on a player piano. "I threw myself down on my knees in the seclusion of my room," she wrote in her autobiography, "and prayed, "really" prayed to God for the first time in my life: 'Why have I been born over a century too late? Why hast Thou given me realization of him and yet put all these years in between?'"

After World War I, still seeking how best to serve Beethoven, Miss Slade felt an "infinite longing" when she visited his birthplace and grave, and, finally, at the age of thirty-two, caught up with Romain Rolland, who had partly based his renowned 'Jean Christophe' on the composer. But Rolland had written a new book now, about a man called Gandhi, "another Christ," and before long Miss Slade was quite literally falling on her knees before the Mahatma in India, "conscious of nothing but a sense of light." Although one would never guess this from the film, she soon (to quote Mehta's impression) began "to get on Gandhi's nerves," and he took every pretext to keep her away from him, in other Ashrams, and working in schools and villages in other parts of India. She complained to Gandhi in letters about discrimination against her by orthodox Hindus, who expected her to live in rags and vile quarters during menstruation, considering her unclean and virtually untouchable. Gandhi wrote back, agreeing that women should not be treated like that, but adding that she should accept it all with grace and cheerfulness, "without thinking that the orthodox party is in any way unreasonable." (This is as good an example as any of Gandhi's coherence, even in his prime. Women should not be treated like that, but the people who treated them that way were in no way unreasonable).

Some years after Gandhi's death, Miss Slade rediscovered Beethoven, becoming conscious again "of the realization of my true self. For a while I remained lost in the world of the spirit.... " She soon returned to Europe and serving Beethoven, her "true calling." When Mehta finally found her in Vienna, she told him, "Please don't ask me any more about Bapu (Gandhi). I now belong to van Beethoven. In matters of the spirit, there is always a call." A polite description of Madeleine Slade is that she was an extreme eccentric. In the vernacular, she was slightly cracked.

Sir Richard Attenborough, however, isn't cracked at all. The only puzzle is how he suddenly got to be a pacifist, a fact which his press releases now proclaim to the world. Attenborough trained as a pilot in the RAF in World War II, and was released briefly to the cinema, where he had already begun his career in Noel Coward's superpatriotic 'In Which We Serve. ' He then returned to active service, flying combat missions with the RAF. Richard Attenborough, in short—when Gandhi was pleading with the British to surrender to the Nazis, assuring them that "Hitler is not a bad man"—was fighting for his country. The Viceroy of India warned Gandhi grimly that "We are engaged in a struggle," and Attenborough played his part in that great struggle, and proudly, too, as far as I can tell. To my knowledge he has never had a crise de conscience on the matter, or announced that he was carried away by the war fever and that Britain really should have capitulated to the Nazis—which Gandhi would have had it do.

Although the present film is handsomely done in its way, no one has ever accused Attenborough of being excessively endowed with either acting or directing talent. In the '50's he was a popular young British entertainer, but his most singular gift appeared to be his entrepreneurial talent as a businessman, using his movie fees to launch successful London restaurants (at one time four), and other business ventures. At the present moment he is Chairman of the Board of Capital Radio (Britain's most successful commercial station), Goldcrest Films, the British Film Institute, and Deputy Chairman of the BBC's new Channel 4 television network. Like most members of the nouveaux riches on the rise, he has also reached out for symbols of respectability and public service, and has assembled quite a collection. He is a Trustee of the Tate Gallery, Pro-Chancellor of Sussex University, President of Britain's Muscular Dystrophy Group, Chairman of the Actors' Charitable Trust and, of course, Chairman of the Royal Academy of Dramatic Art. There may be even more, but this is a fair sampling. In 1976, quite fittingly, he was knighted, by a Labour government, but his friends say he still insists on being called "Dickie."

It is quite general today for members of the professional classes, even when not artistic types, to despise commerce and feel that the state, the economy, and almost everything else would be better and more idealistically run by themselves rather than these loutish businessmen. Sir Dickie, however, being a highly successful businessman himself, would hardly entertain such an antipathy. But as he scrambled his way to the heights perhaps he found himself among high-minded idealists, utopians, equalitarians, and lovers of the oppressed. Now there are those who think Sir Dickie converted to pacifism when Indira Gandhi handed him a check for several million dollars. But I do not believe this. I think Sir Dickie converted to pacifism out of idealism.

His pacifism, I confess, has been more than usually muddled. In 1968, after twenty-six years in the profession, he made his directorial debut with 'Oh! What a Lovely War, ' with its superb parody of Britain's jingoistic music-hall songs of the "Great War," World War I. Since I had the good fortune to see Joan Littlewood's original London stage production, which gave the work its entire style, I cannot think that Sir Dickie's contribution was unduly large. Like most commercially successful parodies—from Sandy Wilson's 'The Boy Friend' to Broadway's 'Superman, ' 'Dracula, ' and the 'Crucifier of Blood'—'Oh! What a Lovely War' depended on the audience's (if not Miss Littlewood's) retaining a substantial affection for the subject being parodied: in this case, a swaggering hyperpatriotism, which recalled days when the empire was great. In any event, since Miss Littlewood identified herself as a Communist and since Communists, as far as I know, are never pacifists, Sir Dickie's case for the production's "pacifism" seems stymied from the other angle as well.

Sir Dickie's next blow for pacifism was 'Young Winston' (1973), which, the new publicity manual says, "explored how Churchill's childhood traumas and lack of parental affection became the spurs which goaded him to a position of great power." One would think that a man who once flew combat missions under the orders of the great war leader—and who seemingly wanted his country to win—could thank God for childhood traumas and lack of parental affection if such were needed to provide Churchill in the hour of peril. But on pressed Sir Dickie, in the year of his knighthood, with 'A Bridge Too Far, ' the story of the futile World War II assault on Arnhem, described by Sir Dickie—now, at least—as "a further plea for pacifism."

But does Sir Richard Attenborough seriously think that, rather than go through what we did at Arnhem, we should have given in, let the Nazis be, and even—true pacifists—them occupy Britain, Canada, the United States, contenting ourselves only with "making them feel unwanted"? At the level of idiocy to which discussions of war and peace have sunk in the West, every hare-brained idealist who discovers that war is not a day at the beach seems to think he has found an irresistible argument for pacifism. Is Pearl Harbour an argument for pacifism? Bataan? Dunkirk? Dieppe? The Ardennes? Roland fell at Roncesvalles. Is the 'Song of Roland' a pacifist epic? If so, why did William the Conqueror have it chanted to his men as they marched into battle at Hastings? Men prove their valour in defeat as well as in victory. Even Sergeant Major Gandhi knew that. Up in the moral never-never land which Sir Dickie now inhabits, perhaps they think the Alamo led to a great wave of pacifism in Texas.

In a feat of sheer imbecility, Attenborough has dedicated 'Gandhi' to Lord Mountbatten, who commanded the Southeast Asian Theatre during World War II. Mountbatten, you might object, was hardly a pacifist—but then again he was murdered by Irish terrorists, which proves how frightful all that sort of thing is, Sir Dickie says, and how we must end it all by imitating Gandhi. Not the Gandhi who called for seas of innocent blood, you understand, but the movie-Gandhi, the nice one. The historical Gandhi's favourite mantra, strange to tell, was 'Do or Die' (he called it literally that, a "mantra"). I think Sir Dickie should reflect on this, because it means, dixit Gandhi, that a man must be prepared to die for what he believes in, for, Himsa or Ahimsa, death is always there, and in an ultimate test men who are not prepared to face it lose. Gandhi was erratic, irrational, tyrannical, obstinate. He sometimes verged on lunacy. He believed in a religion whose ideas I find somewhat repugnant. He worshipped cows. But I still say this: he was brave. He feared no one.

On a lower level of being, I have consequently given some thought to the proper mantra for spectators of the movie 'Gandhi. ' After much reflection, in homage to Ralph Nader, I have decided on Caveat Emptor, "buyer beware." Repeated many thousand times in a seat in the cinema it might with luck lead to om, the Hindu dream of nothingness, the Ultimate Void.

THE UNTOUCHABLES: SUBORDINATION, POVERTY AND THE STATE IN MODERN INDIA

Untouchability has played an important role in Indian history and still affects many millions of Indians. The Untouchables focuses on its connections with poverty and state politics, with a primarily political and historical focus, but also looks at its social construction and effects on the lives of individuals. With a broad approach not burdened with too much theory, it will interest scholars, students, and lay readers of history, politics, religion, economics, sociology, and other disciplines.

Mendelsohn and Vicziany begin with the vexed question of the identity of "the Untouchables" and an explanation for their choice of that term for their title, over Harijan, Dalit, or Scheduled Caste. (They use all these terms and others in the text.) There has been a long-running debate over the nature of Untouchable identity and its relationship with Hindu culture. For Mendelsohn and Vicziany the key issue is

> "*whether the Untouchables share a social situation that is sufficiently common to be the basis or potential basis for their mobilisation as a distinct unit for some important purposes.... There is indeed something of a `hard bar' separating Untouchables from the rest of Indian society, and Untouchables themselves have come to see that bar as the basis for a certain amount of common consciousness and action.*"

The category as it exists now may be a recent construction, a response to British actions and Muslim/Hindu rivalry, but it was constructed on long-standing foundations: evidence from the Bhakti literary tradition shows that Untouchable ritual subordination existed in medieval times.

Recent violence against Untouchables-the so-called "Harijan atrocities"-has brought the issue of Untouchability to prominence. Mendelsohn and Vicziany argue "that the incidence of violence involving Untouchables has increased significantly over the post-Independence period". The violence can be divided into "traditional" forms and others that are responses to Untouchable resistance to ritual subordination, often taking the form of organised retaliatory violence by caste Hindus, sometimes abetted by the police and state apparatus. There are marked regional variations in such violence and it is often tied up with broader political violence, associated with mainstream electoral contests as well as with class conflict and Naxalite revolutionaries.

Early Untouchable politics involved Hindu reform movements, often motivated by the threat, however nugatory, of Untouchable conversion to Christianity or Islam. Early organisation by Untouchables themselves was on a caste and regional basis, and relationships between different Untouchable castes were often difficult. The 1930s saw key struggles between Gandhi and Ambedkar, most notably over whether Untouchables would have separate electorates or joint electorates with reserved seats. Congress was the only national organisation with a large Untouchable following, but Gandhi failed to gain their commitment. Ambedkar, an Untouchable himself, developed a deeper analysis of Untouchability, but lacked a workable political strategy: his conversion to Buddhism in 1956, along with millions of followers, highlighted the failure of his political endeavours.

In the years since 1956 Ambedkarite political organisations have been riven by internal conflicts, notably between young, modernist, and urban elements and older, rural, and often Buddhist ones. But Ambedkar's legacy remains fruitful. Maharashtra and Karnataka have produced a Dalit literary movement, while there have been political success in northern India. In Uttar Pradesh, the Bahujana Samaj party lead by Kanshi Ram has, through alliances of convenience with other parties, attained minority government, installing Mayawati as Chief Minister. Though their achievements in power were limited, this illustrates how Dalits are now using their voting power directly rather than as simple vote banks at the service of mainstream parties.

Public policy on Untouchability has been "abstract and unrealistic" but not completely ineffective. One strand has been action against adverse discrimination. Discrimination against Untouchables is still widespread in rural areas in the private sphere, in ritual matters such as access to eating places and water sources. It has largely disappeared, however, in urban areas and in the public sphere, in rights of movement and access to schools. Mendelsohn and Vicziany argue, however, that this has been part of a broader movement towards a new civic culture rather than the result of legislative action: "court enforcement of the anti-disabilities legislation has not been a powerful force in bringing about an abatement of the practice of Untouchability".

Compensatory discrimination has been more controversial. One success of Ambedkar's was the creation of quotas within public service for Scheduled Castes, though targets set after Independence are only being attained now. Complaints about this system are that it benefits an elite group of well-off Untouchables, that particular castes or regions benefit more, and that those in office do little to help their fellows. Compensatory discrimination in education, through scholarships and reserved places, has had some effects but has generally been poorly implemented. Despite this, basic literacy amongst Untouchables is gradually catching up to that of the broader population.

Brief biographies of some Scheduled Caste politicians, national and state, show that they have indeed come from the better off among their communities. But their advantages have often been very slight: family ownership of a cow, for example, or a small plot of land-just enough to alleviate the desperation of poverty and allow an opportunity for education. Along with public service reservations, scholarships (however small and corruptly administered) and the "Harijan hostels" associated with colleges have helped them overcome the barriers of poverty and Untouchability. While Scheduled Caste politicians have not been effective in representing Untouchables generally, Mendelsohn and Vicziany find little evidence of a "Harijan elite".

Other public policy initiatives of key importance to the Untouchables have been the anti-poverty programs: famine prevention, land reform, food-for-work schemes, and the Integrated Rural Development Program, among others. Apart from the first, these have had limited success. There has been considerable regional variation in alleviation of Untouchable poverty. Along with the population generally, Untouchables in Kerala score extremely well on social indicators such as literacy, education, health, and fertility, but they face high unemployment and lack of opportunity. For contrast Mendelsohn and Vicziany look in detail at the village of Behror, located in a relatively affluent "Green Revolution" area mid-way between Delhi and Jaipur. Different Untouchable communities here exhibit great variation in their employment patterns and economic success.

The Faisalabad stone quarries, just outside Delhi, provide an example of the new Untouchable proletariat being created through urbanisation and migration: eight out of ten workers there are Untouchable and most of the rest are tribals. A case to have welfare legislation enforced and end bonded labour was taken to the Supreme Court by activist Swami Agnivesh, but ostensible success was vitiated by the failure of governments and employers to implement court directives and by an excessive focus on bonded labour. And union organisation amongst Untouchables faces many obstacles.

The negotiations between Gandhi, Ambedkar, and the British in the late 20s and early 30s had a key role in shaping subsequent Untouchable history. But the greatest changes have been gradual, brought about by improvements in education and possession of the franchise. Mendelsohn and Vicziany foresee no end to Untouchable poverty: with the decline of ritual discrimination, "Untouchables will become decreasingly differentiated from other Indians" in their poverty.

4

ECONOMIC PROGRESS OR SOCIAL CHANGES

I think it necessary here to discuss the question as to what should be initiated first, whether economic progress or conversion? I do not agree with the view that economic progress should precede. Untouchability is a permanent handicap on your path of progress. And unless you remove it, your path cannot be safe. Without conversion, this hurdle cannot be removed. So, if you sincerely desire that your qualifications should be valued, your education should be of some use to you, you must throw away the shackles of untouchability, which means that you must change your religion. However, for those who need this Mahar Watan, I can assure them that their Mahar Watan will not be jeopardized by their conversion. In this regard, the Act of 1850 can be referred. Under the provisions of this Act, no rights of person or his successors with respect to his property are affected by virtue of his conversion.

POONA PACT

A second doubt is about political rights. Some people express fear as to what will happen to our political safeguards if we convert. But I feel, it is not proper to depend solely on political rights. These political safeguards are not granted on the condition that they shall be ever lasting. They are bound to cease sometime. According to the communal Award of the British Government, our political safeguards were limited for 20 years. Although no such limitation has been fixed by the

Poona Pact, nobody can say that they are everlasting. Those, who depend upon the political safeguards, must think as to what will happen after these safeguards are withdrawn on the day on which our rights cease to exist. We will have to depend on our social strength. I have already told you that this social strength is wanting in us. So also I have proved in the beginning that this strength cannot be achieved without conversion.

POLITICAL RIGHTS

Under these circumstances, one must think of what is permanently beneficial. In my opinion, conversion is the only way to eternal bliss. Nobody should hesitate even if the political rights are required to be sacrificed for this purpose. Conversion brings no harm to the political safeguards. I do not understand why the political safeguards should at all be jeopardized by conversion. Wherever you may go, your political rights and safeguards will accompany you. I have no doubt about it.

If you become Muslims, you will get the political rights as Muslims. If you become Christians, you will get the political rights as Christians, if you become Sikhs, you will have your political rights as Sikhs. In short, our political rights will accompany us.

So nobody should be afraid of it. On the other hand, if we remain Hindus and do not convert, will our rights be safe? You must think carefully on this. Suppose the Hindus pass a law whereby the untouchability is prohibited and its practice is made punishable, then they may ask you, 'We have abolished untouchability by law and you are no longer untouchables.

Looking through this perspective, conversion becomes a path for strengthening the political safeguards rather than becoming a hindrance. If you remain Hindus, you are sure to lose your political safeguards. If you want to save them, leave this religion. The political safeguards will be permanent only by conversion. The Hindu religion does not appeal to my conscience. It does not appeal to my self-respect. However, your conversion will be for material as well as for spiritual gains.

Some persons mock and laugh at the idea of conversion for material gains. I do not feel hesitant in calling such persons as stupid.

CONVERSION BRINGS HAPPINESS

I tell you all very specifically, religion is for man and not man for religion. To get human treatment, convert yourselves.

CONVERT-For getting organized.

CONVERT-For becoming strong.

CONVERT-For securing equality.

CONVERT-For getting liberty.

CONVERT-For that your domestic life may be happy.

I consider him as leader who without fear or favour tells the people what is good and what is bad for them. It is my duty to tell you, what is good for you, even if you don't like it, I must do my duty. And now I have done it.

It is now for you to decide and discharge your responsibility.

THE CASTE NOTION AND THE NATION

Ambedkar counterpoised the concept of nation as against the concept of caste, which was the pre-eminent mode of social organisation in India. For him, the idea of a nation was not just political sovereignty. A nation was a people who were socially bound as one. India however was divided by caste groups and people were unable to think in any other terms except as caste groups or caste sub-groups.

"The Hindus often complain of the isolation and exclusiveness of a gang or a clique and blame them for antisocial spirit. But they conveniently forget that this antisocial spirit is the worst feature of their own Caste System. One caste enjoys singing a hymn of hate against another caste as much as the Germans did in singing their hymn of hate against the English during the last war. The literature of the Hindus is full of caste genealogies in which an attempt is made to give a noble origin to one caste and an ignoble origin to other castes. The Sahyadrikhand is a notorious instance of this class of literature. This antisocial spirit is not confined to caste alone.

It has gone deeper and has poisoned the mutual relations of the sub-castes as well. In my province the Golak Brahmins, Deorukha Brahmins, Karada Brahmins, Palshe Brahmins and Chitpavan Brahmins, all claim to be subdivisions of the Brahmin Caste. But the antisocial spirit that prevails between them is quite as marked and quite as virulent as the antisocial spirit that prevails between them and other non-Brahmin castes. There is nothing strange in this. An antisocial spirit is found wherever one group has 'interests of its own' who shut it out from full interaction with other groups, so that its prevailing purpose is protection of what it has got. This antisocial spirit, this spirit of protecting its own interests is as much a marked feature of the different castes in their isolation from one another as it is of nations in their isolation.

The Brahmin's primary concern is to protect 'his interest' against those of the non-Brahmins and the non-Brahmin's primary concern is to protect their interests against those of the Brahmins. The Hindus, therefore, are not merely an assortment of castes but they are so many warring groups each living for itself and for its selfish ideal. There is another feature of caste, which is deplorable. The ancestors of the present-day English fought on one side or the other in the war of the Roses and the Cromwellian War. But the descendants of those who fought on the one side do not bear any animosity—-any grudge against the descendants of those who fought on the other side.

The feud is forgotten. But the present-day non-Brahmins cannot forgive the present-day Brahmins for the insult their ancestors gave to Shivaji. The present-day Kayasthas will not forgive the present-day Brahmins for the infamy cast upon their forefathers by the forefathers of the latter. To what is this difference due? Obviously to the Caste System. The existence of Caste and Caste Consciousness has served to keep the memory of past feuds between castes green and has prevented solidarity."

Ambedkar devoted much effort to illustrate this in great detail. This is no surprise. Ambedkar was the chairman of the Drafting Committee of Constituent Assembly that drafted the Indian Constitution, which has lasted up to date with several amendments. He, like other leaders of the independence movement, was aware of the deep division within the Indian society. Nehru, the first Prime Minister of India was very much saddened by this historic reality. In the famous book-The Discovery of India-which he wrote from prison, where he was confined to by the British Raj, there are several references to this tragic historic reality. Mahatma Gandhi was deeply aware of the problem and knew that future of India would very much depend on this issue.

In fact all the great thinkers, poets and writers of India have said something or other strongly on the issue. However, it fell on Ambedkar, the beloved leader of the Untouchables, who also belonged to this group, to analyse this problem in its full details and suggest a path to its solution. Ambedkar's writings have now been brought out in fourteen thick volumes. All his writings directly or indirectly refer to the issue of caste and the nation.

Ambedkar demonstrated how the absence of solidarity led to the weakening of a people, making them indifferent and fear-ridden; as a result cooperation becomes impossible.

> "*Indifferentism is the worst kind of disease that can infect a people. Why is the Hindu so indifferent? In my opinion this indifferentism is the result of Caste System which has made Sanghatan and cooperation even for a good cause impossible*"

The notional foundation of Sanghatan and cooperation is at the heart of Ambedkar's views on the concept of the nation. He, as an eminent jurist, realised that this foundation cannot merely be a juridical one. The juridical conception of the nation are based on the theory of sovereignty which based on the classical legal theory of contract. However, Sanghatan and cooperation are social realities, not merely legal or political ones. Their existence or not is a ground reality.

Thus the notions of Sanghatan and cooperation have to be derived from the ground reality of a given society at a given time. India as a legal entity, a colony under British Raj for most his lifetime and later an independent sovereignty with a constitutional framework, in the formulation of which he participated, was one thing. The ground reality of India as a society was quite another.

A democratic constitution however liberal, could not create this ground reality. The ground reality was primarily a social issue and not a political or a juridical issue. Here, the notions must be derived from the ground reality and if different sets of notions were to be introduced it had to be done by a change in the ground reality, which would involves everyone in society. What then was at issue was not the contract, but consensus. The consensus is not an abstraction; it is a social reality.

In fact Ambedkar's thought can be divided into two parts. Why he thought there was a fundamental impediment-caste-which prevented Indian people from reaching a consensus regarding any important aspect of their social life, and the solutions he proposed to get rid of this great impediment.

THE CONCEPT OF POWER INVOLVED IN THIS DISCOURSE

The concept of power that Ambedkar had to discuss in dealing with the above mentioned two issues were not juridical notions of sovereignty and of the sovereign individual who passed his power to the state, but the issue of social power as actually found in the existing Indian society. He clearly saw the illusion of political power, when divorced from the social bases of power, when such great leaders such as Gandhi and Nehru were unable to achieve any of the fundamental ambitions they had set out to achieve, on the use of Indian independence for altering the nature of Indian society.

Ambedkar engaged in many debates with both the Socialists and people who held right wing views, as well as those who held the view that economic development was the solution to the social division of castes.

> *"One may contend that economic motive is not the only motive by which man is actuated. That economic power is the only kind of power no student of human society can accept. That the social status of an individual by itself often becomes a source of power and authority is made clear by the sway, which the Mahatmas have held over the common man. Why do a millionaire in India obey penniless Sadhus and Fakirs? Why do millions of paupers in India sell their trifling thickets, which constitute their only wealth and go to Benares and Mecca? That, religion is the source of power is illustrated by the history of India where the priest holds a sway over the common man often greater than the magistrate and where everything, even such things as strikes and elections, so easily take a religious turn and can so easily be given a religious twist. Take the case of the Plebeian of Rome as a further illustration of the power of religion over man. It throws great light on this point. The Plebs had fought for a share in the supreme executive under the Roman Republic and had secured the appointment of a Plebeian Consul elected by a separate electorate constituted by the Commitia Centuriata, which was an assembly of Plebeian. They wanted a Consul of their own because they felt that the Patrician Consuls used to discriminate against the Plebeian in carrying on the administration. They had apparently obtained a great gain because under the Republican Constitution of Rome one Consul had the power of vetoing an act of the other Consul. But did they in fact gain anything? The answer to this question must be in the negative. The Plebeian never could get a Plebeian Consul who could be said to be a strong man and who could act*

independently of the Patrician Consul. In the ordinary course of things the Plebeian should have got a strong Plebeian Consul in view of the fact that his election was to be by a separate electorate of Plebeian. The question is why did they fail in getting a strong Plebeian to officiate as their Consul? The answer to this question reveals the dominion which religion exercises over the minds of men. It was an accepted creed of the whole Roman populous that no official could enter upon the duties of big office unless the Oracle of Delphi declared that he was acceptable to the Goddess. The priests who were in-charge of the temple of the Goddess of Delphi were all Patricians. Whenever therefore the Plebeian elected a Consul who was known to be a strong party man opposed to the Patricians or 'communal' to use the term that is current in India, the Oracle invariably declared that he was not acceptable to the Goddess. This is how the Plebeian were cheated out of their rights. But what is worthy of note is that the Plebeian permitted themselves to be thus cheated because they too like the Patricians, held firmly the belief that the approval of the Goddess was a condition precedent to the taking charge by an official of his duties and that election by the people was not enough. If the Plebeian had contended that election was enough and that the approval by the Goddess was not necessary they would have derived the fullest benefit from the political right which they had obtained. But they did not. They agreed to elect another, less suitable to themselves but more suitable to the Goddess which in fact meant more amenable to the Patricians. Rather than give up religion, the Plebeian give up material gain for which they had fought so hard. Does this not show that religion can be a source of power as great as money if not greater?" He goes on to say.

"Religion, social status and property are all sources of power and authority, which one man has, to control the liberty of another. One is predominant at one stage, the other is predominant at another stage. That is the only difference. If liberty is the ideal, if liberty means the destruction of the

dominion which one man holds over another then obviously it cannot be insisted upon that economic reform must be the one kind of reform worthy of pursuit. If the source of power and dominion is at any given time or in any given society social and religious, then social reform and religious reform must be accepted as the necessary sort of reform.

One can thus attack the doctrine of Economic Interpretation of History adopted by the Socialists of India. But I recognise that economic interpretation of history is not necessary for the validity of the Socialist contention that equalisation of property is the only real reform and that it must precede everything else. However, what I like to ask the Socialists is this: Can you have economic reform without first bringing about a reform of the social order?"

In this aspect of economic interpretation of power, Ambedkar's views expressed in the text published in 1937 and many other texts, which are a very integral to his analysis of caste, bear similar perspectives as the views of Foucault expressed in his lectures in 1971, on Truth and Power.

"What is at stake in all these genealogies is the nature of this power which has surged into view in all its violence, aggression and absurdity in the course of the last forty years, contemporaneously, that is, with the collapse of Fascism and the decline of Stalinism. What, we must ask, is this power-or rather, since that is to give a formulation to the question that invites the kind of theoretical coronation of the whole which I am so keen to avoid-what are these various contrivances of power, whose operations extend to such differing levels and sectors of society and are possessed of such manifold ramifications? What are their mechanisms, their effects and their relations? The issue here can, I believe, be crystallized essentially in the following question: is the analysis of power or of powers to be deduced in one way or another from the economy? Let me make this question and my reasons for posing it somewhat clearer. It is not at all my intention to abstract from what are innumerable and

enormous differences; yet despite, and even because of these differences, I consider there to be a certain point in common between the juridical, and let us call it, liberal, conception of political power (found in the philosopher of the eighteenth century) and the Marxist conception, or at any rate a certain conception currently held to be Marxist. I would call this common point economism in the theory of power. By that I mean that in the case of the classic, juridical theory, power is taken to be a right, which one is able to possess like a commodity, and which one can in consequence transfer or alienate, either wholly or partially, through a legal act or through some act that establishes a right, such as takes place through cession or contract. Power is that concrete power which every individual holds, and whose partial or total cession enables political power or sovereignty to be established. This theoretical construction is essentially based on the idea that the constitution of political power obeys the model of a legal transaction involving a contractual type of exchange (hence the clear analogy that runs through all these theories between power and commodities, power and wealth). In the other case-I am thinking here of the general Marxist conception of power-one finds none of all that. Nonetheless, there is something else inherent in this latter conception, something which one might term an economic functionality of power. This economic functionality is present to the extent that power is conceived primarily in terms of the role it plays in the maintenance simultaneously of the relations of production and of class domination which the development and specific forms of the forces of production have rendered possible. On this view, then, the historical raison d'etre of political power is to be found in the economy. Broadly speaking, in the first case we have a political power whose formal model is discoverable in the process of exchange, the economic circulation of commodities; in the second case, the historical raison d'etre of political power and the principle of its concrete forms and actual functioning, is located in the economy. Well then, the problem involved in the researches to which I refer can, I believe, be broken down in the following manner: in the first place, is power always in a subordinate position relative to the economy? Is it always in the service of, and ultimately answerable to, the economy? Is its essential end and purpose to serve the economy? Is it destined to realize, consolidate, maintain and reproduce the relations appropriate to the economy and essential to its functioning? In the second place, is power modelled upon the commodity? Is it something that one possesses, acquires, cedes through force or contract, that one alienates or recovers, that circulates, that voids this or that region? Or, on the contrary, do we need to employ varying tools in its analysis-even, that is, when we allow that it effectively remains the case that the relations of power do indeed remain profoundly enmeshed in and with economic relations and participate with them in a common circuit? If that is the case, it is not the models of functional subordination or formal isomorphism that will characterize the interconnection between politics and the economy. Their indissolubility will be of a different order, one that it will be our task to determine."

In fact the whole study of caste by Ambedkar, which takes many volumes to fully study, falls under what Foucault describes as genealogy. Forced by the need to explain the theory and practice of caste, which could not be explained in terms of the usual economic and social theories, Ambedkar was forced to explain them in other ways. The learned jurist who had obtained many degrees from several western universities, was not able to rely on any of the theories he learned to explain the Indian caste system. What he wrote might fall under what Foucault later called subjugated knowledge.

"On the other hand, I believe that by subjugated knowledge one should understand something else, something which in a sense is altogether different, namely, a whole set of knowledge that have been as inadequate to their task or

insufficiently elaborated: naive knowledge, located low down on the hierarchy, beneath the required level of cognition or scientificity. I also believe that it is through the re-emergence of these low-ranking knowledge, these unqualified, even directly disqualified knowledge (such as that of the psychiatric patient, of the ill person, of the nurse, of the doctor-parallel and marginal as they are to the knowledge of medicine-that of the delinquent etc.), and which involve what I would call a popular knowledge (le saviour des gens) though it is far from being a general commonsense knowledge, but is on the contrary a particular, local, regional knowledge, a differential knowledge incapable of unanimity and which owes its force only to the harshness with which it is opposed by everything-surrounding it-that it is through the reappearance of this knowledge, of these local popular knowledge, these disqualified knowledge, that criticism performs its work."

He further goes on to say, "What emerges out of this is something one might call a genealogy, or rather a multiplicity of genealogical researches, a painstaking rediscovery of struggles together with the rude memory of their conflicts. And these genealogies, that are the combined product of an erudite knowledge and a popular knowledge, were not possible and could not even have been attempted except on one condition, namely that the tyranny of globalising discourses with their hierarchy and all their privileges of a theoretical avant-garde was eliminated.

Let us give the term genealogy to the union of erudite knowledge and local memories, which allows us to establish a historical knowledge of struggles and to make use of this knowledge tactically today. This then will be a provisional definition of the genealogies which I have attempted to compile with you over the last few years."

In fact, the work of both Ambedkar and Grundtvig, are works that of genealogies, though they did not think of their work in that way. It is important to note this aspect when considering the contributions made to education within the context of discourse on power. Grundtvig beautifully combines erudite knowledge with folk memories. Folk School was a meeting place where erudite knowledge and folk thinking were to mix and merge, where academic and popular forms of thinking were to be fused. That was the living dialogue, and the genuine enlightenment.

GANDHI: PATRON SAINT OF THE INDUSTRIALIST

During the years of the Indian independence movement, a leading Indian industrialist, G. D. Birla, was Mahatma Gandhi's most generous financial supporter. While Birla has been described as a devotee of Gandhi, the relationship between the two men was more one of collaboration than of one-sided devotion. Gandhi's campaigns were made possible by drawing from Birla's vast financial resources while Birla benefited not only from the social and religious prestige which his association with Gandhi brought him, but his economic role and position as a wealthy capitalist was strengthened and glorified. Gandhi gave his blessing to the abundant wealth of Birla with his teaching on trusteeship, a concept which asserted the right of the rich to accumulate and maintain wealth, as long as the wealth was used to benefit society. Gandhi apparently borrowed the concept of trusteeship from the writings of the American millionaire, Andrew Carnegie, who had used trusteeship to promote capitalism over socialism.

The close relationship between Gandhi and G. D. Birla did not escape scrutiny. B. R. Ambedkar, a leader of the untouchable castes, accused Gandhi of pretending to support the cause of the oppressed while actually supporting the forces of social conservatism. Lord Linlithgow, the Viceroy of India, questioned the Gandhi-Birla connection. Linlithgow, who had blamed Gandhi for the sabotage and violence of the Quit India Movement of 1942, had suspicions that Birla, as representing big business, was actually the hidden hand behind the violence. Investigations by the governments of both colonial and independent India into Birla's economic and political association with Gandhi and the Congress failed to bring criminal indictment. Nevertheless, the relationship between the two men had consequences for the future of India and deserves attention. Gandhi and Birla, both strong defenders of social conservatism, shared objectives that were not brought out openly. In the shadow of Gandhi's public persona and popular teachings, Gandhi and Birla were able to weave conservative policies into the social, political, and economic fabric of independent India.

Ghanshyam Das Birla (1894-1983) was from a Marwari merchant family of Pilani in Rajasthan. His grandfather, Seth Shivanarain Birla, set out for Bombay on a camel in 1862. In Bombay, Shivanarain began trading in seeds and bullion. His only son, Baldeodas, joined him in the business at age thirteen in 1875. The Birla's trading business thrived and the family established an export-import business in Calcutta. In Bombay the family moved into trading in cotton, wheat, rape-seed and silver. G. D. began his apprenticeship in the family business at age thirteen. G. D. was sixteen when he started his own brokerage. G. D. 's business took him into contact with the British. He was offended by their racial arrogance. Birla wrote, "I was not allowed to use the lift to go up to their offices nor their benches while waiting to see them. I smarted under these insults and this created in me a political interest."

When G. D. was in his early twenties he found himself a wealthy man. World War I had produced great profits in his trading business. He was also a wanted man. G. D., in his frustration with the British had become involved with the Bara Bazaar Youth League, a group that engaged in terrorist activities against the British. Birla denies participating in terrorism, but in 1916 he was accused of stealing a shipment of armaments. He went into hiding for several months until friends could have the charges dropped against him.

Birla, restored to his business, decided to steer clear of terrorism. He would meet the British on the playing fields of business. There were British businessmen though who did not want him to play. When the Birlas attempted to open a jute factory in Calcutta, a British competitor started buying up all the land adjacent to the plot on which the Birlas were to build their factory, forcing the Birlas to move elsewhere. The Birlas were not deterred. G. D. and his brothers prospered in the jute business, as well as in their other enterprises. At the beginning of World War II, the Birlas were worth $3. 3 million. By the end of the war, they had holdings of $20 million. Before independence in 1947 the Birlas had 20 companies. Today they own 175 businesses and are prominent in textiles, sugar, jute, automobiles, bicycles, boilers, calcium carbides, industrial alcohol, linoleum, woollens, flax, ghee, margarine, and also starch, confectionery, banking, and insurance. The Birlas owned several newspapers including the Hindustan Times and a large interest in radio. In the summer of 1993, the Birla fortune was $1. 5 billion. G. D. Birla's political activities were a factor in the success of the Birla empire.

G. D. Birla's association with Mahatma Gandhi began in 1915. Gandhi had just returned to India from South Africa as a hero for championing the rights of Indian workers. In Calcutta, where Gandhi was to make a speech, Birla arranged a grand reception for him. Birla related his first impressions of Gandhi:

> At this first meeting he appeared rather queer.... I was rather puzzled about him when I first saw him, and then gradually I came to know him.... He gave us a new conception of politics. We felt him a saint as well as a politician.... That meeting was thirty-two years ago, and since then I have been associated with him and have been giving him such service as I can.

The service that Birla provided amounted to supplying practically every financial need Gandhi brought to him. Gandhi had other sources of income, including the assistance of the industrialist Jamnalal Bajaj, as well as the accumulated donations from multitudes of poor supporters, but Birla was the major financier. Birla's brothers also contributed to Gandhi, but sometimes G.D.'s gifting was seen by them as an extravagance. Birla rarely refused any financial request on Gandhi's part and Gandhi's requests were numerous. The following request from Gandhi was not atypical:

> My thirst for money is simply unquenchable. I need at least Rs. 2, 00, 000—for khadi, untouchability and education. The dairy work makes another Rs. 50, 000. Then there is the Ashram expenditure. No work remains unfinished for want of funds, but God gives after severe trials. This also satisfies me. You can give as you like for whatever work you have faith in.

With Birla's beneficence Gandhi was able carry on his massive political campaigns, as well as to maintain a semblance of poverty and simplicity in lifestyle, while enjoying almost limitless financial resources.

While Gandhi appeared to share the living standards of the typical Indian villager in his Ashram, the annual expenditure of his Ashram was 100, 000 rupees, a considerable sum in pre-Independence rupees. In a similar vein, Gandhi was known for his humility in insisting on travelling by third-class trains. To get a seat in a crowded third-class car was difficult, so when Gandhi and his entourage travelled, the entire third-class car, cars, and sometimes even the whole train was paid for to ensure Gandhi's comfort. When Gandhi attempted to make a symbolic action by temporarily moving into an untouchable colony in Delhi, half the residents were moved out before his visit and the shacks of the residents torn down and neat little huts constructed in their place. The entrances and windows of the huts were screened with matting, and during the length of Gandhi's visit, were kept sprinkled with water to provide a cooling effect. The local temple was white-washed and new brick paths were laid. In an interview with Margaret Bourke-White, a photo-journalist for Life magazine, one of the men in charge of Gandhi's visit, Dinanath Tiang of the Birla Company, explained the improvements in the untouchable colony, "We have cared for Gandhiji's comfort for the last twenty years."

Gandhi put forward the illusory image of poverty and simplicity while he was actually living very comfortably. We can only speculate whether this image-making was political posturing on Gandhi's part or whether the amenities were forced on him by the practicalities of operating a massive movement. When Gandhi was questioned by the journalist Louis Fischer about the percentage of his budget which was funded by the rich, Gandhi told him practically all of it was, adding, "In this Ashram, for instance, we could live much more poorly than we do and spend less money. But we do not and the money comes from our rich friends." Gandhi was not oblivious to the expense laid out for him.

We can also only speculate on whether certain statements Gandhi made were representative of his opinions or whether they, too, could have been political tactics. Gandhi was well known for espousing seemingly contradictory positions. As a result it is a difficult task to decide what Gandhi's true positions were. For example, Birla criticized Gandhi for his public support of the Swaraj party. Birla did not care for the party due to its violent propensities. Gandhi responded:

I shall talk to you about the Swaraj party when we meet. I do not want you to change your view because by justifying your views I seek to justify my position as well.

Apparently Gandhi had reasons for publicly seeming to support a party which he admitted in private he was against. Similarly, Gandhi voiced radical views against capitalism and industrialism in his public speeches and writing:

Industrialism is, I am afraid, going to be a curse for mankind.... Industrialism depends entirely on your capacity to exploit.

To change to industrialism is to court disaster... The one great change to make is to discard foreign cloth, and reinstate the ancient cottage industry of hand spinning. We must thus restore our ancient and healthgiving industry if we would resist industrialism. I do not fight shy of capitalism. I fight capitalism... I do picture a time when the rich will spurn to enrich themselves at the expense of the poor.

These radical positions do not seem to correspond to other elements in Gandhi's life and thought, especially his close relationship with the industrialists. Margaret Bourke-White, having read Gandhi's seemingly revolutionary writings, was very puzzled to learn that for a quarter of a century Gandhi had spent much of his time living in G. D. Birla's palatial mansion in Delhi, where he was later assassinated.

Margaret Bourke-White's investigations into working conditions at one of Birla's mills in Delhi revealed a equally puzzling attitude on Gandhi's part to Birla's labour practices. Bourke-White was present when Gandhi was fasting in December 1947. During his fast, all the trade-unions sent delegations with peace pledges and pleas for Gandhi to end the fast. One trade-union, the largest union in India, did not send delegates. The textile workers union, whose chief employer was Birla, was noticeably absent. On December 8, shortly before Gandhi was to begin his fast, workers at Birla's textile mill in Delhi went to the manager asking for a cost of living bonus to meet rising prices. When their requests were answered with gunfire and rifle butts, the workers sent a delegation of five workers to see Gandhi at the Birla House. According to Bourke-White, Gandhi refused to see them. On an earlier occasion, the workers at Birla's Delhi mill wrote to Gandhi directly to complain of bad working conditions. Instead of answering the letter or questioning Birla about the matter, Gandhi forwarded the letter to Birla. Birla responded by telling Gandhi that the workers were lying. Margaret Bourke-White visited Birla's mills and found conditions to be appalling. The squalid living quarters Birla provided for his workers were no better than those at mills belonging to owners who were not devotees to Gandhi. She wondered why Gandhi never visited the mills, as it would have been easy for him to do so. In none of the voluminous correspondence between Birla and Gandhi is Gandhi critical of the working conditions in Birla's mills.

Birla once defensively wrote Gandhi, not in response to rebuke from Gandhi, but to reports that conditions were bad in his mills. Birla tells Gandhi that he is improving conditions in one factory and hopes to do so in others. He blames any atrocities at his mills on the mill managers, claiming he cannot control them. While it would seem natural for the Mahatma to take an interest in Birla's workers, Gandhi refrained from criticizing or questioning Birla personally. In other cases, Gandhi did not shy away from public criticism of companions who did not abide by his views. He frequently complained about his longtime friend Pandit Madan Mohan Malaviya. Gandhi had called for a boycott of all British education. Malaviya, the founder of Banaras Hindu University, refused to comply. In one of many attacks against Malaviya's position, Gandhi accused him of the greatest Adharma (unrighteousness).

> I do not want to go into why this Empire in Satanic. But an Empire which has been guilty of the atrocities in the Punjab, which killed children six or seven years old... to study in the schools of such an Empire is, to my mind, the greatest adharma of all. To Panditji, an elder brother to me, this seems to be Dharma.

Though Gandhi continued to say he respected Malaviya, in reality there was a break in their friendship. In Gandhi's thirty-two year friendship with Birla, he never publicly criticized Birla's actions. Gandhi at times would make suggestions to Birla, but if Birla failed to follow them, Gandhi did not complain. Gandhi did not have the upper hand in the relationship. He considered Birla one of his mentors and would act on his advice. In Gandhi's letters to Birla he does not lecture him, except with regard to dietary matters. Their correspondence is remarkably free from spiritual concerns, quite unlike the writing which Gandhi puts forward to the public. In Birla's collection of his correspondence with Gandhi, one letter by Gandhi stands out in addressing spiritual matters. Birla writes that he cannot remember the context or for whom the letter was meant. Though the letters between Gandhi and Birla are very amicable, the subject matter concerns mostly mundane affairs of finances and strategy.

When Gandhi disagreed with Birla, he found a way of avoiding argument. In one instance, Gandhi publicly complained that people were buying mill-produced khadi under the mistaken impression that it was homespun. Birla understood this as an indirect criticism of his textile industry, which was producing milled khadi, and gave quick retort to Gandhi's complaint:

Do you not think that you are unnecessarily exaggerating the results of the khadi propaganda?... You could find this out yourself if you send hawkers with mill-made as well as shuddha khadi who may ask some villagers to select their choice after explaining the latter properly about the quality as well as the price of the cloth, I have not the least doubt that if you made the experiment you will find that 90% of the consumers will pick up the cheaper and more lasting of the two stuffs. Mill khadi is popular because people find it cheap, durable besides it being Swadeshi make.

Gandhi answered a week later: "I got both your letters. But even today there is not time for reply." Gandhi never allowed the khadi issue to become an object of contention between himself and Birla. Instead he found a place for mills in the khadi movement. Later Gandhi wrote to Birla:

I am convinced that the boycott will be successful only through khadi. This does not mean that the mills have no place in the scheme at all. The mills can have their deserved place by recognizing the worth of khadi. The conception of God envelopes all Gods.

Gandhi was clearly making concessions to Birla in incorporating textile mills into his homespun khadi movement. Gandhi was as much interested in pleasing his patron as Birla was in pleasing his saint.

A useful model for examining the give and take of the Gandhi-Birla relationship is that of the patron and publicist as presented by the historian C. A. Bayly. Bayly examines the relationship between wealthy patrons and leaders of reform movements such as the Hindi movement and the cow-protection movement in the late 1880s. Bayly uses for example the patronage of Madan Mohan Malaviya, a leader of the Hindu revivalist movement, the Hindu Mahasabha, by the wealthy magnate Ram Charan Das. Bayly holds that the goal of the patron-publicist relationship was not exclusively concerned with protection of the patron's financial interests:

> Two forms of relationship can be seen between patron and publicist, as also between various levels of political activity. One was the relationship between patron and publicist designed to protect material interests, or to promote them within new political arenas—the vakil relationship. The other concerned the protection or enhancement of particular conceptions of status conceived within the bounds of revived Hinduism—the Dharmik relationship. It is difficult to separate them.

Desire for enhanced religious standing in the community, which affected all avenues of social interactions, from marriage arrangements to business deals, was an important element of the patron-publicist relationship. Religious patronage was a means to enhance social and economic status in the community. Avenues of religious patronage went beyond the traditional practices of temple construction and maintenance, feeding of Brahmans, sponsoring of festivals, etc. With the advent of religious reform movements in the 1800's, sponsoring such causes as the Hindi movement or the cow-protection movement became a religious and status-enhancing act. Elements of some of the earlier religious reform movements, such as the use of the vernacular and revived cultural identity, as well as the political undertones and organizational capabilities of the movements, later played a role in the growth of nationalism. These causes were sponsored by the wealthy, whose economic and social standing profited therefrom. Later, the relationships of patrons and publicists became an important element of Congress.

Aspects of the Birla-Gandhi relationship can be described by Bayly's model. Birla's fame and social standing did not rest on his raw wealth alone. Birla did not neglect to develop his reputation for generous religious patronage. He is well known for his religious gifting, particularly in the construction of magnificent temples. Birla admitted that he did not construct the temples from personal piety, "Frankly speaking, we build temples but we don't believe in temples. We build temples to spread a kind of religious mentality." Birla's financial support of the publicist Gandhi, as a form of religious patronage, would serve him well.

The mere association with Gandhi conferred on Birla a measure of Gandhi's religious stature. It is easy to see that Birla's generous patronage of Gandhi could have been perceived as a sign of devotion and Gandhi's acceptance of that patronage as a sign of approval of Birla. Gandhi's role in the independence movement was as much religious as it was political. He was the Mahatma, the Great Soul. Gandhi captured the hearts and imaginations of his fellow Indians by drawing upon a wealth of traditional Hindu symbolism. The political entity that Gandhi called for would be a Ramarajya, a kingdom likened unto that of the righteous Lord Rama.

The British, Gandhi often said, were the equivalent of the evil demon Ravana, who Lord Rama and his entourage defeated. Gandhi, not only discarded his Western garb and lifestyle to appear to identify with the Indian masses, but also to take upon himself the attitude of the Brahmacari, the holy renunciant. He renounced material possessions, sexual relations, and held to a strict vegetarian diet as part of his regime of holiness. At the same time he was the guiding inspiration to a massive political movement. According to Bayly's model, Gandhi would be the exemplar publicist.

As Birla's publicist, Gandhi was able to deftly weave Birla's interests into a seemingly spiritual context. A blatant example of this is found in Gandhi's support for Birla's position against government regulation of prices. On several occasions Gandhi brought up the need for decontrol in his sermons during his evening prayer meetings. Gandhi also allowed the issue of decontrol to be promoted in his newspaper Harijan, a publication that was supposedly devoted to the needs of the oppressed. As part of the campaign for decontrol, Gandhi's son, Devadas, as managing editor of the Hindustan Times, Birla's chief New Delhi newspaper, also published an editorial calling for decontrols. When Margaret Bourke-White questioned Birla about decontrols, he responded: "I never was in favour of controls. I am not built that way.

The greatest virtue of capitalism is free competition." He went on to add that since the recent decontrol of sugar prices, the price of sugar had gone down. Gandhi followed this line of argument in his prayer meetings. Bourke-White's investigation of decontrol found that it was true that the price of sugar went down for the for the wealthy, who could buy on the black market. As for the man on the street, the price of sugar had doubled. Though in theory prices could go down for poor consumers with decontrol, in this case, it was the wealthy consumers and industrial producers who prospered.

Gandhi did not have anything against wealth. He was not inclined towards socialism and taught that there should be no forced redistribution of wealth in India. Gandhi called for social justice and alleviation of suffering, but believed that change brought about by government intervention would be ineffective. Change must first come in the individual heart. The wealthy should not be coerced into sharing their wealth; they should do it voluntarily.

Gandhi taught that the wealthy should be trustees of their wealth, using only what was necessary for their own use and distributing their surplus for the benefit of society. Gandhi's idea is very much like the ideas of trusteeship that were being expounded in England and America in the late 1800s and early 1900s. Andrew Carnegie, a self-made American millionaire, had published a series of articles between 1886 and 1899 that sought to justify private wealth in the industrial society increasingly burdened with social concern and unrest.

Although some conservative Christian spokesmen had condemned corporate oppression, financial dishonesty, and growing poverty, many American and British religious leaders supporting the capitalistic economic system saw these social realities as prices that must be paid for progress. Carnegie in his essays set "in authoritative form the ideas that many Christian authors and most of the church press had been preaching for at least a generation." In England the articles were reprinted and commented upon in the Fortnightly Review, Nineteenth Century, Saturday Review, and Pall Mall Gazette. The articles received much attention, including a review and praise by the British Prime Minister, William E. Gladstone. Carnegie believed that the articles were better-received in England, because England was "more clearly face to face with socialist questions." Carnegie's articles offered an alternative to socialism. He stressed individual effort and responsibility instead of government control. He urged the wealthy to adopt the principle of trusteeship:

This then, is held to be the duty of the man of wealth: To set an example of modest, unostentatious living, shunning display or extravagance; to provide moderately for the legitimate wants of those dependent upon him; and, after doing so, to consider all surplus revenues which come to him simply as trust funds, which he is called upon to administer... the man of wealth thus becoming the mere trustee and agent for his poorer brethren, bringing to their service his superior wisdom, experience, and ability to administer, doing for them better than what they would or could do for themselves.

Gandhi was a student in England from 1888 to 1891, at the time some of Carnegie's articles were published. As the articles were a subject of some controversy at the time they were published and afterwards, it is possible that Gandhi was exposed to these ideas that served to promote capitalism over socialism. Gandhi's teachings are remarkably similar to Carnegie's:

The rich man will be left in possession of his wealth, of which he will use what he reasonably requires for his personal needs and will act as a trustee for the remainder to be used for society.

Carnegie made a list of worthy causes on which surplus wealth should be spent which included educational institutions, hospitals, churches, etc. To provide for the required surplus wealth, Carnegie called for unbridled capitalism: He who manages the ships, the mines, the factories, cannot withdraw his capital, for this is the tool with which he works wonders; nor can he restrict his operations, for the cessation of growth and improvement in any industrial undertaking marks the beginning of decay.

Birla's lifestyle and actions could almost be used to illustrate Carnegie's ideas. Birla was known for his unostentatious living and philanthropy. Rajendra Prasad, the first President of India, in the foreword to G. D. Birla's book In the Shadow of the Mahatma, puts forward Gandhi's version of trusteeship and points to G. D. Birla as being a worthy trustee. The beneficiaries of Birla's patronage curiously match Carnegie's list of the institutions deserving of surplus wealth:

It has been one of Gandhiji's teachings that those who are blessed with wealth should regard themselves as Trustees and treat their wealth as trust property for the benefit of others. The large number of institutions which are to be seen in so many parts of the country in the shape of educational institutions or religious temples and Dharmshalas or Hospitals with their apex at Pilani and Delhi are testimony to the fact that Birlas have imbibed this part of Gandhiji's teachings in no small manner. They have earned abundantly and likewise spent also generously and abundantly on every good cause.

All this, whatsoever moves on the earth, is to be hidden in the Lord (the Self). When thouhast surrended all this, then thou mayest enjoy. Do not covet the wealth of others.

Perhaps by making such a claim Gandhi hoped to give credence to the concept of trusteeship in the eyes of the Indians. Attributing the basis of contemporary ideas or practices to ancient texts, even while the connection is spurious, is not an uncommon means of legitimization. This is not to say that it was impossible for Gandhi's idea of trusteeship to be original or inspired by Hindu tradition. The Manu smirti, for instance, contains a verse in a section on the duties of castes, which encourages the vainya caste to accumulate wealth for the benefit of others:

He (a vaishya) should expend the greatest effort in justly increasing his goods, and he should also take pains to bestow at least food on all creatures.

Theoretically, the verse could be developed into the idea of trusteeship. But Gandhi did not bring forward such an explicit text on which to claim trusteeship was founded. Judging from the popularity of Carnegie's writings and the simultaneity of Gandhi's stay in England with the publication of Carnegie's "Gospel of Wealth," it is highly probable that Gandhi borrowed from Carnegie's ideas on trusteeship.

Gandhi's first application of trusteeship was with regard to Britain's trusteeship of the colonies well before Gandhi called for independence. While Gandhi changed his mind about the ability of the British to be beneficent trustees, he did not change his mind about the trusteeship of capitalists in India.

Gandhi's support for capitalists is expressed in his writing concerning industrial workers. On one hand, Gandhi suggested in Young India that mill owners should provide the following improvements for their workers:

1. The hours of labour must leave the workmen some hours of leisure.
2. They must get facilities for their own education.
3. Provision should be made for an adequate supply of milk, clothing and necessary education for their children.
4. There should be sanitary dwelling for the workmen.
5. They should be in a position to save enough to sustain themselves during their old age.

In the same article Gandhi makes a strong statement of the intellectual superiority of the capitalist over the workers:

> When labour comes fully to realise its strength, I know it can become more tyrannical than capital. The millowners will have to work dictated by labour if the latter could command the intelligence of the former. It is clear, however, that labour will never attain to that intelligence. If it does, labour will cease to be labour and become itself the master. The capitalists do not fight in the strength of money alone. They do possess intelligence and tact.

In another article Gandhi worries that increased wages and reduced work loads will be squandered by the workers:

> It is now time to examine the use we should make of increasing wages and hours saved. It would be like going into the frying pan out of the fire to use the increase in wages in the grog-shop and the hours saved in gambling dens. The money received, it is clear should be devoted to education of our children, and the time saved to our education. In both these matters the millowners can render much assistance.

Gandhi implies that the workers are incompetent to spend their wages properly and that the mill-owners are better able to use the increase in wages to provide milk, reading rooms and harmless amusements and games for the workers. Gandhi counsels the workers that it would be a sin to request higher wages and less hours if they were unable to controls their passions. Higher wages and reduced hours, according to Gandhi, required clean minds and hearts. Gandhi does not grace the capitalists with a lecture to the effect that increased profits require a clean heart. According to Gandhi's version of trusteeship, the capitalists had a right to their profits owing to their superior abilities. They were to make decisions that would benefit their less able workers.

Birla, while prospering from his textile mills and making use of Gandhi to promote his own industrial interests, daily wore khadi and occasionally worked at the spinning wheel. At Gandhi's suggestion he had been active in the Harijan upliftment movement. Though Gandhi and Birla are supposed to be strong supporters of the untouchables there is a noticeable lack of emotion or enthusiasm about the issue in their letters. The Harijans are spoken of as a cause, perhaps one that they would not want pushed too far. Gandhi did not want to abolish the caste system that had assigned the Harijans to their degraded position. B. R. Ambedkar, an untouchable leader, was strongly critical of Gandhi's motives and policies regarding untouchable castes, including the euphemistic designation of untouchables as Harijans. Ambedkar was also critical of Gandhi's connection with businessmen:

> *If the Bania is financing the Congress it is because he realized and Mr. Gandhi has taught him—that money invested in politics gives large dividends.*

Gandhi's call for Harijan upliftment, like Gandhi's ideas on abolition of capitalism and industry would be revolutionary if put into actual practice. But Gandhi's lofty teachings were otherworldly and seemingly unattainable, perhaps purposely so. That most people would not follow them literally was understood, even by Gandhi. Birla once wrote of the exaggerated expectations Gandhi had aroused in the untouchable castes:

> *Especially among the educated Harijans, hopes have been encouraged which could under no circumstances be fulfilled. Many educated Harijans seem to be under the impression that the society of ours is going to create a millennium.*

Ambedkar accused Gandhi of exploiting social problems, such as the plight of the untouchables, for political gain, while actually preventing social change. Ambedkar pointed out for example that Gandhi had publicly supported a bill for temple-entry for Harijans, but when election time came, he, along with Congress withdrew support for the bill.

Birla realized that behind all the revolutionary rhetoric, Gandhi was socially conservative. Gandhi might make public statements against industrialism, but he was no threat to Birla's industrial interests; he was a boon. Birla, as Gandhi's patron, basked in the aura of Gandhi's popularity, while Gandhi went about securing Birla's interests. Among Birla's chief concerns was Indian independence.

There had been times that Birla had profited from his relations with the British, and for some time had served as a go-between for Gandhi and British officials. But developments in British economic policies in India in 1937 had not been favourable to Birla and other industrialists:

> *The (British) refusal to change the rupee ratio, the willingness to sacrifice large-scale Indian interests in Burma, new encroachments of foreign capital in some profitable fields, austerity budgets and... open hostility to India's industrialization and to planning combined to produce a marked shift in the traditionally cautious line pursued by big business towards the government.*

Resentment on the part of industry grew against the government and led to closer ties with Congress. B. R. Tomlinson, a historian, credits a group of industrialists, which included G. D. Birla, Sir Purshottamdas Thakurdas, and J. R. D. Tata, with presenting in 1944 the most complete survey of India's postwar economic requirements, as well as detailed planning to achieve them.

Tomlinson writes that the industrialists began to regard Congress, rather than the British, "as the body best able and most willing to secure for them a place in the domestic economy and polity they desired." From 1944 onwards, business interests openly supported Congress. It was clear that big business, including Birla, would stand to profit by independence.

There was a major obstacle remaining in Birla's path. Jawaharlal Nehru, as president of the Congress in 1936, put forward two proposals. The first was to establish a joint anti-imperialist front. He was willing to yoke himself to any sympathetic party for this cause, including Madan Mohan Malaviya, whom Nehru had criticized for the communal politics of his Nationalist Party. Nehru's other proposal was the affiliation of trade and peasant unions to the Congress. Nehru in his presidential speech at the Lucknow Congress presented his plea for radical changes in the status quo of India:

> *I see no way of ending the poverty, the vast unemployment, the degradation and the subjection of the Indian people except through socialism. That involves vast and revolutionary changes in our political and social structure, the ending of vested interests in land and industry, as well as the feudal and autocratic Indian States system. That means the ending of private property, except in a restricted sense, and the replacement of the present profit system by a higher ideal of cooperative service.*

The outcome of the Lucknow Congress was that Nehru's idea of yoking the Congress to the unions was gently pushed aside to a committee who was to consider the matter. Satyamurti, a Congressman from Madras, announced that it was the triumph of Gandhi over socialism.

Birla had earlier tried to bring Nehru into his camp. When Nehru was having severe financial difficulties, Birla had offered him a handsome monthly allowance, such as the Birla family was providing Gandhi and other Congress leaders. Nehru was angry with the offer and refused it. Now Birla expressed his pleasure with Gandhi's victory over Nehru:

> *Mahatmaji kept his promise and without his uttering a word, he saw that no new commitments were made. Jawaharlalji's speech in a way was thrown into the waste paper basket because all the resolutions that were passed were against the spirit of his speech.*

A disappointed, but undeterred Nehru went on tour to promote his proposals. In Bombay, he was met with hostility by businessmen. On 20 May 1936, The Times of India published a response to Nehru's speech signed by twenty-one Bombay businessmen:

> *We are convinced that there is a grave risk of the masses of the country being misled by such doctrines into believing*

> *that all that is required for the improvement of their well-being is a total destruction of the existing social and economic structure. The inculcation of any such ideas into the mind of unthinking millions of this country would lead to a situation in which not only the institution of private property but the peaceful observance of religion, and even personal safety, are likely to be jeopardized. The business communities and the propertied classes of this country played not a small part in the furtherance of the national movement for the achievement of political freedom and have supported all practical measures for the amelioration of the lot of the toiling masses of this country.*

Birla himself avoided a public confrontation with Nehru. In a letter to one of the signers of the Bombay businessmen's manifesto, he criticized the open display of hostility towards Nehru's policies:

> *You have rendered no service to your caste men. It is curious how we businessmen are so short-sighted.... It looks very crude for a man with property to say that he is opposed to expropriation in the wider interest of the country.*

Birla's preferred method was to quietly strengthen the opposition to Nehru by bolstering the non-revolutionary, right-wing elements in the anti-British camp. He left it to Vallabhbhai Patel, Rajendra Prasad, Rajagopalachari, and Gandhi to criticize Nehru for taking it on himself to try to push forward his minority viewpoint against propertied interests to the forefront of Congress policies.

Gandhi's friendship with Birla endured until Gandhi's assassination at the Birla mansion in Delhi in January 1948. Gandhi has come to be remembered as a saint and leader of the Indian nationalist movement. He is not remembered as a supporter of capitalism and social conservatism. History's memory of Birla is somewhat fainter. After all, an industrialist is an industrialist. It is noted to his credit that he was also a devotee of Gandhi. This recollection distorts what transpired between Gandhi and Birla, as well as neglects their mutual influences. The relationship between the two men was too complex to be reduced to simple manipulation on the part of either. Theirs was a friendship involving an interplay of nationalism, social conservatism, the exigencies of business, politics, and patronage, as well as shared membership in mercantile castes, religion, and genuine affection.

The relationship between Gandhi and Birla reveals that Gandhi in many ways supported capitalism and policies that were favourable to the industrialists, particularly in respect to his teachings on trusteeship. It cannot be denied that Gandhi and Birla had a hand in the fact that after independence there was no social revolution and the socialist aspirations of Nehru were discouraged. When one reads a letter from Birla written as early as 1942 calling for the formation of Pakistan, and further mentioning that Gandhi told Birla at that time that he was willing to be converted to the idea, ones wonders if the full extent of Birla's influence is yet to be told.

Birla once defended himself for not being the ideal trustee to Margaret Bourke-White. In response to her questions about the contrast between his industrial policies and Gandhi's ideal of trusteeship, Birla responded, "I am an industrialist and a mill owner. He is a saint." Birla did not claim to be a saint and did not feel he had to live up to Gandhi's ideal of trusteeship. Gandhi as a saint had the luxury of being idealistic. He did not have to implement the ideas which won him mass appeal. Nor did he have to make sure his devotees implemented them. Gandhi's relationship to Birla reveals a less public side of the Mahatma. In G. D. Birla's words, Gandhi's letters to him were not those of "a great man or Mahatma but of a saintly man and the outpourings of a friendly soul." Through their correspondence, we see a Gandhi who is far less the saint of history's imagination and much more a man, subject to biases and ideologies of his social milieu.

5

GANDHI'S NONVIOLENT REVOLUTION

Gandhi's Experiments in South Africa Nonviolent Campaign for Indian Independence Soul Force and Nonviolence.

Gandhi continues what the Buddha began. In the Buddha the spirit of love set itself the task of creating different spiritual conditions in the world; in Gandhi it undertakes to transform all worldly conditions. Albert Schweitzer, Indian Thought and Its Development If man will only realize that it is unmanly to obey laws that are unjust, no man's tyranny will enslave him. Mohandas Gandhi, Hind Swaraj Nonviolence is the law of our species as violence is the law of the brute. The spirit lies dormant in the brute, and he knows no law but that of physical might. The dignity of man requires obedience to a higher law-to the strength of the spirit. Mohandas Gandhi, Young India August 11, 1920 For self-defence, I would restore the spiritual culture. The best and most lasting self-defence is self-purification. Mohandas Gandhi, 1924 Those who say that religion has nothing to do with politics do not know what religion means. Mohandas Gandhi, Autobiography A nonviolent revolution is not a program of seizure of power. It is a program of transformation of relationships ending in a peaceful transfer of power. Mohandas Gandhi, 1942.

Mohandas Karamchand Gandhi was born on October 2, 1869 at Porbandar in western India. His father was prime minister of the very small state, and his mother was a religious

Vaishnavite. At the age of 13 Mohandas was married to a girl his own age and began an active sex life. In his autobiography he admitted that as a boy he secretly ate meat with his friends so that they could become strong like the English. After some local education it was decided that he should go to England to study law. He gained his mother's permission by promising to refrain from wine, women, and meat, but he defied his caste's regulations which forbade travel to England. He joined the Inner Temple law college in London.

In searching for a vegetarian restaurant he discovered its philosophy in Henry Salt's A Plea for Vegetarianism and became convinced. He organized a vegetarian club and met people with theosophical and altruistic interests. He discovered the Bhagavad-Gita in Edwin Arnold's poetic translation, The Song Celestial, and offered his limited knowledge of Sanskrit to others. This Hindu scripture and the Sermon on the Mount later became his bibles and spiritual guidebooks. He memorized the Gita during his daily tooth brushing and often recited its original Sanskrit at his prayer meetings.

GANDHI'S EXPERIMENTS IN SOUTH AFRICA

By the time Gandhi returned to India in 1891, his mother had died. He was not successful at breaking into the legal profession because of his shyness. So he took the opportunity of representing an Indian firm in Natal, South Africa for a year. South Africa, which was notorious for racial discrimination, gave Gandhi the insults which awakened his social conscience. He refused to remove his turban in court; he was thrown out of a first-class railway compartment; he was beaten for refusing to move to the footboard of a stage-coach for the sake of a European passenger; and he was pushed and kicked off a footpath by a policeman.

As a lawyer Gandhi did his best to discover the facts and get the parties to accept arbitration and compromise in order to settle out of court. After solving a difficult case in this way he was elated and commented, "I had learned to find out the better side of human nature and to enter men's hearts. I realized that the true function of a lawyer was to unite parties riven asunder. "He also insisted on receiving the truth from his clients; if he found out that they had lied, he dropped their cases. He believed that the lawyer's duty is to help the court discover the truth, not to try to prove the guilty innocent.

At the end of the year during a farewell party before he was to sail for India, Gandhi noticed in the newspaper that a bill was being proposed that would deprive Indians of the vote. His friends urged him to stay and lead the fight for their rights in South Africa. He founded the Natal Indian Congress in 1894, and their efforts were given considerable notice by the press. While he was visiting India, Gandhi wrote a green pamphlet entitled The Grievances of the British Indians in South Africa. When he returned from fetching his family from India in January 1897, the South Africans tried to stop him from landing by bribing and threatening the ship-owner Dada Abdulla Sheth; but Dada Abdulla was Gandhi's client, and finally after a long quarantine period Gandhi was allowed to disembark. The waiting mob recognized Gandhi, and some whites began to hit his face and body until the Police Superintendent's wife came to his rescue. The mob threatened to Iynch him, but Gandhi escaped in a disguise and remained in protective police custody for a few days. Later he refused to prosecute anyone, holding to the principle of self-restraint in regard to a personal wrong; besides, it had been the community leaders and the Natal government who caused the problem.

Gandhi felt it was his duty to support the British during the Boer War; so he organized and led an Indian Ambulance Corps to nurse the wounded on the battlefield. Even this effort was somewhat delayed by race prejudice; but when three hundred free Indians and eight hundred indentured servants volunteered, the whites were impressed. Gandhi was given a medal for his service in the Boer War. In 1902 he travelled in India, and with Gokhale's support his resolution for the Indians in South Africa was passed by the Indian Congress in Calcutta.

Gandhi served the Indian community in Johannesburg, and during the plague of 1904 he got Indian money sterilized so that they could get nursing services. He was instrumental in publishing Indian Opinion weekly in English, Gujarati, Hindi, and Tamil from the hundred-acre Phoenix Farm community he founded. Attracted to the simple agricultural life, Gandhi was influenced by John Ruskin's Unto This Last, which he translated into Gujarati. He readily agreed with Ruskin's idea that the good of the individual is contained in the good of all; but the value of labour in tilling the soil or in handicrafts was a revelation to Gandhi. He recruited another Indian ambulance unit during the Zulu Rebellion and was made a sergeant major. Gandhi experimented with celibacy during his thirties, and in 1906 he took the Brahmacharya vow for the rest of his life. That year Gandhi led a delegation to London and met with the Secretary of State for India, John Morley, to present the case for Indians' rights in South Africa. Gandhi also met with Winston Churchill, who promised to help.

His first use of civil disobedience on a mass scale began in September 1906 when the Transvaal government wanted to register the entire Indian population and passed what the Indians called the "Black Act." In response they held a mass meeting in the Imperial Theatre of Johannesburg; some were so angry at the humiliating ordinance that they threatened a violent response if put to the test. However, with Gandhi's advice they all decided as a group to refuse to comply with the registration provisions. Gandhi suggested that they take a pledge in the name of God; even though they were Hindus and Muslims, they all believed in one and the same God. Every one of the nearly three thousand Indians present took the solemn pledge. Gandhi decided to call this technique of refusing to submit to injustice satyagraha, which means literally "holding to the truth." One week after the pledge, Asiatic women were excused from having to register.

When the Transvaal government finally put the Asiatic Registration Act into effect in 1907, only 511 out of 13, 000

Indians registered. Gandhi and several other Indians were arrested. He was given two months without hard labour, and he spent the time reading. During his life Gandhi would spend a total of 249 days in South African jails and 2, 089 days in Indian jails. Gandhi declared to his followers that a Satyagrahi must be fearless and always trust his opponent, "for an implicit trust in human nature is the very essence of his creed. "Satyagraha thus by its honest purity appeals to the best in the adversary and exposes the true situation for all to see.

It uncovers concealed motives and reveals the truth.
It puts the best possible interpretation
on the opponent's intentions and thereby
gives him another chance to discard baser impulses.
If he fails to do so,
his victims see more clearly and feel more intensely,
while outsiders realize who is wrong.

On February 3, 1908 General Jan Christiaan Smuts promised Gandhi that he would repeal the Transvaal Asiatic Registration Act if they would accept the compromise and register. Gandhi explained the agreement to a meeting, and a majority agreed to register. However, Gandhi's former client Mir Alam Khan accused him of selling out to General Smuts and swore he would kill any man who gave his fingerprints. A week later Gandhi went to register, and the tall Mir Alam knocked him out. Gandhi was kicked and beat by Mir Alam and his companions until he was rescued by passing Europeans. Gandhi was taken to the home of Baptist minister Joseph Doke, where he gave his fingerprints and recovered from his injuries.

General Smuts then introduced a bill to validate the voluntary certificates but not to repeal the Black Act. So on August 16, 1908 three thousand Indians gathered outside the Hamida Mosque in Johannesburg to hear Gandhi make a speech before they burned about two thousand registration certificates. Mir Alam apologized to Gandhi, and they shook hands. Some Chinese burned their certificates too. Two days later the government started deporting new Asiatic immigrants for not knowing a European language. On October 7 Gandhi was arrested for not having his certificate and for refusing to be fingerprinted. He asked for the maximum punishment and was sentenced to a fine or two months hard labour; he chose the latter.

While reading in jail, Gandhi discovered Thoreau's "Civil Disobedience." He was already familiar with the works of Tolstoy and was "overwhelmed" by The Kingdom of God is Within You as he "began to realize more and more the infinite possibilities of universal love. "Gandhi distinguished satyagraha from "passive resistance," which had been used by religious Non-conformists and suffragettes in England and sometimes inflicted injuries and damage. In Satyagraha in South Africa Gandhi wrote that passive resistance had been used along with the use of arms; but satyagraha is the negation of brute force and avoids any injury to the opponent while being willing to suffer in one's own person. As other examples of satyagraha he gave Jesus Christ, the early Christians, and the Russian Doukhobors cited by Tolstoy.

The protest movement for Indian rights in South Africa continued to grow; at one point out of the 13, 000 Indians in the province 2, 500 were in jail, while 6, 000 had fled Transvaal. In being civil to the opponents during the disobedience, Gandhi developed the use of Ahimsa, which means "non-hurting" and is usually translated "nonviolence." Gandhi followed the precept, "Hate the sin and not the sinner." Since we are all one spiritually, to hurt or attack another person is to attack oneself. Though we may attack an unjust system, we must always love the persons involved. Thus Ahimsa became his method in the search for truth. People said that Gandhi was a saint who was losing himself in politics, but he considered himself a politician trying his hardest to be a saint.

Gandhi was sent to London again in 1909, but he felt that suffering in jail did more good than spending money in England seeing politicians and journalists. After meeting extremists who insisted that India could never win its independence without violence, on his return voyage Gandhi wrote the dialog Hind Swaraj, which means "Indian Self-Rule." Based on the conversations he had in London, in this diatribe against the corruption of Western civilization Gandhi suggested that India could gain its independence by nonviolent means and self-reliance. He rejected brute force and its oppression and declared that soul force or love is what keeps people together in peace and harmony. History ignores the peaceful qualities but notices the interruptions and violations which disrupt civilization. He concluded the dialogue by declaring that his life was henceforth dedicated to attaining Indian self-rule.

Aided by a donation of 1500 pounds and the 1, 100-acre farm bought and built by architect Hermann Kallenbach, Gandhi named this Ashram Tolstoy Farm. He exchanged a few letters with the great Russian novelist before he died and continued to write and edit the journal Indian Opinion in order to elucidate the principles and practice of satyagraha.

Three issues brought the quest for Indian rights in South Africa to a crisis-there was a three-pound annual tax on former indentured servants; Asian immigration was banned; and in March 1913 a law went into effect invalidating all but Christian marriages. When Gandhi explained the new law to his wife Kasturbai, she and others crossing the border into Transvaal in protest were arrested on September 15, 1913. Gandhi could not figure out how to feed the striking miners that gathered around him at Newcastle; so after warning them about the horrors of European-run jails, at the end of October he led them from Natal into Transvaal so that they could be "safely deposited in jail." He was followed by 2, 037 men, 127 women, and 57 children. After they crossed the border, they were not arrested. Gandhi was arrested and paid bail to return to his army; he was arrested again and released and arrested once more, all within four days. The pilgrims headed toward Tolstoy Farm but were deported back to the Newcastle mines, where they were imprisoned. Gandhi was sentenced to three months' hard labour, but the strikes and demonstrations went on with about 50. 000 indentured labourers on strike and thousands of free Indians in prison.

The Christian missionary Charles F. Andrews donated all his money to the movement. Gandhi and the other leaders were released and announced another march. However, Gandhi refused to take advantage of a railway strike by white employees and called off the march in spite of Smuts' broken pledge in 1908. Gandhi explained, "Forgiveness is the ornament of the brave. "After six months of negotiation the issues were finally resolved by Smuts and Gandhi at the end of June in 1914, and the Indian Relief Act went into effect in July. All marriages regardless of religion were valid; the tax on indentured labourers was cancelled including arrears; and Indians were allowed to move more freely. General Smuts expressed his respect for Gandhi and his gentle but powerful methods, which had made him realize which laws had to be repealed. Gandhi summarized in Indian Opinion the power of the satyagraha method and prophesied how it could transform modern civilization.

It is a force which, if it became universal,
would revolutionize social ideals and do away with despotisms
and the ever-growing militarism
under which the nations of the West are groaning
and are being almost crushed to death,
and which fairly promises to overwhelm
even the nations of the East.

NONVIOLENT CAMPAIGN FOR INDIAN INDEPENDENCE

Meanwhile India was still suffering under British colonial rule. Gandhi arrived in England during the first week of the World War, and again he supported the British by raising and leading an ambulance corps; but he became ill and returned to India in January 1915. The great poet Rabindranath Tagore gave Gandhi the title "Mahatma," meaning "Great Soul," and in May 1915 Gandhi founded the Satyagraha Ashram for his family and co-workers near the textile city of Ahmedabad in Gujarat. When a family of untouchables asked to live in the Ashram, Gandhi admitted them. Orthodox Hindus believed this polluted them. Funds ran out, and Gandhi was ready to live in the untouchable slums if necessary; but an anonymous benefactor donated enough money to last a year. To help change people's attitudes about these unfortunate pariahs, Gandhi renamed them "Harijans" or "Children of God." Later he called his weekly magazine Harijan also.

In a speech at the opening of Benares University on February 6, 1916 Gandhi said he was ashamed to be speaking in English but questioned whether the anarchists' use of assassination and bomb-throwing was honourable. Yet he agreed that Indians must take power into their hands to gain self-government. Actually Gandhi had not planned to say these things but did so after he was interrupted by the opposition of Theosophist Annie Besant.

Gandhi began wearing home-spun khadi in order to encourage self-sufficient village industries and thus help alleviate poverty in India. In April 1917 Gandhi went to Bihar to learn how suffering indigo workers in Champaran were being exploited by exorbitant fees of landlords. He was arrested and ordered to leave; but as he insisted on staying, he was put in jail. However, the officials soon realized that the Mahatma was the only one who could control the crowds. Assistants helped by carefully documenting the grievances of several thousand peasants, and reforms were won again by civil disobedience. The textile workers of Ahmedabad were also economically oppressed.

Gandhi suggested a strike; when the workers were weakening in their resolve, he went on a fast to encourage them to continue the strike. Gandhi explained that he did not fast to coerce the opponent but to strengthen or reform those who loved him. He did not believe in fasting for higher wages, but he fasted so that the workers would accept the system of arbitration to resolve the conflict, which they did.

In the spring of 1918 Gandhi was persuaded by the British to help raise soldiers for a final victory effort in the war. Charlie Andrews criticized Gandhi for recruiting Indians to fight for the British. Gandhi spoke to large audiences but gained hardly any recruits. He was experimenting with a limited raw-food diet and became sick. Even after the war the Rowlatt Act continued the strict laws against sedition. Despite India's cooperation with Britain during the war, they did not receive Dominion Status, and civil liberties were being curtailed.

Guided by a dream or inner experience, Gandhi decided to call for a one-day hartal or general strike on all economic activity. Many signed the satyagraha pledge, and Gandhi suggested making "a continuous and persistent effort to return good for evil. "Before that day in Old Delhi, Gurka troops opened fire on a march and killed five Hindus and four Muslims. On April 6, 1919 all Indians stopped working. Gandhi spoke and said that machine-guns would no longer afflict them. Two days later he was arrested trying to go to Delhi. News of his arrest led to civil disobedience. Gandhi was allowed to return to Ahmedabad, which he found under martial law because mill workers had killed a British officer, burned government buildings, extorted money, captured weapons, plundered shops, and attacked private houses. Gandhi realized that now he must protest the behaviour of his own people, and he announced a penitential fast for three days, calling off the campaign and declaring he had made a "Himalayan miscalculation. "

In an infamous incident at Amritsar on April 13, 1919 Brigadier General Reginald Dyer, reacted to the killing of three Englishmen by an Indian mob by prohibiting public meetings and then ordering his soldiers to fire into the crowd at an outdoor gathering, killing 379 and wounding 1, 137 with only 1, 650 bullets. The Hunter Report quoted Dyer's own report that he was less concerned with dispersing the crowd and more intent on "producing a sufficient moral effect from a military point of view. "General Drake-Brockman of Delhi also made the statement, "Force is the only thing that an Asiatic has any respect for. "The Hunter Report concluded that the moral effect was quite opposite from the one intended; General Dyer was censured and later relieved of his command.

Gandhi was given editorial control over two weeklies without advertisements-Young India in English and Navajivan in Gujarati and later Hindi. More than seven thousand delegates attended the Amritsar Congress the last week of 1919. Gandhi agreed to support the Muslim Khilafat movement without requiring them to stop slaughtering cows. Instead of civil disobedience, he proposed a nationwide campaign of nonviolent noncooperation with the British government. For the peasant this meant not paying taxes and not buying liquor because the government gained revenue from its sale. Gandhi wrote to the Viceroy, returning his war medals.

In October 1920 at the annual Indian Congress 14, 000 delegates enthusiastically agreed on noncooperation with the British and to end untouchability. Gandhi promised that noncooperation would bring about self-government in one year. At the beginning of 1921 Motilal Nehru, D. R. Das, Vallabhbhai Patel, and thousands of others abandoned their law practices and British courts as students, teachers, and professionals went into the villages to teach literacy and noncooperation.

Gandhi travelled throughout India addressing mass meetings, and imported fabrics were burned. He urged people to spin and weave their own cloth while boycotting British products, and he designed a Congress flag with a spinning wheel in the centre. When the Prince of Wales (Edward VIII) visited Bombay in November 1921, protests degenerated into mob violence with looting. Some policemen were beaten to death; in three days of riots 58 Bombay citizens were killed, and four hundred were injured. Gandhi went on a fast to end the violence. In December the arrests began. By the time Congress met in the last week of 1921 there were 20, 000 in jail. Some nationalist patriots urged rebellion. Although Gandhi believed that cowardice is worse than violence, he still believed that nonviolent action is better than both. Six thousand delegates approved Gandhi's resolution for civil disobedience of all government laws, especially those banning public meetings.

Gandhi planned a massive nonviolent campaign in Bardoli, a county of 87, 000; but news of how an Indian mob had murdered 23 constables by burning their police station reached him on February 8, 1922, the day it was to begin. Although this incident occurred 800 miles from Bardoli, he once again cancelled the campaign, this time before it had started; instead, he fasted for five days in penance. Yet the British Viceroy ordered Gandhi's arrest, and on March 10, 1922 Gandhi was given his only judicial trial by the British. He made no apology for his noncooperation, which he admitted was legally seditious. To Justice Robert Broomfield he said,

I do not ask for mercy.
I do not plead any extenuating act.
I am here, therefore, to invite and cheerfully submit to
the highest penalty that can be inflicted upon me
for what in law is a deliberate crime
and what appears to me to be the highest duty of a citizen.

He explained, "In my opinion, noncooperation with evil is as much a duty as is cooperation with good. "Broomfield sentenced him to six years and hoped the government would reduce the term. Gandhi was in fact released after 22 months after he had an appendectomy.

Perhaps the greatest block to Indian unity and self government was the religious conflict between Hindus and Muslims. In 1924 an anti-Muslim book led to riots and the murder of its author. After 36 Hindus were killed at Kohat, Gandhi fasted for three weeks. He pleaded for unity in diversity, religious tolerance, and love for one another. After he approved of killing stray dogs, Gandhi was accused of abandoning Ahimsa. He was blamed for killing a maimed calf that was suffering from an incurable disease at his Ashram; but he considered that action nonviolent because the unselfish purpose was to relieve the pain of the calf.

During the late 1920s Gandhi wrote An Autobiography, which he subtitled "The Story of My Experiments with Truth." This book is quite candid and humble in the way he examined his faults and his efforts to overcome them. In the preface he indicated that his goal was spiritual liberation (Moksha). In his speeches he pointed out his five-point program on the fingers of his hand: equality for untouchables, spinning, no alcohol or opium, Hindu-Muslim friendship, and equality for women. They were all connected to the wrist, which stood for nonviolence. Finally in 1928 he announced a satyagraha campaign in Bardoli against a 22% increase in British-imposed taxes. Refusing to pay taxes, the people had their possessions confiscated, and some were driven off their land; but they remained nonviolent. It lasted several months, and hundreds were arrested. Finally the government gave in and agreed to cancel the tax increase, release all prisoners, and return confiscated land and property; the peasants agreed to pay their taxes at the previous rate.

The Indian Congress wanted self-government and considered war for independence. Gandhi naturally refused to support a war but declared that if India was not free under Dominion Status by the end of 1929, then he would demand independence. Consequently on January 26, 1930 he asked people to celebrate Independence Day, and he proclaimed a manifesto that India must sever its connection with Britain and attain complete independence.

Gandhi announced an eleven-point program that included reducing land revenue by fifty percent, abolishing the salt tax, prohibiting alcohol, passing a tariff to protect against foreign cloth, enacting a coastal reservation bill to help Indian shipping, revaluating the rupee, reducing military expenditures by at least fifty percent, reducing salaries of civil servants by half, releasing all political prisoners except for murder, abolishing or controlling the Criminal Investigation Department that was targeting Congress, and issuing firearms for self-defence under popular control.

Then on March 2, 1930 Gandhi wrote a long letter to Viceroy Irwin informing him that civil disobedience would begin on March 11. He noted how ruinously expensive was the British military administration that was exploiting them. Even the salt from the sea was taxed. He believed that nothing but organized nonviolence could stop the organized violence of the British government. Civil disobedience would begin with a few people from his Satyagraha Ashram, but others might choose to join. Gandhi explained, "My ambition is no less than to convert the British people through nonviolence, and thus make them see the wrong they have done to India. I do not seek to harm your people. "Gandhi decided to disobey the Salt Laws, which forbade Indians from making their own salt, because this British monopoly especially struck at the poor.

Beginning with 78 members of his Ashram, Gandhi led a 240-mile march to the sea that took 24 days. Thousands had gathered at the start, and several thousand joined them on the march. First Gandhi and then others all along the seacoast gathered some salt water in pans to dry it. In Bombay the Congress had pans on the roof; 60, 000 people assembled, and hundreds were arrested. At Karachi, where 50, 000 watched the salt being made, the crowd was so thick that the police could make no arrests. The jails were filled with at least 60,000 offenders. Amazingly enough there was practically no violence at all; the people did not want Gandhi to cancel the movement. Gandhi was arrested before he could invade the Dharasana Salt Works, but the poet Sarojini Naidu led 2, 500 volunteers and warned them not to resist the blows of the police. According to an eye-witness account by the United Press reporter Webb Miller, they continued to march in hour after hour and were beaten down with steel-shod lathis by the 400 police; but they did not try to fight back, and the injured were dragged away by women. The poet Tagore declared that Europe had lost her moral prestige in Asia. Soon more than 100, 000 Indians were in prison, including almost all the leaders.

Gandhi was called to meet with Viceroy Irwin eight times. Lord Irwin wanted the civil disobedience ended, but Gandhi demanded an inquiry into the police brutality. Finally on March 5, 1931 they signed the Delhi Pact that treated India as an equal with England and provided for constitutional issues to be discussed at a Round Table Conference in London. Civil disobedience was called off; prisoners were released; and salt manufacture was permitted on the coast.

Gandhi travelled to London, where he met Charlie Chaplin, George Bernard Shaw, and Maria Montessori among others. Not having seen a movie, Gandhi did not know who Chaplin was; but his criticisms of modern civilization may have influenced his film Modern Times. Gandhi spoke for a half hour on radio to the United States about a nonviolent way better than brute force to fight for freedom that is more consistent with human dignity. He appealed to the conscience of the world to rescue his people, who were dying in order to regain liberty.

In discussing relations with the British he said he did not want isolated independence but voluntary interdependence based on love. However, the British Labour Party had been replaced by a coalition led by Ramsay MacDonald, and they used the Indian minorities problems to divide the Indian Congress. In his final speech at the Conference on November 30, 1931 Gandhi said he still wanted complete independence and warned, "Today you have to fight the school of terrorists which is there with your disciplined and organized terrorism, because you will be blind to the facts or the writing on the wall."

Back in India at the beginning of 1932, communication with the Viceroy broke down over the threat of civil disobedience, and Gandhi was arrested. As during the salt campaign, the old Regulation XXV of 1827 was used to detain him indefinitely without a trial. While in the Yeravda jail Gandhi fasted on behalf of the Harijans because they had been given a separate electorate. It was to be a "fast unto death" unless he could awaken the Hindu conscience. On September 21, 1932 millions of Indians fasted with him for 24 hours. Three days later the Yeravda Pact was signed, and it was ratified the next day.

After an overwhelming vote in favour of it, Hindu temples were opened to untouchables for the first time. Gandhi replaced Young India with the weekly Harijan. Still concerned about the Harijans, he fasted for three weeks in May 1933; British officials, afraid he might die, released him from prison. In August 1933 he was arrested again and was sentenced to one year. On the seventh day of his fast he was released unconditionally in a very precarious condition. After he recovered, Gandhi went on a speaking tour and raised money for the Harijans (untouchables), travelling more than 12, 000 miles. In May 1934 the All-India Congress endorsed Gandhi's proposal to call off the civil disobedience campaign except for specific grievances.

By the time the second world war was approaching, Gandhi had been confirmed in his pacifist principles. He pointed out how Abyssinia could have used nonviolence against Mussolini, and he recommended it to the Czechs and China. He suggested, "If it is brave, as it is, to die to a man fighting against odds, it is braver still to refuse to fight and yet to refuse to yield to the usurper. "As early as 1938 he exhorted the Jews to stand up for their rights and die if necessary as martyrs so that a degrading manhunt could be turned into a calm and determined stand. Gandhi even recommended the British use nonviolent methods to fight Hitler; no longer could he support any kind of war or killing. On December 24, 1938 he wrote,

How can nonviolence combat aerial warfare,
seeing that there are no personal contacts?
The reply to this is that behind the death-dealing bomb
there is the human hand that releases it,
and behind that still is the human heart
that sets the hand in motion.
And at the back of the policy of terrorism
is the assumption that terrorism if applied in a sufficient
measure

will produce the desired result,
namely, bend the adversary to the tyrant's will.
But supposing a people make up their mind
that they will never do the tyrant's will,
nor retaliate with the tyrant's own methods,
the tyrant will not find it worth his while
to go on with this terrorism.

He even wrote an open letter to Hitler himself, asking him not to go to war. In April 1939 Gandhi prophesied that before the war ended, the democracies would have adopted the tactics of the Fascists and Nazis, including conscription and methods of force to compel and exact obedience.

Calling for mass satyagraha in defiance of the ban on propaganda against the war, Gandhi promised Congress he would stay out of jail; but his disciple Vinoba Bhave was arrested in October 1940, and about 15, 000 were in prison by May 1941. The next year Gandhi wrote, "Supposing that the women and the children of Europe became fired with the love of humanity, they would take the men by storm and reduce militarism to nothingness in an incredibly short time. "He suggested ways to resist the Japanese nonviolently, though he also said that if India had a national government, it should ally itself with the United Nations against the Fascist powers. He criticized the Japanese for attacking China and predicted that their ambition would fail and might prevent the "world federation and brotherhood without which there can be no hope for humanity."

Gandhi was concerned that the British presence would invite the Japanese to invade India. So on July 14, 1942 the Congress Working Committee adopted the famous "Quit India" resolution, and on August 7 the massive nonviolent struggle began under the leadership of Gandhi. Two days later he and the other leaders were arrested, and Congress was declared illegal. The paper Harijan was put under a ban and was not allowed to publish again until 1946. Thus for three and a half years we have little or no writing from Gandhi. While he was detained at the Aga Khan palace, he complained that the government was spreading rumours that he was encouraging violent activities.

He announced a three-week fast to seek justice from God because the government had denied him justice. Although the Viceroy warned him that he would consider a fast by Gandhi "political blackmail" and would let him die, Gandhi disagreed and began fasting on February 10, 1943. If he had not taken some lime juice with his water, he probably would have died. Gandhi's release from prison on May 5, 1944 has been called the end of the Gandhian era.

When the war ended, Gandhi hoped for a real peace based on freedom and equality for all races and nations. He contrasted nonviolence to the horrible violence of the atomic bomb, and he called the use of this weapon on Japan cowardice. In his last years he became more of a socialist, because he believed that inequality breeds violence while equality produces nonviolence. He went on a pilgrimage to Noakhali to help the poor.

Independence for India was now imminent, but the Muslim leader Jinnah was holding out for the creation of a separate state of Pakistan. In a last-ditch effort to salvage Indian unity, on April 1, 1947 Gandhi proposed that Jinnah and his Muslim League control the new government; but this was considered impractical as partition became inevitable. Two weeks later the last viceroy Mountbatten and Gandhi did get Jinnah to sign with them the following statement:

We denounce for all time the use of force to achieve political ends,
and we call upon all the communities of India,
to whatever persuasion they may belong,
not only to refrain from all acts of violence and disorder,
but also to avoid both in speech and writing,
any word which might be construed as an incitement of such acts.

Gandhi prayed for unity and tolerance, and he even read from the Qur'an at his prayer meetings. Hindus attacked him because they thought he was partial to Muslims; but Muslims demanded he let them have Pakistan.

Gandhi went to Calcutta to calm the Hindu-Muslim strife and violence, and on August 15, 1947, the long-awaited independence day for India, he fasted and prayed there instead of going to the ceremonies at Delhi. On the first of September he fasted again, and he only broke it three days later after municipal officials assured him that there had been no violence for 24 hours. The princely state of Kashmir was invaded by Muslim tribesmen and Pakistani troops.

The Hindu maharajah asked to join the Indian Union and said he intended to appoint the Muslim Sheikh Abdulla prime minister, whose National Conference party also appealed to India to repel the invaders. On October 29, 1947 India announced the accession of Kashmir and sent in troops. Gandhi was criticized for approving this action; but he believed it was justified in these circumstances because not to stand one's ground to defend oneself against an aggressor would be cowardice. Although he may not help one retaliate, Gandhi believed that he must not let a coward find shelter behind the guise of nonviolence.

His last fast began on January 13, 1948, and on the third day the Indian cabinet followed Gandhi's advice and agreed to pay the forty million pounds from united India's assets that they had withheld from Pakistan because of Kashmir. Gandhi's kidneys were not functioning well, and on January 18 Congress got the Hindus, Muslims, Sikhs, Christians, Jews, and other religious groups to sign a peace agreement; on that day he ended his fast. Although this religious hatred saddened Gandhi, India had gained her independence, accomplishing the greatest nonviolent revolution in the history of the world. Finally Gandhi was assassinated by a small Hindu conspiracy on January 30.

1948 at a prayer meeting; with his last breath the Mahatma chanted the name of God.

SOUL FORCE AND NONVIOLENCE

Albert Einstein considered Gandhi to be the most enlightened statesman of the age and declared:

Gandhi had demonstrated that a powerful human following
can be assembled not only through the cunning game
of the usual political maneuvers and trickeries
but through the cogent example
of a morally superior conduct of life.

Einstein also predicted, "The problem of bringing peace to the world on a supranational basis will be solved only by employing Gandhi's method on a large scale. "The Encyclopedia Britannica summarizes Gandhi's significance with the statement, "He was the catalyst if not the initiator of three of the major revolutions of the 20th century: the revolutions against colonialism, racism, and violence. "What was his philosophy of nonviolent soul-force, and what instructions did he give in the use of these methods?

Satyagraha means literally holding on to the truth. The Hindu understanding of Sat is more than conceptual truth but means also being, existence, reality; ultimately we realize that our spiritual beingness is the essence of truth as a reality greater than any concept of the mind. Thus the term "soul-force" conveys the idea of employing our spiritual energies. For Gandhi this truth or spiritual reality is the goal, and the means to the goal must be as pure and loving as possible. He noted that we may always control the means but never the ends.

Thus the means must be as good as the goal. Ahimsa therefore is the way of acting without hurting anyone or inflicting oneself against another spiritual being. We may hate an injustice for the harm that it brings to people, but we must always love all the people involved out of respect for human dignity. Satyagraha attempts to awaken an awareness of the truth about the injustice in the perpetrators, and by Ahimsa this is done without hurting them. Since humans are subject to error and we cannot be sure we are judging accurately, we must refrain from punishing. Thus Ahimsa is an essential safeguard in the quest for truth and justice.

Gandhi explained that satyagraha is not a method of the weak, like passive resistance, but it is a tool for the strong that excludes the use of violence in any shape or form. Satyagraha is insisting on the truth and can be offered in relation to one's family, rulers, fellow citizens, or even the whole world. Gandhi elucidated three necessary conditions for its success:

1. The Satyagrahi should not have any hatred in his heart against the opponent.
2. The issue must be true and substantial.
3. The Satyagrahi must be prepared to suffer till the end for his cause.

Gandhi emphasized self-suffering rather than inflicting suffering on others. By undergoing suffering to reveal the injustice the Satyagrahi strives to reach the consciences of people. Satyagraha does not try to coerce anyone but rather to convert by persuasion, to reach the reason through the heart. Satyagraha appeals to intelligent public opinion for reform. In the political field the struggle on behalf of the people leads to the challenging of unjust governments or laws by means of noncooperation or civil disobedience. When petitions and other remedies fail, then a Satyagrahi may break an unjust law and willingly suffer the penalty in order to call attention to the injustice. However, one does not hide or try to escape from the law like a criminal, rather one openly and civilly disobeys the law as a protest, fully expecting to be punished. In Hind Swaraj Gandhi wrote, "It is contrary to our manhood if we obey laws repugnant to our conscience. "By eliminating violence satyagraha gives the opponent the same rights and liberties.

Satyagraha requires self-discipline, self-control, and self-purification, and satyagrahis must always make the distinction between the evil and the evildoer. They must overcome evil with good, hatred with love, anger with patience, falsehood with truth, and violence with Ahimsa. This takes a perfect person for complete success, and therefore training and education are essential to even make it workable. Gandhi emphasized that every child should know about the soul, truth, love, and the powers latent in the soul. Both men and women and even children may participate, and it demands the courage that comes from spiritual strength and the power of love. Surely it takes more courage to face the weapons of death without fighting than it does to fight and kill. From his experience Gandhi believed that those who wished to serve their country through satyagraha should observe chastity, adopt poverty, follow truth, and cultivate fearlessness. It is through fearlessness that we can have the courage to renounce all harmful weapons, filling and surrounding ourselves with the spiritual protection of a loving and peaceful consciousness.

Gandhi listed detailed rules to guide the Satyagrahi. One should harbour no anger but suffer the anger of the opponent, putting up with assaults without retaliating but not submitting out of fear of punishment nor to any order given in anger. One should not resist arrest by a person in authority nor resist confiscation of property; but if one is the trustee for the property of another, one may refuse to surrender it. One should not swear or curse or insult the opponent nor join cries that are contrary to the spirit of nonviolence. Civil resisters may not salute the Union Jack (a flag), but they should not insult it nor officials. If officials are being assaulted, one should protect them by risking one's life. In prison one should behave with decorum and observe discipline that is not contrary to self-respect; one should not consider oneself superior to other prisoners nor observe any distinction. One should not fast to gain conveniences. Gandhi believed that civil resisters who have chosen to join the corps should obey all orders of the leader. One should trust the care of dependents to God. One should not cause communal quarrels; but in the event of a disagreement should support the party clearly in the right.

Noncooperation is a comprehensive policy used by people when they can no longer in good conscience participate in or support a government that has become oppressive, unjust, and violent. Although satyagrahis do not attack the wrongdoer, it is their responsibility not to promote or support the wrong actions. Thus non-cooperators withdraw from government positions, renounce government programs and services, and refuse to pay taxes to the offending government. While challenging the power of the state in this way non-cooperators have the opportunity to learn greater self-reliance. Gandhi held that noncooperation with an unjust government was not only an inherent right but as much a duty as is cooperation with a just government.

Most of the time Gandhi and his followers were involved in constructive programs, and he considered these the most important part of nonviolent action. For Gandhi they included Hindu-Muslim friendship or communal unity, removing untouchability or racial discrimination, abstaining from alcohol and drugs, practising spinning, weaving, and other village industries, sanitation, schooling and adult education, uplift of women, education in hygiene and health, cultivating one's language, working for economic equality, forming labour unions, helping the poor, rural people and lepers, and improving the education and lives of students.

Ahimsa or nonviolence is absolutely essential to Gandhi's civil disobedience. Satyagrahis are expected to give their lives in efforts to quell violence if it erupts. Gandhi interpreted Ahimsa broadly as refraining from anything at all harmful. This principle can be hurt by every evil thought, by undue haste, by lying, by hatred, by wishing ill to anybody, or by our holding on to what the world needs. Thus even greed and avarice can violate Ahimsa. Nonviolence has a great spiritual power, but the slightest use of violence can taint a just cause. The strength is not physical but comes from the spiritual will. Nonviolence implies self-purification, and the spiritual power the nonviolent person has is always greater than one would have by using violence.

The end of violence is always defeat, but nonviolence is endless and is never defeated. The following is Gandhi's summary of the implications of nonviolence:

1. Nonviolence is the law of the human race and is infinitely greater than and superior to brute force.
2. In the last resort it does not avail to those who do not possess a living faith in the God of Love.
3. Nonviolence affords the fullest protection to one's self-respect and sense of honour, but not always to possession of land or movable property, though its habitual practice does prove a better bulwark than the possession of armed men to defend them. Nonviolence, in the very nature of things, is of no assistance in the defence of ill-gotten gains and immoral acts.
4. Individuals or nations who would practice nonviolence must be prepared to sacrifice (nations to the last man) their all except honour. It is, therefore, inconsistent with the possession of other people's countries, *i.e.*, modern imperialism, which is frankly based on force for its defence.
5. Nonviolence is a power which can be wielded equally by all-children, young men and women or grown-up people, provided they have a living faith in the God of Love and have therefore equal love for all mankind. When nonviolence is accepted as the law of life it must pervade the whole being and not be applied to isolated acts.
6. It is a profound error to suppose that while the law is good enough for individuals it is not for masses of mankind.

Gandhi's struggle was so overwhelming and significant, because he challenged the institutional violence of the modern state. He not only recommended refusing military service but also refusing to pay taxes to a militarized state. In addition to citizens' not cooperating with an evil government, a neutral country also has the obligation to refuse to support or assist a military state or aggressor.

Gandhi suggested a nonviolent army that could engage in constructive activities, lessen tensions, and sacrifice their lives to calm mobs and end riots. He described the qualifications for such a peace brigade in 1938. One must have a living faith in nonviolence and the courage to die without anger, fear, or retaliation. The peace messenger must have equal respect for all religions. This work for peace is done locally alone or in groups. Peace messengers will cultivate contacts with people through personal service. One must have integrity and be strictly impartial. Peace brigades should be aware of brooding conflicts and anticipate conflicts before they break out into conflagrations. Volunteers can be drawn from various walks of life. A distinctive dress would enable the brigade to be recognized without difficulty. The cost of training and equipping such a peace brigade or even an army of satyagrahis would be insignificant compared to the huge expenses of the modern military establishment.

Gandhi envisioned a nonviolent state which would protect itself by not cooperating with any aggressor. He was concerned that the democracies would adopt the forceful methods of the Fascists; but true democracy must ultimately be nonviolent, for violence is an obvious restriction of liberty. He observed that the science of war leads to dictatorship, but the science of nonviolence leads to democracy. In 1946 Gandhi asserted that a true democracy will not rely on an army. It is a poor democracy that depends on military assistance because military force interferes with the free growth of the mind and smothers the soul.

Gandhi criticized America for its treatment of the Negro. He observed that armaments are used for greedy exploitation and that the competition and desire for material possessions and the great power's imperialistic designs are the biggest blocks to world peace. Also they must shed their fear of destruction; then by disarmament peace can be attained. Gandhi warned that if the mad arms race continued, it would result in unprecedented slaughter. If a victor remains, the victory will be a living death for that nation. The only escape from this impending doom is by boldly and unconditionally accepting nonviolence with all its glorious implications. His concept of sarvodaya urged us to go beyond family and country to consider the good of all, and he recommended a world governing body which would recognize the equal independence of each nation. He believed that religion means being friendly to one's opponents because being friendly to friends is just business. Gandhi said that the golden way is to be friends with the world and regard the whole human family as one.

HARIJAN SEVAK SANGH

Mahatma Gandhi (1869-1948) dreamt of a nonviolent society comprising of the entire human race. Such a society can rest only upon a nonviolent world order where the nations will spread out as petals of the same flower. The march of the human race from a confictridden society is inevitably towards that end through a process of rise and fall, falters and movements, stagnation and speed.

But the Gandhian ideology holds out a bold promise to bring it within our reach in a foreseeable time span as a reality for the coming generation. The maxim around which the Gandhian world order is woven is that the world has enough for everybody's need but not enough for everybody's greed. Thus, an element of sharing of the global resources consistent with economic justice for all, is the substance of the concept that Gandhiji has left for posterity.

The world today finds itself imbedded in a situation of unbridled competition amongst nations for economic market upon which a bid for political hegemony is super-structured. What has become urgently necessary today is to carve out a legitimate space of cooperation from the realm of competition. That is what Ghandhiji stood for. In the vision of Gandhiji he tried to find out an instrument which could rid the world at large from such economic ups and downs and promise perennial sustenance to every man in every nook and corner of the globe.

Mahatma Gandhi conceived a nonviolent society and it is for the people of this century to march towards it in steady steps. It basically means eradication of poverty of the masses, lifting up the population groaning below the level of subsistence around the world and a rational utilisation of world's resources so that a basic minimum is guaranteed to all.

Gandhiji was totally against such injustice to the posterity and he always propagated the creed that we must give back to nature what we have drawn from it. This approach alone can make for an ecological balance.

The Gandhian ideology aims at conservation of the non-renewable resources of the world at large and a constant endeavour to add to these resources to sustain the human race. That is why he recommends a way of life in keeping with nature and not living based on wild consumerism which only wastes away the resources given by nature and erodes the base that sustains the society.

In the field of political philosophy, the greatest contribution of Gandhi is to pave the way for a system which eschews conflict at the grass-root level of the political administration. According to him, every village shall be a republic, self-sufficient, self-reliant and self-propelling.

Every vital decision in the administration of the village community should be on the basis of a consensus and not by majority of votes which perpetuate a tyranny of the majority over the minority. This is an approach which will take the democratic society to the next higher social order. In addition, village communities should give first preference to the most needy in the distribution of its resources at its disposal. This philosophy of "Unto thc laet" is the basic foundation of the Gandhian political concept. The village polity thus envisaged by Gandhiji is known as "Gram Swaraj"-Village republic..

Gandhism commends itself to the whole world, because a nonviolent society does not exit in isolation and also because violence somewhere contaminates easily elsewhere. The theory of trusteeship, one of the fundamental tenets of Gandhian though is the opposite of economic conflict born out of competition and survival of the fittest.

As we entered the new millennium, let us carry the promise of a nonviolent society for the posterity on the path of Gandhism. Let Gandhism be taken not as a dogma but as an investigating process which will blossom an experiments go on, an experiment which will assume more relevance as more and more nations take to it.

Mohandas Karamchand Gandhi, popularly know as Mahatma Gandhi and Bapuji is well known all over the world for his unique concept of non violence determining interpersonal, intra-national and international relationship for promotion of peace throughout the world. This very concept won national freedom for India without bloodshed. Gandhiji had equally unconventional economic and social theories for upliftment of the poor through eradication of poverty. Gandhiji discounted the efficacy of class confrontation and recommended trusteeship of the rich people for promotion of economic wellbeing of the poor. Keen to remove untouchability and other social evils of the contemporary Indian society, Gandhiji motivated so called higher caste people to show compassion and humane behaviour towards the so called people of lower castes including the untouchables. He firmly believed that gentle persuasion could move mountains while violence achieve very little and provoke more violence. Gandhiji's target group was lowest of the lower echelons of Indian society most of whom was considered untouchables by the higher castes. Thus he developed the concept and programme of Antoday-unto the last. To offer them honour and a place in the society, he called the untouchables "Harijan" meaning Man of God. He dedicated his life for the emancipation.

He founded Harijan Sevak Sangh (HSS), in 1932 to give institutional shape to his ideas and he could gather all the eminent social reformers of the time around him to launch and develop the Sangh as one of the pioneering national level voluntary movements of the country. Amongst these personalities who acted as friends, philosoper and guide of the Sangh were G. D. Birla, Thakkar Bapa, Rameshwari Nehru, Dr. B. R. Ambedkar. Since its inception the Sangh has been tirelessly working. Gandhiji's ideas were ably taken over by Sant Vinoba Bhave (1895-1982) who carried the mantle of Gandhiji after his demise in 1948 and gave a unique direction for regeneration of rural India. His concept of land reforms through Bhoodan and Gramdan revolutionized the contemporary land holding system and concomitant oppression of the marginal and landless peasantry of the country.

Ms. Nirmala Deshpande, the present President of the All India Harijan Sevak Sangh is the spiritual daughter of Acharaya Vinoba Bhave and she took the ideas of Gandhiji and Vinoba Bhave to its logical conclusion. She learned social work at the feet of Vinoba Bhave and herself became a legendary name in the annals of social development in India. Under her leadership ideas and ideals of Mahatma Gandhi and Acharya Vinoba Bhave were disseminated throughout the length and breadth of the country. She relied mainly on conscientisation of the downtrodden and ultimately empowering them to bring about their own emancipation. Hence, she constituted Akhil Bharat Rachnatmak Samaj, a national level confederation of constructive workers and organisations to implement the ideas of Gandhiji and Vinoba Bhave.

It was followed by her taking over the mantle of Harijan Sevak Sangh founded by Gandhiji himself to which she infused unprecedented dynamism and transformed it into a national movement for emancipation of the downtrodden. Her battle for social equity and universal peace crossed national boundaries and she established Association of People of Asia which promoted people to people contact with Pakistan and other neighbouring countries in order to usher in a ambience of peace and tranquillity in the tension-ridden subcontinent. Her message has travelled wider contributions in the arena of international peace and harmony.

The Bengal branch of the Sangh was promoted and patronised by Bengal's stalwarts like Dr. Bidhan Ch. Roy, Dr. P. C. Ghosh and P. C. Sen all former Chief Ministers of the State and other social activist like Acharya P. C Roy and Dr. Satish Ch. Dasgupta eminent scientists, Sakti Ranjan Basu and Sitaram Shaksharia. Up to 1978 the activities of the Sangh in Bengal were on a low key. Prof. Sankar Kumar Sanyal, the young student leader, advocate Calcutta High Court & Industrial Consultant turned into an eminent social activist of the state was picked up by P. C. Sen, former Chief Minister of West Bengal, Shibnath Banerjee and Shakti Ranjan Bose, the well-known socialist in the mould of Jai Prakash Narayan and Khitish Roy Chowdhury and others.

In this way Prof. Sanyal had the privilege of working as General Secretary of various organisations under the illustrious presidentship of Nirmala Deshpande, Prafulla Chandra Sen, Shakti Ranjan Bose, Khitish Roy Chowdhury, Pannalal Dasgupta, Rakhal Chandra Dey and Dr. Phulrenu Guha, all eminent freedom fighters & Gandhian stalwarts of the country. Prof. Sanyal took up the responsibility as the Hon'y Secretary of the Bengal branch of the Sangh and within a few year transformed the Bengal branch into a dynamic institution having activities in all the 18 districts of the State. He established 210 branch/associate bodies all over the State and through them galvanised the rural poor including the Harijans and Tribals into a fighting force for their own emancipation. Empowerment through education and self-employment were his basic tools of development which he relentlessly pursued. His dynamic leadership and creative vision soon transformed the Sangh into a vibrant and forward looking organisation from its moribund state and made it a fighting instrument for the upliftment of the downtrodden.

During this period Jai Prakash Narayan and his disciples veered round to problems of political turmoil of the day and started organising the people for changing the character of political power. Most of orthodox Gandhianslike Vinoba Bhave and his disciple Nirmala Deshpande stuck to their Gandhian beliefs in nonviolence and peace and parted company of the emerging socialists.

Simultaneously he spread the operations of HSS, Bengal throughout the state and thus attracted the attention of renowned Sarvodaya leaders of the country, Mr. Nirmala Deshpande. He then joined the national mainstream of Gandhian movement under the outstanding leadership of Ms. Nirmala Despande and ultimately became Vice President of All India Harijan Sevak Sangh and of Akhil Bharat Prakrihick Chikitsha Parishad (All India Nature Cure Federation) the General Secretary of Akhil Bharat Rachantmak Samaj (All India Constructive Workers' Conference), Rural Development Consortium and also of and many other organisations.

Prof. Sanyal had the opportunity to visit many foreign countries and discussed with many stalwarts in the field of international Peace about the role of Gandhian concept of nonviolence in establishing permanent peace in the world. But during the International year of Peace in 1986, he was profoundly motivated by the words of Mahatma Gandhi which said that "with every true friendship we build more firmly the foundation on which the peace of the world rests.

Thought by thought and act by act with every breath we build the kingdom of nonviolence that is the true home of the spirit of man". Since then Prof. Sankar Kumar Sanyal has been relentlessly striving to establish an international organisation under the Chairmanship of Ms. Nirmala Despande, who is the heir in the true sense of both Mahatma Gandhi and Acharya Vinoba to act as a global coordinating council seeking to orchestrate the institutions, individuals and efforts oriented towards nonviolent transformation of society as envisaged by Mahatma Gandhi. The present Gandhi International Mission is a step in that direction.

6

CASTES AND INDIAN SOCIETY

INTRODUCTION

Caste as a religious concept is recognized by Oxford Dictionary as "each of the hereditary classes of Hindu society, distinguished by relative degrees of ritual purity or pollution and of social status, "and as" any exclusive social class." Anthropologists use the term more generally, to refer to a social group that is endogamous and occupationally specialized; such groups are common in highly stratified societies with a very low degree of social mobility. In its broadest sense, examples of caste-based societies include colonial Latin America under Spanish and Portuguese rule, apart from India prior to 1947. Caste systems are traditional, hereditary systems of social stratification, enforced by law or common practice, based on classifications such as occupation, race, ethnicity, etc.

Etymology of the English Word Caste: The word caste is derived from the Romance word casta (seen in Portuguese, Spanish, and Italian), which (in addition to representing the same concept as English caste) can mean "lineage" or "race". It comes from Romance casto, which can mean "pure" or "chaste" (the word chaste itself is ultimately cognate). Casto is derived from Latin castus, which also meant "pure" or "chaste".

Castes in Africa: Countries in Africa who have societies with caste systems within their borders include Mali, Mauritania, Senegal, Gambia, Guinea, Guinea-Bissau, Ivory

Coast, Niger, Burkina Faso, Cameroon, Ghana, Liberia, Sierra Leone, Algeria, Nigeria, Chad, Ethiopia and Somalia.

The Osu caste system in Nigeria and southern Cameroon are derived from indigenous religious beliefs and discriminate against the "Osus" people as "owned by deities" and outcastes. Caste systems in Somalia mandate non-Arab descended "outcastes" such as Midgan-Madhiban, Yibir, Tumal and other groups deemed to be impure and are ostracized from society. Similarly, the Mandal societies in Senegal, Gambia, Guinea, Sierra leone, Liberia, Ivory Coast and Ghana have caste systems that divide society by occupation and ethnic ties. The Mandal caste system regards the "Jonow" slave castes as inferior. Similarly, the Wolof caste system in Senegal is divided into three main groups, the Geer (freeborn/nobles), jaam (slaves and slave descendents) and the outcasted neeno (people of caste).

Other caste systems in Africa include the Borana caste system of NE Kenya with the Watta as the lowest caste, the "Ubuhake" castes in Rwanda and Burundi, and the "Hutu" undercastes in Rwanda who committed genocide on the "Tutsi" overlords in the now infamous Rwandan Genocide.

Balinese Caste System: The Balinese caste system resembles the Indian system with a fourfold division of society. Sudras make up 97% of the society.

Castes in India: The original meaning of caste, which was also known as Varna, was determined by one's spiritual qualities and occupation according to the Vedas. Over time, the caste system became a traditional, hereditary system of social stratification.

The traditional hereditary system of social stratification of India, in which all social classes exist in thousands of endogamous groups is termed jati. The jati system, usually with politically and economically derived hierarchies, has been followed across the Indian subcontinent with regional variations across India, Pakistan, Bangladesh and Nepal. Different religious denominations have traditionally followed different kinds of jati stratification. While the prevalence of the jati system has declined significantly over the course of the twentieth century, remote and rural areas of the subcontinent continue to subscribe to jati and jati segregation.

Caste, on the other hand is a theoretical construct of the Brahmin scholars to describe and categorise (Varna) the complex social arrangement of which they were themselves a part. In the absence of any other better word, Varna was translated as caste by the Europeans, with its connotations of racial purity. Contrary to popular belief, historically there was a great deal of mobility and intermingling between Indian castes, other than Brahmins, largely based on economic or political status of the concerned group.

The Brahmins were enjoined by their scriptures and texts, including the Manu Smriti, to live in poverty and to shun possessions and temporal power and instead devote themselves to study and teaching of scriptures and other knowledge, pure conduct and spiritual growth. In fact, they usually subsisted on alms from the rest of the society, including the so called backward caste of "Shudras". This is an important point in understanding the difference between caste and class. Caste became an important element of Indian politics after the British used the entirely theoretical construct of varna, now caste, as the basis of classifying the Indian population, especially the Hindus, in the population censuses of late 19th Century.

This became more specific in the 1901 Census, because the Indian population, not being aware of what the Brahmins thought of them, by and large did not understand what was meant by "caste" and gave their occupation, religion, education etc. as their "caste". In the 1901 Census, the people were asked to slot themselves, or were slotted by enumerators, as members of the specific castes of Brahmin, Khshatriya, Vaishya, Sudra etc. This was ostensibly done to simplify an otherwise difficult to slot society, with subtle hierarchies, for the purposes of better statistical manipulation.

Thus, a purely theoretical construct of "varna" or "caste" now became a living entity and got embedded in the minds of intellectuals and common people alike as an "ancient" system of social segregation. It did not take much time to become a significant political issue in India and members of certain castes often form Votebanks that subscribe to special interest political parties.

CASTE SYSTEM AMONG HINDUS

The Indian caste system, prevalent also among local Muslims and Christians, exhibits some differences from those of other countries. Elsewhere, the separation between one group and the other is usually along racial lines. Within India, that is not so. Nor is there any discernable dichotomy (white/black or high/low) because the caste system forms a continuum that defies such ready definition. While many lower-caste people live in conditions of great poverty and social disadvantage, many upper-caste Brahmins too are poor and now disadvantaged politically. Efforts by the Indian government to emancipate the lower castes with affirmative action like reservations in education, jobs and promotions have achieved some success, although the benefits have tended to be cornered by the well-off "Creamy Layer" of lower castes.

The concept of 'upper' and 'lower' caste is therefore a matter of social standing and assimilation rather than anything based on wealth or influence. Even in this age, some castes do not allow other caste members, whom they consider to be "lower" to touch them, and would have washed themselves or their possessions if they had been touched by someone from a "lower" caste. In some parts of India, there was the practice of defining the physical distance one should keep from persons of another caste. As a result of this, children who attended a school where children of lower castes were present had to bathe in running water before returning home. In some parts of the world, as well as in India, such discrimination still exists, though it is punishable by law and unconstitutional in India. The Indian constitution was drafted by Ambedkar, himself of low-caste origins, who is regarded as an emancipator of the Dalits.

Loss of caste could occur if individuals strayed from the norms of behaviour expected of them; for instance, if one married a person belonging to another caste. Despite the prosletysing efforts of Christian missionaries, the fact is that converts rarely achieve emancipation from the caste system to gain an equal social standing with people of privilege. Even among converts, matrimony between members of different castes is rare, although it is not unknown.

A detailed analysis of the caste system, Castes in India: Their Mechanism, Genesis and Development in India was presented by Dr. B. R. Ambedkar in his doctoral paper at the Columbia University.

MYTHICAL ORIGIN OF CASTES

This is a unique verse as it is the only one in the ancient Brahminical Veda scriptures that has a mention of Varna. This may seem rather strange, given the preponderance of caste in India. But once we recognise that the Indian society was Jati based and the Varna system was a later Brahminical interpretation of that society, this anomaly becomes understandable.

In the Puranas, it is said that the creative force of the universe, Brahma, created some humans from his mouth-they became reciters of the Veda and became the Brahmins. Then he created other humans from his arms, they became the Kshatriyas, bearers of arms, the warrior and ruling class. Brahma then created some from his abdomen, who became the Vaishyas or merchants.

Finally, Brahma created humans from his feet. They served the other castes even as the feet serve the man; they came to become the Sudras (manual labourers and artisans). Thus, the whole universe is held to be one organic entity, the body of the almighty.

Most scholars are agreed that the caste system was not rigid, including in the early vedic times. Change of one's caste could be effected by all except Brahmins, by changing one's vocation and acquiring new skills, or gaining economic or political power.

JATI

Major castes were subdivided into hundreds of sub-castes or jatis. Castes were based on occupation. Endogamous marriage (including polyandry) and other association within caste was strongly enforced.

- Sub-castes within a group of jat ("birth" as opposed to varna) were called jati
- Jati members were allowed to marry only with their jati.
- People were born into their jati; this status couldn't be changed, unless through marriage or under rare circumstances.
- Each jati was part of a local system of interdependence with other groups, involving occupational specialization, and was linked in complex ways with networks that stretched across regions.

For example, in Tamil Nadu and Kerala, states of South India, castes based on occupation would include: asari (carpenters), thattar (goldsmiths), muusaari (coppersmiths), karuvar (ironsmiths), ambattar (clothes-washers), parayar (cobblers) and so on.

Modern Developments: With rapid urbanization and education of India's largely rural, agrarian population, the significance of caste has diminished, except in government mediated interventions in the form of quotas and reservations in education, jobs and promotions for the socially "lower", but numerous and thus politically important, castes.

The caste system and its attendant practices have been outlawed and declared punishable offences, but these laws are difficult to implement. There are occasional violations of human rights of Dalits (outcastes-also called untouchables) by the higher castes, including forcing Dalits into their traditional professions. Dalits in rural areas have often been victimized by other castes, many a times themselves politically powerful "Shudras" or "lower castes".

The government of India provides freeships, scholarships, reservations for government jobs and of university seats in programs of higher education (undergraduate and above) for people hailing from Scheduled castes, Scheduled tribes and Other Backward Castes; see Reservation in India. Upper caste Hindus and several secular elements counter-argue that unmeritorious Dalits, especially those from the well off "Creamy Layer" are exploiting this constitutionally obligatory discrimination to their unfair advantage and meritorious candidates are being sidelined. The site Dalitstan (presently taken down), once banned by the Indian government, is an example of anti-Brahmin and anti-Hindu rhetoric by Dalit extremists, allegedly supported by Christian missions.

CASTE SYSTEM AMONG INDIAN MUSLIMS

There is also several caste systems among some Muslims in India. They are broadly divided into two castes, Ashraf and Ajlaf, or oonchi jaat (high caste) and niichi Zaat (low caste). The Muslim Caste System in India was analysed by Ambedkar, who had a very dim view of the rampant discrimination of the Ajlaf castes by the Ashraf castes. In addition to the Ashraf and Ajlaf castes, there exist the Arzal under-caste or the Dalit Muslims who are regarded by the Ashraf and the Ajlaf as ritually impure and are relegated to professions regarded as "menial" such as scavenging and the carrying of night soil.

In addition, Muslims in Bengal organize their society according to social strata called "Quoms", where division of labour is granted by birth,.rather than by economic status. Professions perceived as "lowly" are provided to people of certain ostracized Quoms and higher Quoms get professions perceived as superior. The Quoms are rigidly segregated with little or no intermarriage or cohabitation.

CASTE SYSTEM AMONG INDIAN CHRISTIANS

Converts to Christianity have retained the old caste practices. In particular, Dalit Christians are regarded as an undercaste by upper-caste Christian clergy and nuns and are discriminated against in society.

INDIAN CASTE SYSTEM

History: Some researchers believe that the caste system began with the Indo-Aryan migration to India. However, the theory of Indo-Aryan migration itself is a highly disputed topic. The critics claim that it was formulated to undermine the historical significance of India, and was exploited by the British to show that they had the right to invade India, as the Indians supposedly themselves were invaders.

Although many Hindu scriptures contain passages that can be interpreted to sanction the caste system, they also contain indications that the caste system is not an essential part of the Hindu religion. The Vedas place very little importance on the caste system, mentioning caste only rarely and in a cursory manner.

In the Vedic period, there also seems to no discrimination against the Sudras (which later became an ensemble of the so-called low-castes). Later scriptures such as Bhagavad Gita and Manu Smriti state that the four Varnas are created by God. A varna is a division of the society that consists of many sub-castes or Jatis.

Manu Smriti and some other shastras mention four varnas: The Brahmins (teachers, scholars and priests), the Kshatriyas (kings and warriors), the Vaishyas (traders, landowners and some artisan groups), and Sudras (agriculturists, service providers, and some artisan groups). Another group of untouchables excluded from the main society was called Parjanya or Antyaja.

Passages from these scriptures suggest that the caste system was originally non-hereditary:

According to the Manu Smriti, every caste belongs to one of the four varnas. However, there have been many disputes about the varna of many castes, such as castes being considered Kshatriya by some scholars, while described as Sudra by others. While texts such as the Manu Smriti attempted to rationalize ambiguous castes by placing them in varna-sankaras (*i.e.* mixed varna), the fact remains that Indian society was, and is, composed of numerous geographically diversified but endogamous groups. With many occupational groups practising endogamy within a particular region, as well as numerous sub-divisions within the four main castes, a more complex system of sub-castes and jatis is evident. The jatis have broken up into clans like Agarwal, Iyer, etc.

THE STATUS OF UNTOUCHABLES

The untouchables (now called Dalits) in Hindu society were the people who worked in what were seen as unhealthy, disgusting or polluting jobs. Untouchables used to live separately within a subcultural context of their own, outside the inhabited limits of villages and townships, made pariahs in every sense of the word. No other castes could, or would, interfere with their social life since untouchables were lower in social ranking than even those of the shudras.

In the past, the Dalits suffered from social restrictions in addition to extreme poverty. They were not allowed temple worship with others, nor water from the same sources. Person of higher castes would not interact with them. Untouchables were not allowed to use the same wells as the other castes as that would "pollute" the water and indirectly the other castes who drank it. If somehow a member of a higher caste came into physical or social contact with an untouchable, the member of the higher caste was defiled, and had to bathe thoroughly to purge her/himself of the impurity. Such contact even included the shadow of an untouchable falling on the member of the higher caste. At the same time, the untouchables developed their own rich folk traditions with a lifestyle that was unhampered by the variety of restrictions on the rest of the society.

The inclusion of so-called untouchables into the mainstream was argued for by many social reformers. Mahatma Gandhi called them "Harijans" (people of God). The term Dalit (downtrodden) is used now as the term Harijan is largely felt patronising. Gandhi's contribution toward the emancipation of the untouchables is controversial. This is usually highlighted by the commentary of his contemporary Dr. B. R. Ambedkar, an untouchable himself. Ambedkar was deeply suspicious of Gandhi's motivations and frequently saw his activities as detrimental to the cause of upliftment of his people.

For instance, Gandhi, a Vaishya, was not against the caste system, but tried hard to bring untouchables into the mainstream of society and get the other castes to discard the practice of untouchability. Ambedkar, influenced by liberal thinkers like Voltaire, was interested in the elimination of the caste system and untouchability altogether. To him, Gandhi's efforts solved no problems of the untouchables as they would remain at the bottom of the hierarchy. Ambedkar suggested that the evils of the caste system would be eliminated if the upper castes (especially the Brahmins) would change their behaviour and eventually get rid of the caste system altogether.

Even among Dalits, there's discrimination. The social status of Dalit sub-castes such as Bhangi has long been a source of contention within Indian society. Upper sub-castes among Dalits like Dhobi, Nai etc. do not intearct with Bhangis, the lowest order among the dalits. They are called untouchable among the untouchables. This is an example of deep set roots of caste system in the Indian psyche.

The practice of untouchability has been formally outlawed by the Constitution of India, and has declined heavily in independent India. K. R. Narayanan, a Dalit, became the President of India in 1997.

CASTE SYSTEM AMONG NON-HINDUS

In some parts of India, the Christians are stratified by sect, location, and the castes of their predecessors. Presently in India, more than 70% of Christians are Dalits, but the higher caste Christians (30% by estimates) control 90% of the churches administrative jobs. Out of the 156 bishops, only 6 are from lower castes. Many Dalit Catholics have spoken out against discrimination against them by the Catholic Church. Despite Islam's egalitarian tenets, units of social stratification, termed as "castes" by many, have developed among Muslims in some parts of South Asia. Various theories have been put forward regarding the development of castes among Indian Muslims. Some sources state that the castes among Muslims developed as the result of close contact with Hindu culture and Hindu converts to Islam, while others feel that these developed based on the claims of descent from the prophet Muhammad.

Ashrafs have a superior status derived from their foreign ancestry, while the Ajlafs are assumed to be converts from Hinduism, and have a lower status. In addition, there is also the Arzal caste among Muslims, who were regarded by anti-caste activists like Babasaheb Ambedkar as the equivalent of untouchables. In the Bengal region of India, some Muslims also stratify their society according to 'Quoms'. While some scholars have asserted that the Muslim Castes are not as acute in their discrimination as that among Hindus, Ambedkar argued otherwise, writing that the social evils in Muslim society were "worse than those seen in Hindu society".

CASTE-RELATED VIOLENCE

Independent India has witnessed considerable amount of violence and hate crimes motivated by caste. Ranvir Sena, a caste-supremacist fringe paramilitary group based in Bihar has committed violent acts against Dalits and other members of the scheduled caste community. Phoolan Devi, a bandit-turned-politician belonging to Mallah lower-caste was mistreated and raped by upper-caste Thakurs. She turned a bandit and carried out violent robberies against upper-caste people. In 1981, her gang massacred twenty-two Thakurs, most of whom were not involved in her kidnapping or rape.

Over the years, various incidents of violence against Dalits, such as Kherlanji Massacre have been reported from many parts of India. At the same time, many violent protests by Dalits, such as the 2006 Dalit protests in Maharashtra, have been reported as well.

CASTE POLITICS

Mahatma Gandhi, B. R. Ambedkar and Jawaharlal Nehru had radically different approaches to caste especially over constitutional politics and the status of "untouchables". Till the mid-1970s, the politics of independent India was largely dominated by economic issues and questions of corruption. But since 1980s, caste has emerged as a major issue in the politics of India.

The Mandal Commission was established in 1979 to "identify the socially or educationally backward", and to consider the question of seat reservations and quotas for people to redress caste discrimination. In 1980, the commission's report affirmed the affirmative action practice under Indian law whereby members of lower castes were given exclusive access to a certain portion of government jobs and slots in public universities. When V.P. Singh Government tried to implement the recommendations of Mandal Commission in 1989, massive protests were held in the country. Many alleged that the politicians were trying to cash on caste-based reservations for purely pragmatic electoral purposes.

Many political parties in India have openly indulged in caste-based votebank politics. Parties such as Bahujan Samaj Party (BSP), the Samajwadi Party and the Janata Dal claim that they are representing the backward castes, and rely primarily on OBC support, often in alliance with Dalit and Muslim support to win the elections.

Criticism: There has been strong criticism of the caste system existing in India, both within and outside India.

Gautama Buddha and Mahavira, the founders of Buddhism and Jainism respectively, were against any kind of caste structure. Many Bhakti period saints such as Kabir, Dnyaneshwar, Eknath, Ramananda, Ramanuja and Tukaram rejected all caste-based discrimination and accepted disciples from all the castes. Many Hindu reformers such as Swami Vivekananda and Sathya Sai Baba believe that there is no place for the caste system in Hinduism.

The caste system has also been criticized by many Indian social reformers. Some reformers, such as Mahatma Jyotirao Phule and Iyothee Thass argued that the lower caste people were the original inhabitants of India, and were conquered in the ancient past by Brahman invaders.

Mahatma Gandhi coined the term "Harijan", a euphemistic word for untouchable, literally meaning Sons of God. B. R. Ambedkar, born in Hindu Dalit community, was a heavy critic of the caste system. He pioneered the Dalit Buddhist movement in India, and asked his followers to leave Hinduism, and convert to Buddhism. Periyar Ramasami, a Tamil rationalist fought against the caste practice of Brahmins and was a prominent Anti-Hindu.

The caste system has been often used to criticize Hinduism and India, in general. Kancha Ilaiah, a professor at Osmania University is known for his polemical attacks on Hindus and the caste system. Many Hindus, however point out that the caste system is related to the Indian society, and not Hinduism (as is evident by presence of caste among Indian Christians and

Muslims). Hindu Nationalist organizations such as the Rashtriya Swayamsevak Sangh have actively criticized the caste system.

Some activists consider that the caste system is a form of racial discrimination. The participants of the United Nations Conference Against Racism in Durban, South Africa in March 2001, condemned the discrimination due to the caste system, and stated that caste as a basis for the segregation and oppression of peoples in terms of their descent and occupation is a form of apartheid.

The Indian government denies the claims of equivalency between Caste and Racial discrimination, pointing out that the caste issues as essentially intra-racial and intra-cultural. Indian Attorney General Soli Sorabjee insisted that "The only reason India wants caste discrimination kept off the agenda is that it will distract participants from the main topic: racism. Caste discrimination in India is undeniable but caste and race are entirely distinct.

"..Many scholars dispute the claim that casteism is akin to racism. The view of the caste system as "static and unchanging" has been disputed. Sociologists describe how the perception of the caste system as a static and textual stratification has given way to the perception of the caste system as a more processual, empirical and contextual stratification. Others have applied theoretical models to explain mobility and flexibility in the caste system in India. . According to these scholars, groups of lower-caste individuals could seek to elevate the status of their caste by attempting to emulate the practices of higher castes.

Sociologist M. N. Srinivas has also debated the question of rigidity in Caste. For details see sanskritization. In India, some observers felt that the caste system must be viewed as a system of exploitation of poor low-ranking groups by more prosperous high-ranking groups. In many parts of India, land is largely held by dominant castes high-ranking owners of property that economically exploit low-ranking landless labourers and poor artisans, all the while degrading them with ritual emphases on their so-called god-given inferior status.

Matt Cherry, claims that karma underpins the caste system, and the caste system traditionally determines the position and role of every member of Hindu society. Caste determines an individual's place in society, the work he or she may carry out, and who he or she may marry and meet. According to him, Hindus believe that the karma of previous life will determine the caste an individual will be (re)born into.

VARNASHRAMA DHARMA

Varnashrama Dharma refers to the system of classes of social life and stages of individual life in Hinduism. Varna refers to the belief that most humans were created from different parts of the body of the divinity Purusha and according to which part they were created from it defines their social standing for issues such as who they can marry and what jobs they can do.

The classes of society given in the Hindu scriptures: Brahmana ("scholarly community"), Kshatriya ("warriors or politicians community"), Vaishya ("mercantile community") and Sudra ("service providing community").

Asrama refers to the four stages of individual life prescribed for all Hindus: Brahmacharya ("student life"), Grihastha ("householder life"), Vanaprastha ("anchorite life") and Sannyasa ("renunciate life").

The Hindu tradition holds this system as a Dharma ("sacred law") sanctioned by the scriptures. While the above is the general belief and interpretation by some, there is no mention except at one place in Purusha Sukta (Yajurveda), of various Varnas or castes or classes, either natural or created, in any of the Vedas.

There are views held by some that even the stanza which talks about the four Varnas originating from Face, Hands, Torso and feet of the Hindu deity Purusha appears different from other Slokas and could have been altered at some later stages.

One of the foremost Rishi in Rig Veda is Vishwamitra, who was a King and Kshatriya by birth. Vyasa was of mixed birth between Parasara, a Brahmin and Sathyavathi (a Soodra, fisher woman). Maharishi Matanga was from the Matanga Bhil tribe but was raised as a Brahmana. Hence to attribute caste system to Hindu scriptures is without substance. Only Manu Smriti talks clearly about caste system and their duties.)

The Sanskrit term Varna is derived from the root Vrn meaning "to choose (from a group)." This is contrary to the assumption that 'varna' denotes colour and hence signifies qualities of someone, just as Saguna Brahman means "with qualities. "In the context of social hierarchies, it means "arrangement".

When humans first settled down into agrarian and trading societies, many changes occurred in social relationships with this greater specialisation of labour. People got organised into structures that could be stable and accommodating diverse individuals in diverse occupations. Societies are organic wholes self-sustained by diverse groups with differing occupations that optimise that society's well-being and growth.

The varna system is a functional hierarchy system proposed by the Brahmin texts to describe their society. It is an ideal system that did not exist anywhere in reality, as the Indian society was organised according to Jatis, since time immemorial. The oldest mention of the varna system is in the Purusha sukta of Rig Veda 10. 90 which claims "Brahmana is the mouth of the purusha, rajanya his arms, vaishya is his thighs and shudra arose from his feet"-an obvious reference to the organic (purusha) nature of the society, sustained by the harmonious integration of functional groups (organs) working in unison.

In such organic hierarchies, it is recognised that proper functioning of each part is necessary for the stability of the whole. This led to the importance given to kartavya or "duties" (deontology). Each one is obligated to perform their duties relevant to their position in the system. Proper functioning is of utmost necessity for the stability of the whole structure.

ETYMOLOGY

Varna is a Sanskrit term (varna meaning type, order, colour or faith (faithless), preference, religious affiliation, conviction, or "to choose", or lustre.

- In the Zend Avesta and the Gathas, the word Varana or Varena (from the root Var ("put faith in, to believe in") is used in the sense of preference (or religious affiliation, conviction, faith, religious doctrine, choice of creed or belief). The language of the Gathas (the oldest part of the Avesta) is very similar to the language of the Rig Veda.
- It may also come from the root Var-"choose", as in "svayamvara", "(a girl's) own choice (of a husband)", or from the root vri (which means "one's occupation").
- In the Rig Veda, the word Varna occurs 22 times and means lustre. In 17 out of 22 times it refers to the "lustre" (*i.e.* "one's own typical light") of gods like Soma, Agni or Ushas. In RV 3. 34. 5 and RV 9. 71. 2 it refers to the lustrous colour of the sky at dawn.
- According to Hindu tradition, Varna refers to sounds of speech or language. Western Indologists have wrongly interpreted varna as "a letter of the alphabet". According to Welzer (1994 (229-230)), Varna can be grammatically derived from the term "class" (vide Panini), but it has acquired the incorrect meaning of "colour".

SOCIAL DEVELOPMENT

The caste system is used by Hindus, particularly in India, Bali and Nepal for reasons of determining lineage and is passed down through patrilineal descent. It is based on the older four-varna system varnas which later became attached to the members' families. Sometimes Mlechha (people excluded from caste) are referred to as fifth varna.

JATI

The terms Varna (class) and Jati (caste) are two distinct concepts. Varna ("class") (from Sanskrit, literally "arrangement") is a supposed unification of all the Hindu sub-castes or jatis into either four groups: Brahmin, Kshatriya, Vaishya, Sudra, or into one of several varna-sankaras. Jati (Caste) is an endogamous group. Generally a sub-caste is divided into exogamus groups based on same Gotras. Many of the Hindus could be classified into a specific varna. But not all. During the British rule, several cases went to court to settle the "varna" of a sub-caste. For example, the farmers are sometimes given Kshatriya status because many ruling Chieftains may have risen from them. On the other hand some classified them as Vainya, based on an older occupation of artisans. Orthodox Brahmins may classify them as Sudras, because they do not have a tradition of undergoing through the thread ceremony, that would make them Dvija.

THE TWICE BORN

The first three varnas are seen as 'twice born'. They are allowed to study Vedas. In India and Nepal the sub-castes within a Varna are called Jat or Jati (The varna is also used instead of Jat). Traditionally, each Jati members are allowed to marry only with their Jati members. People are born into their Jati and normally it cannot be changed, though there were some exceptions in Hindu Mythology. For example, sage Vishwamitra was born as a Kshatriya (ruling class) and by deep meditation (tapas) became a venerable Brahmin Rishi (saint). Once someone is born to certain sub-caste or Jati he or she cannot normally change their Jati, although some groups throughout history have risen or fallen according to their deeds. Caste is a permanent attribute among the Hindus.

The occupations of the Vaishya are those connected with trade, the cultivation of the land and the breeding of cattle; while those of a Kshatriya consist in ruling and defending the people, administering justice, and the duties, of the military profession generally and ruling and expounding all Dharma. Both share with the Brahmin the privilege of reading the Vedas. To the Brahmin belongs the right of teaching and expounding the sacred texts vedas. Sudras were the serfs, and performed agricultural labour. Muluki Ain has incorporated the entire ethnic group of Nepal into Caste hierarchy.

INSTANCES IN HINDU TEXTS AND TRADITION

The Rig Veda refers in the Purusha Sukta to the four principal varnas described in Manu's code, *viz.* Brahmins, Kshatriyas, Vaishyas, and Sudras. The term Varna is not associated with Brahmins or Kshatriyas in the Rig Veda, and the term Varna does not occur in the Purusha Sukta. It affirmed that Varnashram Dharma needs to be strictly followed as every soul has been given a specific duty by God. A soul is born into a varna as punishment/reward for its karmic influences-actions in past lives (Hindus believe in reincarnation). The "Purusha Sukta' hymn (Rig Veda 10:90) mentions the varnas and compares them to the body of the "primordial man": "The Brahmana was his mouth, of both his arms was the Rajanya made. His thighs became the Vaishya, from his feet the Sudra was produced." (RV 10:90:12) In the Purusha Sukta hymn the word Varna is not used, and it is the only hymn of the Rig Veda where the words Vaishya and Sudra are used. The Purusha Sukta hymn is considered to be one of the youngest parts of the Rig Veda.

There is an Upanishadic story of a boy who went to a guru to study the various holy Hindu scriptures. His guru asked him what his varna was. Consulting his mother, who was actually a prostitute who didn't really know what her caste was, the boy returned to the guru and told him that he was all castes. He worshipped the Gods, thus fulfilling the duties that are ordinarily a Brahmin's, he earned his keep like a Vaishya, took care of cleaning the house, like a Sudra, and protected his family's interest like a Kshatriya. The guru was pleased and told the boy he was fit to be taught and initiated into the Brahmin's life. The Dharmashastras (a collection of collections of Hindu codes and laws) say that caste is not just determined by birth, but by action in life according to the Dharma of varna-ashram as well.

The Brahmins (priests), The Kshatriyas (warriors, nobility), the Vaishyas (the craftsmen and men of commerce), and the Sudras (agriculture workers; menial workers) were the four varnas. A person of each varna was said to possess certain set of characteristics: the Sudras, they believed, were of the tamasic nature; the Vaishyas were either tamasic or rajasic; the Kshatriyas were believed to be noble, learned and selfless, his or her duty being the administration of the people and fighting of battles against intruders, often very spiritually inclined; and that the Brahmins were religious, pure, Society's bank of knowledge and wisdom for their memory of holy scriptures, the performers of rituals. However, there is a dispute as to which varna holds the greatest spiritual purity. Brahmins are associated with the evil Daksha, an arrogant Brahmin that received the head of a goat, and according to scriptures caused all Brahmins to be cursed by Nandi to never attain the greatest spiritual heights in Hinduism as Daksha insulted Shiva.

Hindu tantrics are a part of Hinduism whose scriptural texts, the Agamic texts known collectively as the Tantras, assert their descent from the Vedas, especially the Atharva Veda. Claiming that the Vedic rituals no longer necessary in Kali Yuga, that the fourth and final epoch of humanity in Hinduism shall see morality ebb to complete dissolution until the end of the earth, the Tantrics see themselves as natural continuations of the Vedas through Hindu yogic practices—and not of any particular caste, yet not Untouchables. Many Hindu yogis and sages have, over the centuries, constantly commented about caste. Shri Chaitanya Mahaprabhu (15th century), the powerful Bhakti of Krishna also denounced caste. He famously distributed the Hare Krishna Mantra to non-brahmins all around India, claiming this was the True path to Moksha.

Kanakadasa of the 15th century also denounced Casteism. He believed that Life in every human being is Divine, and that only the ignorant wrought injustice against their own brethren by practising the caste system.

RIG VEDA AND MANU SMRITI

In Sanskrit, Varna means colour, as in quality (just as the term "Shaguna Brahman") One of the hymns of the Rig Veda, one of the holiest Hindu scriptures, gives the following enumeration in the famous Purusha Sukta (RV 10. 90):

Its rough translation is: "What became of his (the Cosmic Spirit's) face or mouth? What became of his two arms? What became of His two thighs? What were (the products of) the two feet called? From His face (or the mouth) came the Brahmanas. From His two arms came the rajanya (the Kshatriyas). From His two thighs came the vaishyas. From His two feet came the shudras." In the Purusha Sukta hymn the word Varna is not used, and it is the only hymn of the Rig Veda where the words Vaishya and Sudra are used. The Purusha Sukta hymn is considered to be one of the youngest parts of the Rig Veda. Manu Smriti is often quoted in reference to the Varna-caste system. The Manu Smriti is a later work that does not form a part of Hindu Scriptures, so it is of questionable relevance. Use of the Manu Smriti by the British colonialists has been used by politicians and sociologists to denigrate those of the Hindu faith.

The Manu Smriti claims that by the time it was written, Hinduism included another class (untouchables) of people without a position in any of the four Varnas and therefore associated with the lowest of the jobs. The upper castes, who were supposed to maintain ritual and corporal purity, came to regard them as untouchables. The people of this "fifth varna" are now called Dalits (the oppressed) or Harijans; they were formerly known as "untouchables" or "pariahs". It is very clear that in the early Vedic times, the Varna system (if at all it existed) meant classes with free mobility of jobs and intermarriage. One hymn of the Rig Veda states:

"I am a bard, my father is a physician, my mother's job is to grind the corn."

While intermarriage between Brahmana bridegrooms and Kshatriya princesses was extremely common (even sanctioned by the later Manu Smriti), in many instances, marriages between Kshatriya princes and Brahmana brides was also observed (severely condemned by Manu Smriti). One of such instances is marriage of Yayati, a Kshatriya King, with Devayani, a daughter of the sage Shukracharya.In later times, with the elaboration of ritualism, the caste system became absolutely hereditary (the historians disagree as to when) and the Sudras were not even allowed to hear the sacred word of the Vedas.

This text is not found in Manu Smriti: Request the author to remove this.

> *"If the shudra intentionally listens for committing to memory the Veda, then his ears should be filled with (molten) lead and lac; if he utters the Veda, then his tongue should be cut off; if he has mastered the Veda his body should be cut to pieces."*

A stark contrast to this is a mantra from the White Yajur Veda itself:

> *"I do hereby address this salutary (Vedic) speech for the benefit of humanity-for the Brahmanas, the Kshatriyas, the Sudras, the Vaishas, the kinsfolk and the men of lowest position in society. May I be dear to the learned in this world."*

OPPOSITION WITHIN HINDUISM

Critics point that the effect of the system was to bind certain castes to sources of influence, power and economy while locking out others and thus create more affluence for higher castes and severe poverty for lower castes and the outcast Dalit. In the last 150 years Indian movements arose to throw off the economic and political yoke of the caste system. And replace it with true Varnashrama Dharma, described in the Vedas.

In the religious scripture Mahabharata, Yudhisthira, is questioned by Yama in the form of a Yaksha, about what makes one a Brahmin. Yudhisthira, without hesitation, said that it is conduct alone that makes one a Brahmin.

Ramananda, an ascetic of the Sri Ramanuja's Sri Vaishnava sampradaya, accepted all varna as his disciples. Mirabai, the 15th century mystical poet and Queen of Chittor is known to have ignored varna distinctions and elected the cobbler, Sant Rohidas, as her guru. Annamacharya, a 15th century telugu poet's famous Bramhamokkada song, preaches equality of all in the eyes of God and condemns the caste system as un-Vedic. And proposed a return to traditional varnashrama Dharma. Which promoted equality and stressed the importance of all varnas. Ramakrishna Paramahamsa, the 19th century Hindu religious leader, also did not recognise varna distinctions and took his first alms as a twice-born Brahmin from a Sudra woman.

The late Swami Krishnananda, the successor to Swami Sivananda and former head of Divine Life Society, noted the following about caste in his autobiography:

> "*While the caste system was originally evolved for the necessary classification of human duty in order to preserve the organic stability of society, its original meaning and its philosophical foundation was forgotten through the passage of time, and bigotry and fanaticism took its place through the preponderance of egoism, greed and hatred, contrary to the practice of true religion as a social expression of inner spiritual aspiration for a gradual ascent, by stages, to God Almighty. Vidura, famous in the Mahabharata, was born of a Sudra woman. But he had the power to summon the son of Brahma, from Brahmaloka, by mere thought. Which orthodox Brahmin can achieve this astounding feat? It is, therefore, necessary for everyone to have consideration for the facts of world-unity and goodwill, Sarvabhuta-hita, as*

the great Lord mentions in the Bhagavad Gita. Justice is more than law. No one's body is by itself a Brahmin, because it is constituted of the five gross elements, -earth, water, fire, air and ether. Else, it would be a sin on the part of a son to consign to flames the lifeless body of a Brahmin father. It is, therefore, not proper to victimise a colleague by an action plan of any religious community wedded to fundamentalist doctrines."

Paramahansa Yogananda also opposed what he called to the un-Vedic caste system as we know it today. He taught that the caste system originated in a higher age, but became degraded through ignorance and self-interest. Yogananda said:

"These were (originally) symbolic designations of the stages of spiritual refinement. They were not intended as social categories. And they were not intended to be hereditary. Things changed as the yugas (cycles of time) descended toward mental darkness. People in the higher castes wanted to make sure their children were accepted as members of their own caste. Thus, ego-identification caused them to freeze the ancient classifications into what is called the 'caste system.' Such was not the original intention. In obvious fact, however, the offspring of a Brahmin may be a Sudra by nature. And a peasant, sometimes, is a real saint."

—from Conversations with Yogananda, Crystal Clarity Publishers, 2003.

ASHRAMA

The traditional classification of the stages of a Hindu's life into Brahmacharya ("student life"), Grihastha ("householders life"), Vanaprastha ("anchorite life") and Sannyasa ("renunciate life") has been sanctioned in the Hindu scriptures.

This classification is believed by the Hindus to lead to a fulfilment of the four aims of life, namely Dharma ("righteousness"), Artha ("wealth"), Kama ("sensual gratification") and Moksha ("salvation").

7

DIVISIONS OF CASTES

It is difficult to define how castes are divided. However, there are two main sources:

1. Early British Census Records
2. Interpretations of the Manu Smriti

British Census Officers determined caste hierarchy based on the principle, *e.g.* someone who accepts food and water from another person but the other person does not reciprocate the same way, then the other person is superior to the former. It was contested at many places (a notable example is that the Koris of up who said they won't accept water from Brahmins, and so should be placed higher than them). Because it was met with rampant controversies, arbitration was very common during those days. The most notable arbitration stories are:

1. Caste status of Bhumihar
2. Caste status of Kayastha
3. Caste status of Kurmi
4. Caste status of Yadav

It raised more questions than it answered and subsequent census records varied radically, making it free for all, after some time. Manu Smriti is considered as the most ancient and authentic source regarding origin and hierarchy of castes. Though it answers most of the questions, it is ambiguous at most places. Other accounts which throw light on social structure in past are:

- Arthasastra by Kautilya
- Indica by Megasthenese
- Travel account by Fa-Xien
- Travel account by Alberuni
- Travel account by Ibn Battuta.

Caste division among Muslims was determined according to ancestry. One with ancestry matching with invaders were considered superior to converts. Some castes are based on occupation. For example, goldsmiths, carpenters, and barbers each form separate sub-castes. Often, a sub-caste with a significant number of members will be divided into further sub-castes. This further division may be due to:

- Geographical separation: For example, there are purabia (eastern) and pachchaia (western) sections of some castes.
- Variation in standards of conduct: For example, disagreements over the permissibility of widow marriages have caused some castes to subdivide.

VARNAS (CLASSES) AND JATIS (CASTES)

Although Varna Jati and caste sounds synonymous, they have different connotations. Varna is mentioned as caste equivalent in scriptures. Puranas use it in the context of skin colour too. Puranic deities are often described as belonging to Shwet or "Gaur" meaning white and Shyam meaning black varnas. Scriptures describe Varnas as classification based on profession too. Manu Smriti identified four varnas in Indian society. These are Brahmin, Kshatriya, Vaishya, and Sudra according to origin. However, Lord Krishna in Bhagwadgita says Varna are according to Karma (work) nothing to do with origin.

Theoretically, according to the Manu Smriti, every caste belongs to one of the four varnas (Brahmin, Kshtriya, Vaishya, and Sudra). However, the division of Indian society into four castes was a generalization rarely held in practice. Consequently, there have been many disputes about the varna of many castes, such as castes being considered Kshatriya by some scholars, while described as Sudra by others. While texts such as the Manu Smriti attempted to rationalize ambiguous castes by placing them in varna-sankaras (*i.e.* mixed varna), the fact remains that Indian society was, and is, composed of numerous geographically diversified but endogamous groups.

With many occupational groups practising endogamy within a particular region, as well as numerous sub-divisions within the four main castes, a more complex system of sub-castes and jatis is evident. The jatis have broken up into clans like Agarwal, Iyer, etc. Unlike the varna system of Brahmins, which requires spiritual purity in order to ascend, a jati is able to move up or down the social hierarchy based on the aspirations of its members. Marriages are usually arranged within one's own sub-caste; however, they may occur between two affiliated sub-castes, or two sub-castes that are in the same region, and are as such termed inter-caste marriages. Over time, this grew more and more rigid, until every aspect was determined by birth, with various "justifications" as described below.

To simplify the perspective, often people use the classification based on Four varnas, given in Manu Smriti and other Dharmashastras: The Brahmins (Teachers, Scholars and Priests), The Khshatriyas (Kings and warriors), the Vaishyas (Traders, Landowners and some Artisan groups), and Sudras (Agriculturists, Service providers, and some Artisan groups).

There was another group, which was excluded from the main society, for various reasons, which was called Parjanya or Antyaja; these were the people called untouchables. The varnas (rather than Jatis), was used after the 1902 Census by the British, for consolidation of demographic data into manageable proportions. However no commonly agreed approach for classifying the castes into the four varnas exists, sometimes a caste may claim to be a Brahmin, but others may regard it to be a Vaishya.

In the past, members of different castes would not partake in various activities, such as dining and religious gatherings, together. In addition, the performance of religious rites and rituals were restricted to Brahmins, who were the designated priesthood. In recent years, more egalitarian reforms have enabled lower castes and even non-castes such as the Dalits to become religious clerics. The "Pandaram" priests are an example of an order of Dalit priests, based in Nepal and South India. The Pandaram maintain the same tradition as the Brahmin priests, including the use of the Sanskrit language (traditionally reserved for the Brahmins) for the rituals. While they are not generally as well trained as the Brahmin priests, they are highly respected within their community and are addressed with reverence.

MOBILITY AMONG THE CASTES

Although group mobility was not completely uncommon, individual mobility among castes was generally rare. While mobility among caste groups was not common, it was not unheard of. Groups of lower-caste individuals could seek to elevate the status of their caste by attempting to emulate the practices of higher castes.

The view of the caste system as "static and unchanging" has been disputed by many scholars. Sociolgists such as Bernard Buber and Marriott McKim describe, for instance, how the perception of the caste system as a static and textual stratification has given way to the perception of the caste system as a more processual, empirical and contextual stratification. Other sociologists such as Y. B. Damle have applied theoretical models to explain mobility and flexibility in the caste system in India.

Sociologist M. N. Srinivas has also debated the question of rigidity in Caste. In an ethnographic study of the Coorgs of Karnataka, he observed considerable flexibility and mobility in their caste hierarchies. He asserts that the caste system is far from a rigid system in which the position of each component caste is fixed for all time. Movement has always been possible, and especially in the middle regions of the hierarchy. It was always possible for groups born into a lower caste to "rise to a higher position by adopting vegetarianism and teetotalism" *i.e.* adopt the customs of the higher castes. While theoretically "forbidden", the process was not uncommon in practice. The concept of sanskritization, or the adoption of upper-caste norms by the lower castes, addressed the actual complexity and fluidity of caste relations.

When it comes to stance of a hereditary caste system, the Manu Smriti takes the position:

> *The above verse is believed to sanction support for vocational non-hereditary caste system, suggesting some flexibility in the propagation of the Castes. According to some economists, mobility across broad caste lines may have been "minimal", though sub-castes (jatis) may change their social status over the generations by fission, relocation, and adoption of new rituals.*

Historical examples of mobility in the Indian Caste System among Hindus have been researched. The "Noniya" Caste of salt makers have claimed to the higher status of the "Chauhan Rajput". They have risen well above the untouchable line and their leaders have, in the past, mobilized upwards along the caste hierarchy. There is also precedent of certain Sudra families within the temples of the Shrivaishava sect in South India elevating their caste.

A well-known precedent for mobility in the caste system is that of Shivaji, the founder and monarch of the Maratha Confederacy, who was born into a lower caste but was elevated to a higher caste to facilitate his coronation.

THEORIES ABOUT THE ORIGINS OF THE SYSTEM

The histories of many of the castes are available in form of an oral tradition. Many of these were recorded in the past few centuries. With the archaeological findings in the last one and half centuries, it is now possible to trace the emergence on several of the specific castes to 11-12th century or even a few centuries earlier. For example, Babb has attempted to trace the history of several castes in Rajasthan in his "Archemies of Violence", based largely on narratives recorded in the past few centuries. Prior to the availability of archaeological evidence, the histories of individual castes are often speculative.

One theory is, in its initial period caste system was flexible and it was merit and job based. One could migrate from one caste to other caste by changing one's profession. Evidence in support of it says that Rama's guru Rishi Vashishtha was a shudra and he became Rishi later. Also Rishi Valmiki was a dacoit before becoming a sage. Later, the caste system is said to have become rigid, and caste began to be inherited rather than acquired by merit.

According to 19th century theories, the caste system began with the arrival of the Aryans in India. Indo-Aryan culture arrived in India around 1500 BC, around the time of the collapse of the Indus Valley Civilization. The Indo-Aryans arrived in India from Central Asia. European scholars first supposed that they came as invaders, and were contemptuous of their newly-conquered subjects. This was often romanticized as a struggle between the native dark skinned culture and the invading light skinned one. Before the arrival of the Indo-Aryans, the dominant cultural and linguistic group would have been the Dravidians. The Dravidians were the largest community in India, and are by some scholars identified as the bearers of the Indus Valley Civilization. It was fully developed by 800 BC. It was at first assumed that the Indus Valley Civilization collapsed due to the apparent invasion of the Aryans, but it now seems more likely that the migration of Indo-Aryan culture came about as a result of the diminished power of the Indus Valley Civilization as it was collapsing due to internal pressures, much like the migrations period in Europe was brought on by the weakening of the Roman Empire.

The early Aryans organized among themselves in three groups, much like other Indo-European peoples. The different Jats (sub-castes) who professed different occupations were integrated in different Varnas according to their occupation. According to the invasion theory of caste origin, most of the communities that were in India before the arrival of the Aryans were integrated in the Sudra Varna or were made outcast depending on the professions of these communities. Communities who professed non-polluting jobs were integrated in Sudras Varna. And communities who professed polluting professions were made outcasts or untouchables. Untouchables were not only disallowed to touch the high caste people but they also had to stand at a certain distance from the high castes.

This Aryan Invasion theory is today often claimed to have been formulated to undermine the historical significance of India and its cultural and religious heritage by the British, and subsequently the west.

The British historians were writing under a Biblical time-frame where the world began only around 4000 BC. The theory was also exploited by the British to show that they had the right to invade India, as the Indians supposedly themselves were invaders. It indirectly also implied that the "indigenous" people were incapable of creating their religion or culture and that it was brought by outsiders. Recent genetic studies have supported the idea that the invasion did not occur, showing that most north Indians today are primarily of Indian, not Central Asian, descent suggesting that the influx of Indo-Aryan culture was one primarily of language, not genes.

MODERN STATUS OF THE CASTE SYSTEM

The caste system was first exposed to the modern Western world during the Portuguese occupation and rule of sections of India. Indeed, the word 'caste' in this context is derived from the Portuguese, casta. Later, other European empires, including the British, occupied parts of the subcontinent. The anthropologist Herbert Risley's The Tribes and Castes of Bengal, published in 1892, was one of the first works on the caste system in India written by a Western scholar.

SCHEDULED CASTES, SCHEDULED TRIBES AND OTHER BACKWARD CLASSES

Independent India officially documented castes and sub-castes, primarily to determine those deserving reservation (positive discrimination in education) through the census. The Indian reservation system relies entirely on quotas. The Government lists consist of scheduled castes, scheduled tribes and other backward classes.

Scheduled Castes (SC): Scheduled castes generally consist of former "untouchables" (the term "Dalit" is now preferred). Present population is 16% of total population of India *i.e.* around 160 million. For example, the Delhi state has 49 castes listed as SC.

Scheduled Tribes (ST): Scheduled tribes generally consist of tribal people. Present population is 7% of total population of India *i.e.* around 70 million.

Other Backward Classes (OBC): Other backward classes generally consist of cultivators, pastoralists, artisans, etc. The Mandal Commission has covered more than 3000 castes under OBC Category. According to the Mandal Commission, the present population of OBC's is approximately 52% of the population. The Mandal Commission has since been criticized for fabricating data. The National Sample Survey puts the figure at 32%. For example, Delhi places 53 castes in this group.

There is substantial debate over the exact number of OBC's in India, with census data compromised by partisan politics. It is generally estimated to be sizable, but lower than the figures quoted by either the Mandal Commission or and national Sample Survey. Some Indian states are dominated by caste-based politics. Sometimes converts to other religions, such as Christianity or Islam, retain their caste identity, often due to the economic benefits it carries, and also to retain their ties with the community for social reasons. This practice, however, is often frowned upon by members of the same sub-caste.

CONTEMPORARY CRITICISM OF THE CASTE SYSTEM

There has been strong criticism of the caste system existing in India. Some activists consider that the caste system is a form of racial discrimination. The participants of the United Nations Conference Against Racism in Durban, South Africa in March 2001, condemned the discrimination due to the caste system, and stated that caste as a basis for the segregation and oppression of peoples in terms of their descent and occupation is a form of apartheid.

The Indian government denies the claims of equivalency between Caste and Racial discrimination, pointing out that the caste issues as essentially intra-racial and intra-cultural. Indian Attorney General Soli Sorabjee insisted that "The only reason India wants caste discrimination kept off the agenda is that it will distract participants from the main topic: racism. Caste discrimination in India is undeniable but caste and race are entirely distinct."

In India, some observers felt that the caste system must be viewed as a system of exploitation of poor low-ranking groups by more prosperous high-ranking groups. In many parts of India, land is largely held by dominant castes high-ranking owners of property that economically exploit low-ranking landless labourers and poor artisans, all the while degrading them with ritual emphases on their so-called god-given inferior status.

Matt Cherry, claims that karma underpins the caste system, and the caste system traditionally determines the position and role of every member of Hindu society. Caste determines an individual's place in society, the work he or she may carry out, and who he or she may marry and meet. According to him, Hindus believe that the karma of previous life will determine the caste an individual will be (re)born into.

THE STATUS OF UNTOUCHABLES

The untouchable (or Dalit) in Hindu Society was a person who worked in what were seen as unhealthy, polluting work dealing with the dead bodies and animal carcasses, the collection and disposal of bodily waste, and other jobs that brought him/her into constant contact with what society considered disgusting and even dangerous. These occupations, although they were helpful to the society and improved sanitation, were considered unclean and polluted the individual, and such polluted individuals were considered unfit for physical or social contact with the non-polluted, "purer" sections of society. Untouchables used to live separately within a subcultural context of their own, outside the inhabited limits of villages and townships, made pariahs in every sense of the word. No other castes could, or would, interfere with their social life since untouchables were lower in social ranking than even those of the shudra varna. In the past, extreme poverty drove many untouchables to wear clothing off the bodies of the dead that they handled.

In their home they ate from broken dishes discarded by others. Untouchables suffered from many social restrictions. They were not allowed temple worship with others, nor water from the same sources. Person of higher castes would not interact with them. Untouchables were not allowed to use the same wells as the other castes as that would "pollute" the water and indirectly the other castes who drank it. If somehow a member of a higher caste came into physical or social contact with an untouchable, the member of the higher caste was defiled, and had to bathe thoroughly to purge her/himself of the impurity.

Such contact even included the shadow of an untouchable falling on the member of the higher caste. At the same time, the untouchables developed their own rich folk traditions with a lifestyle that was unhampered by the variety of restrictions on the rest of the society. The inclusion of lower castes into the mainstream was argued for by Mahatma Gandhi who called them "Harijans" (people of God). The term Dalit (downtrodden) is used now as the term Harijan is largely felt patronising.

Gandhi's contribution toward the emancipation of the untouchables is controversial. This is usually highlighted by the commentary of his contemporary Dr. B. R. Ambedkar, an untouchable himself. Ambedkar was deeply suspicious of Gandhi's motivations and frequently saw his activities as detrimental to the cause of upliftment of his people.

For instance, Gandhi, a Vaishya, was not against the caste system, but tried hard to bring untouchables into the mainstream of society and get the other castes to discard the practice of untouchability. Ambedkar, influenced by liberal thinkers like Voltaire, was interested in the elimination of the caste system and untouchability altogether. To him, Gandhi's efforts solved no problems of the untouchables as they would remain at the bottom of the hierarchy. Ambedkar suggested that the evils of the caste system would be eliminated if the upper castes (especially the Brahmins) would change their behaviour and eventually get rid of the caste system altogether.

There is a "sub-caste" that today exists even below even the Dalit: the Bhangi. The social status of the hundreds of thousands of Bhangi (approximately 32, 000 families in Gujarat alone) has long been a source of contention within Indian society. Upper sub castes among Dalits like dhobi, nai etc. do not intearct with Bhangis, the lowest order among the dalits. They are called untouchable among the untouchables. This is an example of deep set roots of caste system in the Indian psyche. Fortunately, now the caste system is relaxing, especially in metropolition and other major urban areas, due to higher penetration of high education, coexistence of all communities and lesser knowledge about caste system due to alienation with rural roots of people. But in the countryside and small towns, this system is still very rigid.

INDIA'S CASTE SYSTEM

Although many other nations are characterized by social inequality, perhaps nowhere else in the world has inequality been so elaborately constructed as in the Indian institution of caste. Caste has long existed in India, but in-the modern period it has been severely criticized by both Indian and foreign observers. Although some educated Indians tell non-Indians that caste has been abolished or that "no one pays attention to caste anymore," such statements do not reflect reality. Caste has undergone significant change since independence, but it still involves hundreds of millions of people. In its preamble, India's constitution forbids negative public discrimination on the basis of caste. However, caste ranking and caste-based interaction have occurred for centuries and will continue to do so well into the foreseeable future, more in the countryside than in urban settings and more in the realms of kinship and marriage than in less personal interactions.

Castes are ranked, named, endogamous (in-marrying) groups, membership in which is achieved by birth. There are thousands of castes and sub-castes in India, and these large kinship-based groups are fundamental to South Asian social structure. Each caste is part of a locally based system of interdependence with other groups, involving occupational specialization, and is linked in complex ways with networks that stretch across regions and throughout the nation. The word caste derives from the Portuguese casta, meaning breed, race, or kind. Among the Indian terms that are sometimes translated as caste are varna, jati, jat, biradari, and samaj. All of these terms refer to ranked groups of various sizes and breadth. Varna, or colour, actually refers to large divisions that include various castes; the other terms include castes and subdivisions of castes sometimes called sub-castes.

Many castes are traditionally associated with an occupation, such as high-ranking Brahmans; middle-ranking farmer and artisan groups, such as potters, barbers, and carpenters; and very low-ranking "Untouchable" leather workers, butchers, launderers, and latrine cleaners. There is some correlation between ritual rank on the caste hierarchy and economic prosperity. Members of higher-ranking castes tend, on the whole, to be more prosperous than members of lower-ranking castes. Many lower-caste people live in conditions of great poverty and social disadvantage.

According to the Rig Veda, sacred texts that date back to oral traditions of more than 3, 000 years ago, progenitors of the four ranked varna groups sprang from various parts of the body of the primordial man, which Brahma created from clay (see The Vedas and Polytheism). Each group had a function in sustaining the life of society—the social body. Brahmans, or priests, were created from the mouth. They were to provide for the intellectual and spiritual needs of the community. Kshatriyas, warriors and rulers, were derived from the arms. Their role was to rule and to protect others. Vaishyas—landowners and merchants—sprang from the thighs, and were entrusted with the care of commerce and agriculture. Sudras—artisans and servants—came from the feet. Their task was to perform all manual labour.

Later conceptualized was a fifth category, "Untouchable" menials, relegated to carrying out very menial and polluting work related to bodily decay and dirt. Since 1935 "Untouchables" have been known as Scheduled Castes, referring to their listing on government rosters, or schedules. They are also often called by Mohandas Karamchand (Mahatma) Gandhi's term Harijans, or "Children of God." Although the term Untouchable appears in literature produced by these low-ranking castes, in the 1990s, many politically conscious members of these groups prefer to refer to themselves as Dalit, a Hindi word meaning oppressed or downtrodden. According to the 1991 census, there were 138 million Scheduled Caste members in India, approximately 16 percent of the total population.

The first four varnas apparently existed in the ancient Aryan society of northern India. Some historians say that these categories were originally somewhat fluid functional groups, not castes. A greater degree of fixity gradually developed, resulting in the complex ranking systems of medieval India that essentially continue in the late twentieth century.

Although a varna is not a caste, when directly asked for their caste affiliation, particularly when the questioner is a Westerner, many Indians will reply with a varna name. Pressed further, they may respond with a much more specific name of a caste, or jati, which falls within that varna. For example, a Brahman may specify that he is a member of a named caste group, such as a Jijotiya Brahman, or a Smartha Brahman, and so on. Within such castes, people may further belong to smaller subcaste categories and to specific clans and lineages. These finer designations are particularly relevant when marriages are being arranged and often appear in newspaper matrimonial advertisements.

Members of a caste are typically spread out over a region, with representatives living in hundreds of settlements. In any small village, there may be representatives of a few or even a score or more castes. Numerous groups usually called tribes (often referred to as Scheduled Tribes) are also integrated into the caste system to varying degrees. Some tribes live separately from others—particularly in the far northeast and in the forested centre of the country, where tribes are more like ethnic groups than castes. Some tribes are themselves divided into groups similar to sub-castes. In regions where members of tribes live in peasant villages with non-tribal peoples, they are usually considered members of separate castes ranking low on the hierarchical scale.

Inequalities among castes are considered by the Hindu faithful to be part of the divinely ordained natural order and are expressed in terms of purity and pollution. Within a village, relative rank is most graphically expressed at a wedding or death feast, when all residents of the village are invited. At the home of a high-ranking caste member, food is prepared by a member of a caste from whom all can accept cooked food (usually by a Brahman). Diners are seated in lines; members of a single caste sit next to each other in a row, and members of other castes sit in perpendicular or parallel rows at some distance. Members of Dalit castes, such as Leather workers and Sweepers, may be seated far from the other diners—even out in an alley. Farther away, at the edge of the feeding area, a Sweeper may wait with a large basket to receive discarded leavings tossed in by other diners. Eating food contaminated by contact with the saliva of others not of the same family is considered far too polluting to be practiced by members of any other castes. Generally, feasts and ceremonies given by Dalits are not attended by higher-ranking castes.

Among Muslims, although status differences prevail, brotherhood may be stressed. A Muslim feast usually includes a cloth laid either on clean ground or on a table, with all Muslims, rich and poor, dining from plates placed on the same cloth. Muslims who wish to provide hospitality to observant Hindus, however, must make separate arrangements for a high-caste Hindu cook and ritually pure foods and dining area.

Castes that fall within the top four ranked varnas are sometimes referred to as the "clean castes," with Dalits considered "unclean." Castes of the top three ranked varnas are often designated "twice-born," in reference to the ritual initiation undergone by male members, in which investiture with the Hindu sacred thread constitutes a kind of ritual rebirth. Non-Hindu caste-like groups generally fall outside these designations.

Each caste is believed by devout Hindus to have its own Dharma, or divinely ordained code of proper conduct. Accordingly, there is often a high degree of tolerance for divergent lifestyles among different castes. Brahmans are usually expected to be nonviolent and spiritual, according with their traditional roles as vegetarian teetotaller priests. Kshatriyas are supposed to be strong, as fighters and rulers should be, with a taste for aggression, eating meat, and drinking alcohol. Vaishyas are stereotyped as adept businessmen, in accord with their traditional activities in commerce. Sudras are often described by others as tolerably pleasant but expectably somewhat base in behaviour, whereas Dalits—especially Sweepers—are often regarded by others as followers of vulgar life-styles. Conversely, lower-caste people often view people of high rank as haughty and unfeeling.

The chastity of women is strongly related to caste status. Generally, the higher ranking the caste, the more sexual control its women are expected to exhibit. Brahman brides should be virginal, faithful to one husband, and celibate in widowhood. By contrast, a Sweeper bride may or may not be a virgin, extramarital affairs may be tolerated, and, if widowed or divorced, the woman is encouraged to remarry. For the higher castes, such control of female sexuality helps ensure purity of lineage—of crucial importance to maintenance of high status. Among Muslims, too, high status is strongly correlated with female chastity.

Within castes explicit standards are maintained. Transgressions may be dealt with by a caste council, meeting periodically to adjudicate issues relevant to the caste. Such councils are usually formed of groups of elders, almost always males. Punishments such as fines and outcasting, either temporary or permanent, can be enforced. In rare cases, a person is excommunicated from the caste for gross infractions of caste rules. An example of such an infraction might be marrying or openly cohabiting with a mate of a caste lower than one's own; such behaviour would usually result in the higher-caste person dropping to the status of the lower-caste person.

Activities such as farming or trading can be carried out by anyone, but usually only members of the appropriate castes act as priests, barbers, potters, weavers, and other skilled artisans, whose occupational skills are handed down in families from one generation to another. As with other key features of Indian social structure, occupational specialization is believed to be in accord with the divinely ordained order of the universe.

The existence of rigid ranking is supernaturally validated through the idea of rebirth according to a person's karma, the sum of an individual's deeds in this life and in past lives. After death, a person's life is judged by divine forces, and rebirth is assigned in a high or a low place, depending upon what is deserved. This supernatural sanction can never be neglected, because it brings a person to his or her position in the caste hierarchy, relevant to every transaction involving food or drink, speaking, or touching.

In past decades, Dalits in certain areas (especially in parts of the south) had to display extreme deference to high-status people, physically keeping their distance—lest their touch or even their shadow pollute others—wearing neither shoes nor any upper body covering (even for women) in the presence of the upper castes. The lowest-ranking had to jingle a little bell in warning of their polluting approach. In much of India, Dalits were prohibited from entering temples, using wells from which the "clean" castes drew their water, or even attending schools. In past centuries, dire punishments were prescribed for Dalits who read or even heard sacred texts.

Such degrading discrimination was made illegal under legislation passed during British rule and was protested against by preindependence reform movements led by Mahatma Gandhi and Bhimrao Ramji (B. R.) Ambedkar, a Dalit leader. Dalits agitated for the right to enter Hindu temples and to use village wells and effectively pressed for the enactment of stronger laws opposing disabilities imposed on them. After independence, Ambedkar almost single-handedly wrote India's constitution, including key provisions barring caste-based discrimination. Nonetheless, discriminatory treatment of Dalits remains a factor in daily life, especially in villages, as the end of the twentieth century approaches.

In modern times, as in the past, it is virtually impossible for an individual to raise his own status by falsely claiming to be a member of a higher-ranked caste. Such a ruse might work for a time in a place where the person is unknown, but no one would dine with or intermarry with such a person or his offspring until the claim was validated through kinship networks. Rising on the ritual hierarchy can only be achieved by a caste as a group, over a long period of time, principally by adopting behaviour patterns of higher-ranked groups. This process, known as Sanskritization, has been described by M.N. Srinivas and others. An example of such behaviour is that of some

Leather worker castes adopting a policy of not eating beef, in the hope that abstaining from the defiling practice of consuming the flesh of sacred bovines would enhance their castes' status. Increased economic prosperity for much of a caste greatly aids in the process of improving rank.

India has a hierarchical caste system in the society. Within Indian culture, whether in the north or the south, Hindu or Muslim, urban or village, virtually all things, people, and groups of people are ranked according to various essential qualities. If one is attuned to the theme of hierarchy in India, one can discern it everywhere. Although India is a political democracy, in daily life there is little advocacy of or adherence to notions of equality.

Castes systems in India and caste like groups—those quintessential groups with which almost all Indians are associated—are ranked. Within most villages or towns, everyone knows the relative rankings of each locally represented caste, and people's behaviour toward one another is constantly shaped by this knowledge. Between the extremes of the very high and very low castes, however, there is sometimes disagreement on the exact relative ranking of castes clustered in the middle. Castes system in India are primarily associated with Hinduism but also exist among other Indian religious groups. Muslims sometimes expressly deny that they have castes—they state that all Muslims are brothers under God—but observation of Muslim life in various parts of India reveals the existence of caste-like groups and clear concern with social hierarchy. Among Indian Christians, too, differences in caste are acknowledged and maintained.

Throughout India, individuals are also ranked according to their wealth and power. For example, there are "big men" (bare Admi, in Hindi) and "little men" (chhote admi) everywhere. "Big men" sit confidently on chairs, while "little men" come before them to make requests, either standing or crouching down on their haunches, certainly not presuming to sit beside a man of high status as an equal. Even men of nearly equal status who might share a string cot to sit on take their places carefully—the higher-ranking man at the head of the cot, the lower-ranking man at the foot.

Within families and kinship groupings, there are many distinctions of hierarchy. Men outrank women of the same or similar age, and senior relatives outrank junior relatives. Several other kinship relations involve formal respect. For example, in northern India, a daughter-in-law of a household shows deference to a daughter of a household. Even among young siblings in a household, there is constant acknowledgment of age differences: younger siblings never address an older sibling by name, but rather by respectful terms for elder brother or elder sister. However, an older sibling may address the younger by name.

Even in a business or academic setting, where colleagues may not openly espouse traditional observance of caste or class ranking behaviour, they may set up effective kinship relations, addressing one another by kinship terms reflecting family or village-style hierarchy. For example, a younger colleague might respectfully address an older colleague as chachaji (respected father's younger brother), gracefully acknowledging the superior position of the older colleague.

PURITY AND POLLUTION

Many status differences in Indian society are expressed in terms of ritual purity and pollution. Notions of purity and pollution are extremely complex and vary greatly among different castes, religious groups, and regions. However, broadly speaking, high status is associated with purity and low status with pollution. Some kinds of purity are inherent, or inborn; for example, gold is purer than copper by its very nature, and, similarly, a member of a high-ranking Brahman, or priestly, caste is born with more inherent purity than a member of a low-ranking Sweeper (Mehtar, in Hindi) caste. Unless the Brahman defiles himself in some extraordinary way, throughout his life he will always be purer than a Sweeper. Other kinds of purity are more transitory—a Brahman who has just taken a bath is more ritually pure than a Brahman who has not bathed for a day. This situation could easily reverse itself temporarily, depending on bath schedules, participation in polluting activities, or contact with temporarily polluting substances.

Purity is associated with ritual cleanliness—daily bathing in flowing water, dressing in properly laundered clothes of approved materials, eating only the foods appropriate for one's caste, refraining from physical contact with people of lower rank, and avoiding involvement with ritually impure substances. The latter include body wastes and execrations, most especially those of another adult person. Contact with the products of death or violence are typically polluting and threatening to ritual purity.

During her menstrual period, a woman is considered polluted and refrains from cooking, worshipping, or touching anyone older than an infant. In much of the south, a woman spends this time "sitting outside," resting in an isolated room or shed. During her period, a Muslim woman does not touch the Quran. At the end of the period, purity is restored with a complete bath. Pollution also attaches to birth, both for the mother and the infant's close kin, and to death, for close relatives of the deceased.

Members of the highest priestly castes, the Brahmans, are generally vegetarians (although some Bengali and Maharashtrian Brahmans eat fish) and avoid eating meat, the product of violence and death. High-ranking Warrior castes (Kshatriyas), however, typically consume non-vegetarian diets, considered appropriate for their traditions of valour and physical strength. A Brahman born of proper Brahman parents retains his inherent purity if he bathes and dresses himself properly, adheres to a vegetarian diet, eats meals prepared only by persons of appropriate rank, and keeps his person away from the bodily exuviae of others (except for necessary contact with the secretions of family infants and small children).

If a Brahman happens to come into bodily contact with a polluting substance, he can remove this pollution by bathing and changing his clothing. However, if he were to eat meat or commit other transgressions of the rigid dietary codes of his particular caste, he would be considered more deeply polluted and would have to undergo various purifying rites and payment of fines imposed by his caste council in order to restore his inherent purity. In sharp contrast to the purity of a Brahman, a Sweeper born of Sweeper parents is considered to be born inherently polluted. The touch of his body is polluting to those higher on the caste hierarchy than he, and they will shrink from his touch, whether or not he has bathed recently. Sweepers are associated with the traditional occupation of cleaning human feces from latrines and sweeping public lanes of all kinds of dirt. Traditionally, Sweepers remove these polluting materials in baskets carried atop the head and dumped out in a garbage pile at the edge of the village or neighbourhood. The involvement of Sweepers with such filth accords with their low-status position at the bottom of the Hindu caste hierarchy, even as their services allow high-status people, such as Brahmans, to maintain their ritual purity.

Members of the Leather worker (Chamar) caste are ascribed a very low status consonant with their association with the caste occupation of skinning dead animals and tanning the leather. Butchers (Khatiks, in Hindi), who kill and cut up the bodies of animals, also rank low on the caste hierarchy because of their association with violence and death.

However, castes associated with ruling and warfare—and the killing and deaths of human beings—are typically accorded high rank on the caste hierarchy. In these instances, political power and wealth outrank association with violence as the key determinant of caste rank.

Maintenance of purity is associated with the intake of food and drink, not only in terms of the nature of the food itself, but also in terms of who has prepared it or touched it. This requirement is especially true for Hindus, but other religious groups hold to these principles to varying degrees. Generally, a person risks pollution—and lowering his own status—if he accepts beverages or cooked foods from the hands of people of lower caste status than his own. His status will remain intact if he accepts food or beverages from people of higher caste rank. Usually, for an observant Hindu of any but the very lowest castes to accept cooked food from a Muslim or Christian is regarded as highly polluting.

In a clear example of pollution associated with dining, a Brahman who consumed a drink of water and a meal of wheat bread with boiled vegetables from the hands of a Sweeper would immediately become polluted and could expect social rejection by his caste fellows. From that moment, fellow Brahmans following traditional pollution rules would refuse food touched by him and would abstain from the usual social interaction with him. He would not be welcome inside Brahman homes—most especially in the ritually pure kitchens—nor would he or his close relatives be considered eligible marriage partners for other Brahmans.

Generally, the acceptance of water and ordinary foods cooked in water from members of lower-ranking castes incurs the greatest pollution. In North India, such foods are known as kaccha khana, as contrasted with fine foods cooked in butter or oils, which are known as pakka khana. Fine foods can be accepted from members of a few castes slightly lower than one's own. Local hierarchies differ on the specific details of these rules.

Completely raw foods, such as uncooked grains, fresh unpeeled bananas, mangoes, and uncooked vegetables can be accepted by anyone from anyone else, regardless of relative status. Toasted or parched foods, such as roasted peanuts, can also be accepted from anyone without ritual or social repercussions. (Thus, a Brahman may accept gifts of grain from lower-caste patrons for eventual preparation by members of his own caste, or he may purchase and consume roasted peanuts or tangerines from street vendors of unknown caste without worry).

Water served from an earthen pot may be accepted only from the hands of someone of higher or equal caste ranking, but water served from a brass pot may be accepted even from someone slightly lower on the caste scale. Exceptions to this rule are members of the Waterbearer (Bhoi, in Hindi) caste, who are employed to carry water from wells to the homes of the prosperous and from whose hands members of all castes may drink water without becoming polluted, even though Waterbearers are not ranked high on the caste scale.

These and a great many other traditional rules pertaining to purity and pollution constantly impinge upon interaction between people of different castes and ranks in India. Although to the non-Indian these rules may seem irrational and bizarre, to most of the people of India they are a ubiquitous and accepted part of life. Thinking about and following purity and pollution rules make it necessary for people to be constantly aware of differences in status.

With every drink of water, with every meal, and with every contact with another person, people must ratify the social hierarchy of which they are a part and within which their every act is carried out. The fact that expressions of social status are intricately bound up with events that happen to everyone every day—eating, drinking, bathing, touching, talking—and that transgressions of these rules, whether deliberate or accidental are seen as having immediately polluting effects on the person of the transgressor, means that every ordinary act of human life serves as a constant reminder of the importance of hierarchy in Indian society.

There are many Indians, particularly among the educated urban elite, who do not follow traditional purity and pollution practices. Dining in each others' homes and in restaurants is common among well-educated people of diverse backgrounds, particularly when they belong to the same economic class. For these people, guarding the family's earthen water pot from inadvertent touch by a low-ranking servant is not the concern it is for a more traditional villager.

However, even among those people whose words and actions denigrate traditional purity rules, there is often a reluctance to completely abolish consciousness of purity and pollution from their thinking. It is surely rare for a Sweeper, however well-educated, to invite a Brahman to dinner in his home and have his invitation unself-consciously accepted. It is less rare, however, for educated urban colleagues of vastly different caste and religious heritage to enjoy a cup of tea together.

Some high-caste liberals pride themselves on being free of "casteism" and seek to accept food from the hands of very low-caste people, or even deliberately set out to marry someone from a significantly lower caste or a different religion. Thus, even as they deny it, these progressives affirm the continuing significance of traditional rules of purity, pollution, and hierarchy in Indian caste system.